*Just Practising*

*Also by David Grant*

Tales From the Animal Hospital
A Year in the Life of the Animal Hospital

# *Just Practising*

## *Early Days as a Country Vet*

**DAVID GRANT**

SIMON & SCHUSTER
A VIACOM COMPANY

First published in Great Britain by Simon & Schuster UK Ltd, 1999
A Viacom company



3 5 7 9 10 8 6 4 2

Simon & Schuster UK Ltd
Africa House
64–78 Kingsway
London WC2B 6AH

Simon & Schuster Australia
Sydney

A CIP catalogue record for this book is available
from the British Library

ISBN 0-684-86063-5

Typeset by SX Composing DTP, Rayleigh, Essex
Printed and bound in Great Britain by
The Bath Press

Although all the stories that feature in this book are true, the names of
pets and owners have been changed to protect their privacy.

For my mother and my family

# *Acknowledgements*

With thanks to Helen Gummer, Ingrid Connell, Katharine Young and all the staff at Simon & Schuster.

# *Chapter One*

Miffy was a small black-and-white Jack Russell terrier. Rather more white than black, with just one black patch left of her spine and another, smaller, covering her right eye, that made her look like a pirate. Or so I liked to think as she and I explored the streets and the parks in Rochester, Kent, where I grew up. Miffy wasn't my dog. I just used to take her for walks. But she was the reason I ever became a vet. I was about eleven and, because my parents both worked, Dad in a factory and Mum in an old people's home, there was never any question of having a dog ourselves. We didn't even have a cat. But when Mrs Anderson, who lived in the next street to us, found her arthritis too bad to give Miffy the daily walks she needed, I took over the job. Not that it ever seemed like a job.

I had just started at the local grammar school and, every day for the next two years, the first thing I did when I got home was to change out of my school uniform and into short trousers that reached the knee (Elvis Presley had just about reached England, but jeans hadn't) and a jumper knitted by my Mum, grab a slice of bread and Marmite and go round to Mrs Anderson's, where Miffy would be waiting for me, her lead already in her mouth, by the kitchen door ready for her daily adventures.

On the whole, doctors deal just with their patients, but with anything to do with animals there's always a human in the story. So it was with Miffy. She really belonged to Mrs

Anderson's daughter, Lesley, who I soon discovered was a vet. When I came back after taking Miffy out for her walk, Miffy would flop down and pant in her basket in the kitchen, and Mrs Anderson would always give me a slice of cake and tell me stories about Lesley and her husband Brian, who had met at veterinary college. She was very proud of her daughter, and rightly so. In those days, it was rare for someone from a working-class background – especially a girl – to become a vet. I heard how they lived in the country and how they had a swimming pool and a tennis court. Mrs Anderson would read out letters from Lesley and I heard all these fantastic tales. But it was only when Miffy died, about two years later, that I had the idea of becoming a vet. She didn't die of anything in particular, just faded away with old age, but I had never felt so sad and I just thought it would be nice to help sick animals. Once I'd decided, that was it. I never thought about being anything else.

I went to the local vets, told them what I wanted to do, and so for the next few years, at most weekends and during the school holidays, I would go round there and help out, anything from cleaning the kennels to watching small animal operations and going out with the vet in his car on farm visits. From then on, everything I did was geared to my becoming a vet. My A-levels wouldn't have been much use for anything else: physics, chemistry, zoology and botany. Four A-levels is a tough load, particularly for somebody who was not a natural academic, and I did have another interest which took up a lot of my free time and energy. I was a sprinter, ending up as captain of the school athletics team and captain of cross-country. Somehow running always seemed a better option than sitting in a library reading books or writing essays, especially in the summer.

Veterinary medicine is very specialized and in the early sixties, as now, there were only six universities where you could do it. In those days you always had an interview and you'd be given a provisional acceptance dependent on your A-level results. I went to interviews at Bristol, Liverpool and London, but I was a rather gauche lad, a working-class boy with no experience of the world, and I was completely overawed by the whole process, not to mention the professors who interviewed me. Not surprisingly, I didn't get a provisional acceptance anywhere, although the Royal College of Veterinary Surgeons, part of London University, said that I should give them a call when I got my results. I know now that I was incredibly lucky, but at the time I just had this blithe optimism that everything would be all right. And it was. Although I only just scraped through my exams, it was enough. I gave London a call and a few days later a letter arrived offering me a place. So with less than three weeks to go before the start of term, I had to organize a grant and find somewhere to live.

It takes five years to train to be a vet. The first three years are mainly theoretical – the first four years I spent in London – then the emphasis changes to practical work. My final year was spent on a campus near Potters Bar, in the countryside just to the north of the city, where most of my time was spent on a farm, becoming familiar with clinical practice. It was a very intensive course, studying nine to five every day, not like an arts degree where you have about half a dozen lectures a week.

For the gauche lad from Kent, it was all a bit of a culture shock. It seemed to me that all my fellow students had either been brought up on a farm or came from well-to-do families. Often both. And much as I enjoyed my summer bike rides through the Kentish countryside, no one could describe me as a country boy. However, I think I sublimated this sense that I didn't really fit in through sport, and my social life largely revolved around that, particularly as in my second year I met a wonderful girl, a hurdler, called Sally, with legs that seemed to go on for ever. She was studying anthropology, and we were soon what is known today as 'an item'. I eventually became captain of the University of London athletics team.

Gradually, as the 'Sixties got underway, things began to change and it mattered less what school you had been to or what your parents did. The music had a lot to do with it and, even now, just hearing one track of an early Beatles, Rolling Stones or Kinks LP can take me straight back to a specific party. Sally was always a great party girl, her long legs and straight blonde hair perfectly suited to the mini-skirts that were every girl's uniform. On the athletics track she might have dressed like any other sportswoman, but once the spikes were off, she could easily have been mis-taken for a model. She was a fan of Biba and on a Saturday morning, if she wasn't down at the athletics track training, sure as hell she would be in Biba's, buying another of those vivid outfits that seemed to be made for her, ready to wow us all, me particularly, at the party that always seemed to materialize every Saturday night. My own clothes were a bit less fashionable. Not for me tight trousers or flowered cravats. Jeans were more my style, though I did have a very nice pair of imported American cowboy boots.

It was a great time to be young. Although I didn't have a record player, I did have a reel-to-reel tape recorder and used to record the top twenty every week off the radio and could then play it in my car, an old Morris that Dad had bought for me for £30.

An integral part of a vet's training is what is called

'seeing practice' – practical experience. During your five years of training you had to spend twenty-six weeks with a veterinary practice. You had to organize this yourself, so that's how I eventually got to meet Mrs Anderson's daughter Lesley and her husband Brian, and I spent several weeks every summer with them in Leicestershire. As I had already had a fair amount of experience of small animals at my local vets in Rochester, it was ideal, as their practice was mainly farm animals. Lesley ran the small animal side of the practice from a room in their house, but it rarely seemed to involve more than an hour's work a day.

My talent as a sprinter turned out to be more use than anything else. I could catch a cow like nobody's business, and for routine but time-consuming work of calf castrations or testing for tuberculosis it saved a huge amount of time. I would catch them and Brian would do whatever had to be done. I learned to leap on the animal, then grab it round the neck and grab its nose. Once you've got its nose, it just stands still.

It's a skill that never left me. In about 1980 I was on a remote farm in Australia. It was like an advert for Australian lager, and I think they saw the opportunity for a bit of sport with this Pommie vet.

'Oh, we've got a calf to castrate,' the senior stockman said to me nonchalantly, the corks around the rim of his bushman's hat bobbing around just like they do in the ads, keeping off the flies.

'Wanna show us how to do it?'

Equally nonchalantly, I said yes. They took me to the stockade, where there was a jersey cow with her calf that needed castrating, and they all sat around the stockade watching to see what I would do. I could practically hear the Clint Eastwood-style music as I went in. Even though it was nearly ten years since I had done any competitive running and the heat was punishing, my legs seemed to know instinctively what to do. I chased around after it, and within seconds had grabbed its nose. It stood there immobilized. Then came the moment I'd been waiting for.

'Well, come on, you bastards. Are you just going to sit there?'

You could see their attitude change completely. The next thing, they were inviting me to go for a drink. This was a mistake. The nearest pub was thirty miles away. But that's another story.

Back in Leicestershire, my ability to outrun just about anything on two legs – or four – cut the time spent on any job by about half, leaving both Brian and me plenty of time to enjoy summer afternoons playing tennis or lazing around at the swimming pool. Although I didn't start playing tennis until I was fifteen, because my parents couldn't afford to buy me a racket, I had become quite a useful player and represented the school.

To be working with animals, with the prospect of a luxurious life style at the end of it, was enough of an incentive to keep me going when things got tough back at college.

Five years of study went by in a blur. I wasn't very good at organizing myself in those days, and whether I did well at something or not depended entirely on how well I was taught. With a really good teacher, I never forgot anything. But where I had to do most of the leg work myself, then that was different. What I needed was spoonfeeding, and sometimes I got it.

The professor of anatomy was a very charismatic man, called Professor Amoroso. He came from Trinidad and had originally qualified as doctor, but had switched to veterinary medicine and was now a world authority on the placenta. Professor Amoroso was very unconventional and could be fearsome. One day I was sitting quietly having a cup of coffee in the canteen when he came and sat down opposite me, then a cussed young lad of twenty, going on fifteen.

'What are you drinking, boy?' he barked. 'Coffee, is it?' I nodded.

'What is in coffee?'

I could answer that.

'Caffeine, Professor.'

'So then, tell me about the physiological effects of caffeine.'

It was like a tutorial.

'It dilates the anterior arterials,' I stammered.

'So. Remember that, boy. Remember that.'

Then he started on about oxytocin.

'Who synthesized it?'

I paused a bit too long.

'It was Duvignieau. Now remember that.'

We're talking about over thirty years ago, yet I remember every single word. He was a hell of a character. Nine months later I went into the final oral exam. And there was Professor Amoroso, next to the external examiner.

'Now then, Mr Grant,' he said, without the hint of a smile. 'Tell me about oxytocin. Who synthesized it?'

I passed.

I never found orals easy, but the final oral was terrifying. I don't know how I managed to walk out of the examination room that Thursday afternoon in December 1967. I felt as if my knees were giving way under me. The first cull of would-be vets happens after three years. About ten of the seventy or so who started with me in 1962 were kicked out then. So you're under phenomenal pressure, because either you're a qualified vet, or you're not. If you're not, you can't have anything to do with the veterinary profession; you just have to find something else to do. And after five years of hard study, that's not a happy prospect.

During the oral I had been asked about a cow with a prolapsed uterus. This was something I had not been spoon-fed but had had to read up myself. Unfortunately I had been interrupted just before turning the crucial page by a friend who thought I was taking life far too seriously and suggested a beer would do me more good than finishing the chapter. I happily went through what I knew, but then the examiner had silenced me with his 'and then what would you do, Mr Grant?' Mr Grant had not the slightest idea. Mr Grant had never turned the page to find out.

The examiner answered for me.

I went down to our students' pub, the Parr's Head in Camden Town, to drown my sorrows and, as I drank my pint with the others, my hand was shaking. It was like intravenous valium when the beer went in. The results were posted the next evening at six o'clock. I could hardly believe my luck when I saw, between Gordon L.M. and Hayes M.E., Grant D.I., Pass. I was a veterinary surgeon.

By chance I had qualified at the height of the biggest epidemic of foot and mouth disease Britain has ever experienced. As a result, the Ministry of Food and Agriculture was desperately short of vets and had asked for volunteers from people in my year who were just qualifying. The results were posted at six o'clock on Thursday, by nine o'clock the next day an emergency registration was held, and by Saturday I was in Oswestry, on the Welsh/English border, on Saturday afternoon I saw my first case of foot and mouth disease.

It hadn't been intended that way. As a new boy, I was sent to patrol what was called a contiguous farm, a farm next to one where foot and mouth had been found, to confirm that it was still clear. But it was obvious when we got there that the disease had spread. Suddenly I was exposed and contaminated.

Foot and mouth is a virus disease of cattle, sheep and pigs. It creates ulcerations in the mouth and the feet and it makes the animals go off their food and waste away, so they're useless economically. It's highly contagious and infectious and it is endemic in parts of Africa and South America. The thinking at the time was that it had come 'on the bone' from infected pig meat. Unless contained, it could devastate the entire British herd.

Suddenly I was one of the great experts. My first case was 400 sheep, all of which were infected. That first afternoon of my new life as a vet, I watched as these poor creatures were all shot and buried by slaughtermen who usually worked in abattoirs. The cows suffered the same fate. It was dreadful. The slaughtermen would walk amongst them and just fire into them, bang, bang, bang, using a captive bolt rather than a free bullet, and they would go down like a ton of bricks. It was like a vision from hell. It was carnage. I saw literally thousand upon thousand of animals destroyed.

I had come into veterinary practice to save sick animals and here I was involved in their wholesale slaughter. But there was nothing else to be done except make sure that the animals were treated with respect and not frightened. The policy was simple. The outbreak had to be contained and the only way to contain it is by killing all the animals in that area so that it can't spread, because there are no animals for it to spread through. Every time there was just one infected cow in the herd, they would kill off the whole herd.

Although there was compensation, it could never make up for the loss. I remember one farmer who had a nervous breakdown. Instead of calling the Ministry when he realized his cattle were infected, he just took to his bed. Only when the doctor called to see him, after friends realized he wasn't well, did anyone know what had happened. By that time it had spread to his sheep and his pigs. I was one of the team of vets sent in. For me it was an education. On one farm I saw acute foot and mouth disease, chronic foot and mouth disease, the whole spectrum. Cows with fever, sick, hunched up and salivating. Cows that were a bit better but had lost a tremendous amount of weight. Even I have difficulty catching healthy sheep, but these were so sick and lame, some with their feet dropping off with ulcers, that they were only just able to stagger around. It was a unique experience. I saw at close hand a disease that hitherto had only been seen by very few vets in the country.

Although, objectively, I suppose it is the worst thing I have ever seen in my life as a vet, in a way we were all distanced from it. It felt like being at war. We even had the uniform, black protective clothing: masks, caps, sou'westers, boots right up to our waists. We looked like spacemen. Some of the farmers were so edgy, they thought vets were transmitting the disease and wouldn't let us on to the farm. But they had to. They were breaking the law if they didn't.

In some ways we were similar to the police. We were based in a police station, and there were huge maps on the wall, like at the Battle of Britain, with red flags for the infected farms and blue for the contiguous farms. It was a real battle, and you felt you were part of it. There was no time for emotion.

It was the first time I really appreciated the skill of sheepdogs. The infected area fanned right out into the Welsh Hills, and I would have to go out with the shepherd, have the sheepdog round up the sheep and watch to see if any of them were lame. If I was uncertain about a particular animal, the dog would pick it off and drive it up close to us. All this done with nothing more than whistles and – to me – unintelligible Welsh. And there was no question where the dogs' loyalty lay. If you went anywhere near the shepherd, even to do up a button on his coat, they'd have you.

I had always thought of myself as a small animal vet, but my experience with foot and mouth made me think it might be sensible to build on my farm animal experience and finally get rid of that chip about being a townie that had so bedevilled me when I was a student.

By the spring of 1968 the outbreak was waning and one day, while making a quick scan through the *Veterinary Record*, I saw an advertisement for a large animal vet in a practice in my beloved Kent. It was over five years since I had left home, and although the practice was some way from Rochester, it was still close enough to enable me to have some home cooking every so often. It also wasn't that far from London, where Sally was working in an advertising agency. Although she had got a good degree, jobs in anthropology were thin on the ground, and she had been lured into the lucrative world of advertising. Having graduated a year before me, she was already speeding her way up the corporate ladder and, at the age of 22, was already an account executive.

The practice was a prestigious one, and still is, and I knew that it was just the place to get the training I knew I needed. Five years' intensive studying had somehow not filled me with confidence in my abilities. I would need to learn so much, and I thought that the best place to start was in a big hospital with plenty of people around to help.

The interview went quite well. At least the nervous boy who had made such a mess of his university entrance interviews could now talk quite knowledgeably about foot and mouth disease, which neither of the two senior partners had any experience of. Frank Archer had been a large animal expert, but now dealt exclusively with small animals. Alan Jenkins, who headed the farm side, would have been happy to talk about nothing else.

The whole thing was far more informal than I had expected. The interview was not held at the hospital, but in a local hotel restaurant over lunch. I had spent the night before in my old bedroom at Rochester and I had begun to have cold feet. Although it was a 50:50 mixed practice, with the farm animal vets doing only an hour a day of small animals, and no operations, it was very much a large animal vet the practice was looking for. However, within half an hour I really wanted the job. Then, of course, I began to worry that a townie was not really what they wanted. And Frank Archer, the small animal partner, clearly didn't suffer fools gladly and was a stickler for detail. During the course of the lunch he sent the fish back twice.

Next came a tour of the hospital itself, and meeting the other two vets who were soon to become partners. The practice itself seemed enormous by the standards I had been used to. I had been attached to three practices in my time as a student and none were anything like as big or as busy as this. There were four consulting rooms, an operating theatre and a separate X-ray room. I was to find out that this was where the impromptu crisis meetings were usually held. The central part was a huge pharmacy where all the drugs were dispensed, to both farmer and small animal clients. There was a mixture of all the modern antibiotics, but also bottle upon bottle of mixtures for bloating cows, colic in horses and remedies for various other ailments. All this was completely new to me.

To the side of the practice there were lovely brand new kennels for in-patients, and at the back some lambing pens. Upstairs was a well-stocked library with all the latest books and periodicals, plus a flat for the resident veterinary nurses. One of them was always on call.

There was a buzz around the place that some years later I would find at the RSPCA Harmsworth hospital, which coincidentally was nearing completion at the time.

While I inspected the library, the two senior partners nipped into the X-ray room for a quick chat, and that was it. The job was mine. £1,500 a year and a car. A fortune. Before the interview I had told myself that under no circumstances was I to make a decision before talking it over with Sally. But somehow all that went out the window. It was the first job interview I'd ever had, and the first job offer. And I took it.

I could see myself now, bowling along country lanes, cheery farmers waving to me over five-barred gates, farmhands doffing their caps and offering me samples of homebrew. And I said yes. The details of rotas and night shifts were just proof that this was it, the real thing, though I didn't take it in. After all, I was starting on Monday. Plenty of time to get the hang of the details then. Perhaps I wasn't such a bad bet after all. Only later did I realize that they were probably desperate and would have taken anyone, as long as they could use a knife and fork and didn't swear too much. It was spring, and the lambing and calving season was just beginning, the most intensive few months in the livestock year.

# *Chapter Two*

Animals, particularly farm animals, have no sense of the working week or the working day. Although I had had some experience of this with Lesley and Brian in Leicestershire, I had never been there in spring. In Leicestershire it had always been summer, and there was always the pool to cool off in. Now, however, I was about to be thrown into the deep end of a much colder pool.

My digs were with Mrs Nightingale, whose large Edwardian house was home to students from the local teachers' training college. The stable block to the right of the house had been turned into two self-contained flats, one of which was mine. The other tenant, who I met when I moved in, was Keith, a representative of a crisp, snack and pie company, whose job seemed mainly to consist of making sure the pubs and off-licences in his territory never ran out of things to eat. In those days proper food was a luxury that most pubs didn't run to. You went to a pub to drink beer. A warmed-up pie, or a sandwich made with processed cheese, was the usual option for those who didn't have a home to go to.

As a result, Keith knew every pub in the area, from former turnpike inns to tap rooms at the far end of country lanes, no bigger than my parents' front room. This was all good news. Even more extraordinary was the fact that the ten students who shared this rambling Edwardian house were all girls.

Although my relationship with Sally was rock solid, the idea of all those girls literally on the doorstep was nonetheless enough to put an added spring in my step that first evening.

My car turned out to be an oldish Ford Anglia, not a model that even in its heyday was likely to turn heads. Its major virtue from a veterinary point of view was that it was reliable, cheap to maintain and had a very large boot. To a vet, a car boot is the equivalent of a doctor's bag, and a brief glance inside it confirmed that it contained everything I would be likely to need on a farm visit. But on this first introductory day, the Anglia was left at the hospital and I eased myself into the passenger seat of Alan Jenkins's Citroën DS, a car that was almost futuristic in design and has since become a classic.

From his name to his devotion to rugby, Alan was the archetypal Welshman, minus the accent. Tall, dark-haired and handsome, he looked more like a banker than a vet. He always wore a suit, and usually sported a flower in his lapel, picked from his substantial garden, the local park, or even the hedgerow. It didn't seem to matter. He and his wife lived in a very grand house. Helen was an ex-policewoman, but now used her energies looking after their two small children. They were a formidable couple. Not that I knew any of this that first Monday morning as the Citroën purred out of the hospital car park and turned north.

We were heading for a case of mastitis, infection and inflammation of the udder. I had seen this many times before, on my seeing practice in Leicestershire, and was confident that I wouldn't make too much of a fool of myself.

The sun was shining and the hedgerows were fresh and green after an early morning shower as I tentatively confessed my worries to my new mentor. My lack of practical experience of cows, and birth generally, had become a major preoccupation for me. I knew how important a live and healthy birth was to a farmer. And what would happen if one came late at night and I was the only vet on call? My biggest worry, however, was a prolapsed uterus, or 'calf bed' as farmers called it. This was a complication of calving that I had only read about in books, but I knew that sooner rather than later I would have to tackle one.

'The thing is, Alan, I haven't actually done many calvings,' I said. In fact, even this was a lie. I hadn't done *any*. It's one thing watching another vet struggling to rotate a badly presented calf, but with only the contortions of his face to go on, the arm doing the work being entirely invisible inside the cow, how are you to know what you're meant to do if it's *your* arm that's stuck up a cow's rear end?

Whether he saw through my half truth I will never know, but he then proceeded to give the best and most succinct seminar on the practical approach to the main problems with calvings. I had had very good lectures at college on the subject, but Alan had the knack of making it seem so simple and straightforward.

'Get a rope around the calf's head,' he said. 'Find the ears, slip it over, then find the teeth and slip it between the jaw. Just make sure you avoid the neck or you'll kill it before it's been born. And keep up a steady pull. Then with a rope on each front leg, pull on one and then the other, just as though you were crawling through a tunnel.'

Crucial to this procedure was lubrication, and the answer to that was soap flakes. Later that day, going through my equipment in the Anglia's boot, I found a brand new box of soap flakes amongst all the instruments and drugs.

The travelling seminar continued as Alan went over the

common things that I was likely to come across during the next few months: calf castrations, de-horning cattle and, in about six months' time when I got my licence from the Ministry, tuberculin testing. This is a test to check that cows are free from tuberculosis. By the time I started doing these tests it would be summer, and it was something I looked forward to – a chance to spend all day on a farm in the open air with no lives or livelihoods at stake.

Our destination was only a mile or so from the coast. It was a smallish place, with about fifty milking cows, one of which had mastitis. The farm had apparently been in the family for generations and was worked now by Bill and his wife, Janet. Their daughter Margaret who, as it turned out, was a very talented painter, made up the team. I was to buy several of her landscape oils over the next few years, but for now I was getting to know the family. The farmhouse itself looked like a picture on a calendar. It must have once been rather grand, beautifully proportioned, lying snugly beside a wonderful copper beech tree that must have been hundreds of years old and was just getting its leaves.

Alan introduced me as the new assistant and together we looked at the patient, called – in the classic English way I soon became familiar with – Buttercup. Only in the very largest herds did farmers dispense with names and resort to numbers. Buttercup had a bit of a fever and I stripped some milk out of the affected and swollen udder, using a small purpose-made siphon.

Treatment in these cases is simple: we took a sample for the practice laboratory, to see which bug was causing the problem, then it was a question of giving the cow an antibiotic injection and putting some antibiotic cream into her udder through one of the teats. Alan got me to do the injection. This was one thing I had done many times in

Leicestershire. It's given right at the back of the animal near the tail. I had learned to tap the site a couple of times with my fist, to get the patient used to the idea of a painless blow, then deftly stick the needle in. Nine times out of ten, the cow wouldn't flinch.

I remember my first ever injection. I had just completed my pre-clinical training and it was the first of my summers in Leicestershire. Brian got me to give an injection of antibiotic to a cow with mastitis, just like today's case. My first attempt wasn't bold enough, just having the effect of making the cow agitated. She was restrained in the milking parlour, and although her head was held firm by a rope, her feet weren't. As I prepared for my second attempt, I well remember her all hunched up and shifting her head from side to side – something I was soon to learn was the cow getting her aim right. The second time the needle went in and, like lightning, her left rear foot swung back, catching me on the top of my thigh. As if it was coming from somewhere else, I heard the sound of my yelp reverberate through the parlour. I had forgotten the most basic point drummed into me during the animal management lectures in my first year at college: get up close to the cow so that, if she does try to kick you, you won't catch the full force. To be honest, I had forgotten that cows can kick. Horses, yes, but cows? Well, I had just found out the hard way. I got the full force right at the end of a wide swing. I was propelled high up in the air, out of the parlour and landed in a pile of manure in the yard. My head went back and I was covered in it. The pain was excruciating, and I was winded. Through a mist I could see Brian the vet and the cowman looking down at me.

'Sorry, Guvnor,' said the cowman, 'I forgot to tell 'ee – Daisy, as you might say, has a bit of a temper on her.'

As Brian helped me up, I could feel him shaking with mirth behind his words of concern. There was nothing for it but to strip off and stick my head under a tap.

Since then I haven't been kicked by a cow. I was quick to learn from my mistakes.

The rest of the morning of my first day in practice was spent doing some pregnancy diagnosis on cows and treating some for lameness before heading back to the practice for lunch. Then Alan and I set off again, this time to the south, to see some sheep. Here the landscape was completely different from the flatlands and marshes nearer to the coast. The high banks were white with cow parsley and occasionally there would be flashes of blue when the Citroën purred through bluebell woods. The windows were open and every so often our noses would be assailed by the unmistakable aroma of wild garlic. Alan had a number of calls to make, and at each farm I was introduced and received with good humour, both by the farmers themselves or their hands. It was obvious that Alan was very popular and I felt that people were so friendly that in a few months it would be me laughing and joking with the cowmen and shepherds.

We got back to town just in time to start evening surgery – and it was time at last to let me loose on the public and their pets. Alan explained that usually the large animal vets would aim to get through their rounds so that they could help out with some consulting in the hospital. On busy evenings there would be four vets consulting, which meant there would be plenty of appointments available, and an end to the day for everyone – at least in theory – at about six-thirty.

After a cup of tea and one of the practice secretary's ginger biscuits, and with a feeling of butterflies in my stomach, I faced my first evening clinic in consulting room four. Mostly it was straightforward vaccinations, but after half an hour of puppy and kitten jabs I was suddenly confronted with a real unwell dog.

Sophie had gone off her food. She was a long-haired dachshund and her owner, Mrs Bell, was beside herself. She was a woman in her sixties and I suspected that Sophie was her entire life. Everything about Sophie showed that Mrs Bell probably spent as much on Sophie's hairstyles and outfits as she did on her own. Her coat was in wonderful condition, and smelt of expensive shampoo. In other circumstances I am sure that Mrs Bell would have insisted on seeing the senior partner, but, although Sophie was five years old, she had never been to the vet before so, for all Mrs Bell knew, I had been working there for years. Dealing with human emotions is a large part of a vet's job, but one that can't be taught. To be standing there with this woman, who reminded me of my primary school headmistress, in floods of tears, was very disconcerting for a lad of twenty-three. What do you do? Spotting a box of tissues on the window sill, I handed her first one, and then, realizing that was not going to be enough, the whole box, and suggested she sit down and take her time.

All I was able to find out in between tears was that Sophie was just moping about and picking at her food. Mrs Bell explained that she lived on her own and had recently retired from the civil service. And, yes, at least that bit of the Grant diagnosis was correct: Sophie was her life.

I went through the textbook examination: history – nothing there, just the moping about. Temperature, pulse, respiration, lymph nodes, mucous membranes, heart, lungs, abdominal paplation, disgustingly normal. With a mounting sense of panic I wondered what to do.

'What do you think is wrong with her?' Mrs Bell asked,

her imploring face now blotched and running with mascara. It was a worrying question, since I didn't have a clue.

I busied myself by looking professional, when Mrs Bell came up with her second penetrating question.

'In your experience, have you ever seen anything like this before?'

I decided the only thing to do was to seek help. As I didn't like to admit that I had very little experience in these matters, I told her I would like to have a second opinion. I found Frank just wrapping up his evening's consultations. And while Mrs Bell made her way through the box of Kleenex in the next consulting room, I went through Sophie's history and my complete lack of findings.

'Have a look and see whether she has any milk. And find out when she was last in season. Sounds like a false pregnancy to me!'

I went back into consulting room four. Sure enough, Sophie had enough milk to feed six pups, but had been in season six weeks before. No pups could be felt. Frank was right. How could he have known? It was one of the mysteries of experience that I would find out for myself years later.

The good news I was able to tell Mrs Bell was that there was nothing to worry about. Some new pills had appeared on the market, just for this particular condition. Frank had pointed them out to me on the shelf in the dispensary, just in case he was right, and I prescribed some and suggested that we would spay Sophie once she was better. My first consultation had lasted thirty minutes and resulted in a happy owner.

'Will you be on duty next week for Sophie's check-up?' was my reward. My confidence level had gone up in leaps and bounds in just one and a half hours. And I had an appetite for the next day.

The new assistant was to be spared any night-time rota for the first week, and it gave me time to settle into my new flat. There's something really nice about settling into a new place, knowing that it will be your home for the next few years. My flat was called the garden flat and was just a bit bigger than a bedsit. My windows overlooked the Nightingales' garden, that was mostly lawn with clumps of daffodils and hyacinths. My living room doubled as a kitchen, with a tiny sink, a couple of gas rings and a stove that I used for grilling bacon. And there was a tiny bedroom and bathroom adjoining. For six pounds a week it was all that I needed. Now, with £1500 a year, I was rich.

As a student I'd lived on a grant of £500 a year and whatever I could earn in the holidays, including work as a tractor driver on a hop farm and packer in a bean canning factory.

There was a knock at the door. Hastily I combed my hair, took a quick look in the bathroom mirror, and opened the door. Perhaps one of the student teachers needed to borrow a tea bag or a cup of sugar. I needn't have bothered. It was only Keith. He had forgotten to tell me that most of the girls didn't get back until the middle of the week, though two, Julia and Angie, were due back tomorrow.

Keith was tall and slim and had a permanent twinkle in his eye. He told me later he thought he looked a bit like George Harrison but, frankly, I never saw it. In order to fit in with my new life, I had decided that I had to look completely professional and in keeping with everyone else. If I wanted to be taken seriously by the farmers and my fellow vets I had to be completely inconspicuous. So my hair was cut short, in a style that was completely without style.

Keith had no such professional constraints and had already allowed his own locks to grow quite long. He clearly saw himself as a bit of a ladies' man, and wore a flowered shirt and a psychedelic tie that would startle a horse.

'What about a beer?' he said. It seemed like the best offer I had had all day. Although Keith's knowledge of Kentish pubs was encyclopaedic, we walked to our nearest, the Spotted Cow, and sampled the very good local ale. He took the opportunity of giving me a 'bird-by-bird' account of the teachers – which ones had boyfriends, what they looked like – but by the end of the evening, and too many beers later, they had all blended into one.

With a start, I realized I hadn't called Sally to tell her how things had gone. Perhaps it was better to leave it until I had more to say. It might not be a good idea to give the impression I was spending my time socializing, particularly as the weekend we had arranged for her to come down was the weekend I was on duty. This was just one of those little details I hadn't taken in when I said yes to the job.

I was already in the dog house with Sally for not discussing the job with her. To be honest, I had thought she would be as excited about it as I was and was quite taken aback by her less than enthusiastic attitude. But as far as Sally was concerned, Kent might as well have been Northumberland. It wasn't London, where she was. I protested that it was only a little over an hour away, and said that I needed a couple of weeks to settle in and then she could come down for the weekend. Of course, I hadn't reckoned on the night rota. But that was in the future.

Although my night duty rota for next week was plunging me into the deep end with five nights on the trot, I would be on second call, which theoretically meant I would only get called out if whoever was on first call was at some distant farm.

'Done many farrowings?' Frank Archer asked as soon as I walked through the door the next morning. The furrow in my face answered for me.

For most of his career, Frank had been a large animal vet, but, for reasons I never really discovered, he now only did small animals, except in emergencies. Frank and Alan were quite different. Of the two, Frank was more dapper – which probably had more to do with the bow tie he always wore than anything else. He had a piercing intelligence, accentuated by his stainless steel glasses and was full of energy. He was always on the go and would never let you get away with anything. Frank was a real workaholic and expected the same commitment from his staff. I can't remember a day at the beginning of my time in the practice when he didn't pick me up on something. And whenever I saw 'DG see FA' written in the diary, I would quake. Sure enough, out would come a great long list of things that I'd done wrong. It didn't last forever, though.

'So, farrowings, David. Ever done one?' I hadn't even seen one. Frank guessed as much, and over the next few minutes gave a potted summary of all that I would need to know about the task. I would have to go on my own, as Alan hadn't got back from an early morning emergency near the coast, and Charles, the other large animal vet, who a few months later would become a junior partner, was miles away doing a tuberculin test.

Frank gave me a quick diagram of the sow's womb, how much oxytocin to give – the drug that would help the womb to contract more efficiently – and a summary of how to pull the piglets out.

Just as I was getting into the Anglia, he shouted through the consulting room window, 'And give her seven ccs of dimycin'. This was the trade name of the antibiotic in vogue for sows with birth difficulties. The effect of this miniature seminar on my confidence was marvellous. Like the seasoned professional I wasn't, I bowled along the Kentish country lanes following the practice secretary's directions to old Paddy Dixon's farm, some twenty miles south of the practice. His wasn't a particularly high-tech enterprise, just a dozen or so breeding sows and a boar, but Paddy was a farmer of the old school and took great pride in his pigs. He didn't believe in short cuts and wasn't pleased to see me, a mere boy, who was obviously as green as they come.

'Where's Mr Jenkins?' was my welcome, as the old Anglia drew up outside his farmhouse. Yesterday's image of a country full of friendly farmers vanished like early morning mist. I explained that Alan was doing a difficult calving up the coast, some thirty miles away.

'But I'm the new assistant, David Grant. Pleased to meet you.'

I smiled broadly with as much confidence as I could muster and proffered my hand in greeting. He shook it unwillingly and promptly wiped his hand on his trousers – something that, judging by a stickiness on my hands, might have been better done before shaking mine. His hands were rough and hard from the daily grind of making ends meet. He had eyes that were so deeply embedded in his head you could hardly see them, though I suspect they were as sharp as an eagle's. He took me round to see Shirley, his prize sow, lying panting in her farrowing crate. She looked pretty exhausted.

'She's been like this since first thing, and nothing's happening. You done many of these?' There was a definite note of suspicion in his voice.

I didn't dare answer, but politely asked if I could have some soap and warm water. With a grunt, he took me to the steam-filled kitchen where Mrs Dixon was winding the handle of an old-fashioned wringer. Washday had come a day late that week.

Thanks to Frank's seminar, all went to plan. Within half an hour I had delivered ten live piglets, injected the oxytocin and the antibiotic, and it was obvious that Shirley had completed the job as she contentedly allowed her newborn litter to suckle. It amazed me how quickly the little piglets had got the message.

'Like a cup of tea and toast?' said Paddy, looking mightily relieved.

I said that, yes, it would be very welcome, but didn't admit the reason, which was that I hadn't felt like breakfast first thing after the heavy session with Keith the night before. As Paddy made his way through the farmyard and motioned me to follow, I decided to hop over the wall of the pen to cut off a corner. A roar of rage told me I had made a mistake. A big mistake. I had jumped into the pen of an extremely large sow, who saw no reason to share it with anyone else, particularly me. With a loud snort, she came at me at a great rate of knots, with her tusks thrust in a businesslike manner in front of her. I had heard tales of the nasty slashing bites of enraged pigs, particularly sows protecting their young, not to mention the damage their tusks could do. With a huge adrenaline rush, I jumped higher than I ever thought possible. But Gladys was just too quick and caught the top of my waders, producing a large hole in the right one.

And I wasn't out of the wood yet. The noise had stirred up the other sows, and I was literally jumping from the frying pan into the fire as I landed in the pen of yet another one, who was no happier to see me than Gladys had been. On the other side of this pen was a huge slick of mud, into which I fell. I was covered from head to toe.

At first Paddy was more worried about his sows than he was about me, but once he knew 'his girls' were all right, he surveyed the sorry state I was in.

'You look like you're gonna need a brandy in that tea of yours,' he chuckled, and I followed him back into the farm kitchen for the first of the very many breakfasts I would have with farmers and their families over the years.

'You must be fit,' he said, as I did the best I could to get the mud off my face by sticking my head under a tap. 'I've never seen jumping like that. You ought to be in the Olympics.'

The ice was definitely broken. It was a pattern I was to see countless times in my first year. Do a good job once, and you're accepted. Have a bit of a misfortune they could talk about down the pub and have a good laugh about, and it would be you they'd be asking for next time.

With a pint of tea (I turned down the offer of brandy) and several slices of hot buttered toast inside me, I waved goodbye to Paddy and Eileen, his wife, and set off back to the hospital, dreading what Frank would say when he discovered what had happened to the boots.

Alan was by now back from his calving and, as soon as I had cleaned up, already had plans for the rest of the morning.

'How did you get on?' he asked.

'Fine,' I replied. 'More or less as Frank predicted.'

'So you think you're going to like pig work?'

'Don't see why not.'

'Good. Because we've got 200 that need vaccinating against erysipelas.'

All the ramifications of this bacterial disease went through my mind. I had never seen it, or done any vaccination.

'Nothing to worry about. The pigman will put down some nuts and while they're scoffing you can do anything you like with them – including jabbing them in the neck!'

Five minutes later I was on my way, armed with syringes and needles and a little over 200 doses of erysipelas vaccine. I was to learn over the next few months that some of the jobs were routine and traditionally the preserve of the new boy. There was a lot of sense in this. At least the greenhorns were bringing in income for the practice while gaining experience with the farmers, getting to know them and making friends. In the main, though, the 'boy's jobs' usually had some downside. I was soon to find out what this was with pig vaccination.

As I drew up outside the pig farm, I knew I was at the right place without checking the address. Pigs, although cleaner animals than they're given credit for, have a smell about them which is pungent and unique. The wind was in the right direction this clear April morning and I had smelt them from half a mile away. Just as well the farm was pretty much isolated. Bert, the pigman, was waiting for me. If he was disappointed that it was me, and not one of the experienced ones, he didn't show it. A man of few words, he said, 'They're in 'ere.'

Bert fetched an old wooden gate from the yard, held it against the exit so that the pigs couldn't escape, and suggested I might as well carry on.

This was a far bigger operation than the Dixons', but my success with the farrowing earlier that morning had given me confidence. I followed him into a large building divided up into lots of pens holding about ten pigs each. The pigs were bedded down on straw, but half the pen was just concrete and this was where the pigs urinated and defecated. Bert approached one pen while I was loading up the syringes and threw some pig nuts on to the clean straw. Immediately the pigs set about eating them with a furious concentration. I was able to move amongst them easily, jabbing each one in the neck with the vaccine. For the most part, each pig feigned complete indifference, with the odd squeal. As I worked on, I got hotter and hotter. It was quite humid in the pens and bumping and bustling about amongst the pigs was hard work. After a while I took off my brown vet's coat, which acts as a general overall.

This was my first mistake. My white shirt seemed to upset a few of them and I sensed a change of atmosphere, a hint of panic. With only about thirty pigs to go, I decided to press on. Then, out of the blue one of the pigs refused to eat the nuts, and when I came over in his direction he shot off into the concrete part of his pen. His brothers and sisters all immediately followed suit, and refused to have anything further to do with the food.

The noise had by now increased to a complete crescendo, with the pigs milling about and jumping all over me. I gradually worked my way to the last pen. But word had obviously got around, and these last ten did just the same: turned up their noses at the nuts and huddled over in the concrete corner. I put my brown coat on again – the white shirt had in any case by this time attracted liberal amounts of pig muck. The first 180 had taken less than an hour, but those last ten pigs took another half an hour and, working as I was at the concrete end – their communal toilet – the inevitable happened and I slipped, ending up in a heap in all the muck. The coat was covered in it. Everything was covered in it. Outside, I stripped to the waist, washed myself as well as I could and then cleaned the worst off my shirt. The coat joined the calving apron and Wellingtons in the boot.

'Thanks very much then, vet'n'ry,' said Bert when it was all over. 'Nice to see you like pigs. Be seein' you again, I 'spect.'

I smiled wanly. Not, I hoped, that soon. I climbed wearily into the Anglia, starting to shiver. It wasn't a cold day by any means, but a dousing under a farmyard tap is not the same as a nice hot shower. I put on the heating as high as I could, to dry out. Steam soon started to fill the car, and with it a smell which seemed to get better as I approached town.

I had arranged to have lunch with Keith and the two students who had come back early. I swung into the car park in front of the house and hooted. Quarter to one – perfect timing. I wasn't due back at the hospital until two. We had planned to go to a small pub on the outskirts of town. Keith came out with two very pretty girls, Angie and Julia, both of whom he had described the night before as 'good fun'. They obviously all knew each other well, as Keith had been at the Nightingales' for nearly a year and the girls were in their second year at the teachers' training college.

Brief introductions over, we all piled into the little grey Anglia and I put her into gear. Immediately a change of expression came over Keith's face and from the back I heard suppressed laughter.

'Excuse me saying so – but what's that smell?' came a giggly voice.

'Er, pigs, I think,' was my honest reply. 'Is it that bad?'

The windows were rapidly wound down and the two girls theatrically held their heads half out of the window until we reached the pub.

I just had time for a half and a sandwich and a quick chat with my new friends before it was time to be getting back. My offer of a lift received no takers. They had decided they would stay on chatting with Keith, even though it was a good twenty minutes' walk back to the house. 'Is it me or my car?' I wondered as I drove back to the hospital. The old inadequacies came flooding back.

The list for the afternoon looked reasonably straightforward. There were two farm visits for cleansing cows, a fertility session at Bob Adams' place twenty miles away – he was one of the most important clients, apparently, so I doubted if I would get that to do – and a tuberculin test to read. That wouldn't be me either, as I hadn't yet got my certificate. It would be the cleansings – another 'boy's job'. Cleansing was a farming term for removing the placenta, or the afterbirth, as it is more commonly known, when it hadn't come away cleanly. I had seen these done as a student. The afterbirth would hang from the back end and was characterized by an extremely ripe smell. The reasons why it didn't get properly expelled at the normal third stage of labour were obscure, but one possible cause was a disease called brucellosis. This usually caused abortion, but sometimes would just show itself as a retained placenta with the potential for an infected womb and subsequent infertility, something which would cost the farmer dear.

As I expected, I soon found myself on the way to the two farms. Alan gave me a few brief instructions. I needed to insert my arm right up the womb and gently peel the placenta away, without tugging too hard, or it would just snap in two. Afterwards came a pessary and perhaps an injection of antibiotic if the cow was running a temperature. The farms were at opposite sides of the practice, so these two jobs would take me the rest of the afternoon, but Alan said I was to try to get back for evening surgery. I sped out north to a smallholding near the coast. It couldn't have been easier. There were only about ten cows in all and Doris had recently given birth. Hanging from her back end was the huge retained afterbirth. I put a mask on, and shoulder-length plastic gloves, just in case it was brucellosis. Old Arthur was extremely amused by the 'Dr Kildare' approach, as he called it. He lived on his own in a house that I don't believe had ever seen a Hoover, or even a woman. But Arthur's pride and joy was a television set, and 'Dr Kildare', starring Richard Chamberlain, was an American hospital series, the first to be seen on British TV. In spite of the sideshow of Arthur's cackling, the afterbirth slid away with just gentle tugging. In went the pessary and I was on my way. Doris looked positively relieved by the procedure and by my leaving. No time to stop and chat.

I had a thirty-mile drive across country to the much bigger farm right to the west of town, about 200 acres owned by Jed Dickens. Alan had warned me that he could be a bit cussed, and had not been pleased to hear that he was getting the new assistant to cleanse his cows. At least it would be a simple job and nothing much could go wrong – or so I hoped. As I checked the map, I suddenly realized what a lovely day it was. The cross-country drive couldn't have been better. No big towns, just village after village, ducks crossing to their pond, a group of schoolchildren and their teacher out for a nature walk giving me a cheery wave.

From the flat marsh lands near the coast, the landscape changed dramatically as I made my way inland, to softly undulating hills and narrow country lanes. In the months that followed I would get to know the lanes as if I had been born in them. In later months these lanes would be transformed into tunnels as the trees overhead put on their thick summer livery of shiny green. It was the beginning of the lambing season – another thing I had no experience of, but was looking forward to. After all, sheep, unlike cows, are not likely to give you a bruise the size of a football for your trouble. In the fields there were already some lambs cavorting about, full of the joys of spring. It was quite magical, and at one clearing I stopped the car and spent ten minutes just watching them jumping and racing about, and breathing in the crisp air. This didn't seem like work and I had to snap myself out of it and press on to Jed Dickens.

His sour face did not bode well. His real name was Jeremiah and, frankly, that would have suited him better.

The farm looked mightily run down, with rusty bits of farm machinery scattered all over the place and an air of decay over everything. Later I heard that things had been quite different when his wife had been alive, but when she had died – ten years before I came along – the life had gone out of him. They had been completely devoted, although there had been no children, so no one to hand the farm on to and no one to keep an eye on him. When Ellie died, I heard more than one person say, it was just like he'd lost a twin. He just fell apart. The farm ticked over, but that was about it.

'Over there,' Jed grunted, indicating a cowshed. Three cows were tied up, each with tell-tale and uniquely smelly afterbirth. I was to learn so many sights and smells which, once seen or smelt, would never leave me. Even now, thirty years later, they are vivid in my mind. I was grudgingly provided with a bucket of lukewarm water, soap and a towel.

As I put on my mask and gloves, he snorted. 'Hurry up. I haven't got all day. The others don't waste time with all this dressing up.'

Three of them made me even more jumpy about brucellosis. Just like at Old Arthur's place, though, I was lucky. The afterbirths came clean away without a struggle.

They wouldn't all be like this. When I had finished and was cleaning up, Jed added, as if in afterthought, 'What do you think to these calves then?'

I had just been getting into my car. I got out and looked at the four calves resting in a pen.

'They look all right to me,' I answered. 'In fact, they look pretty good.' I had just glanced over the top of the pen at them. They were quiet and resting.

'Give my regards to Alan,' he said, 'and tell him it's about time he paid us a visit. I've got some cows that need pregnancy diagnosis.'

I wasn't going to argue with the gruff old man, because the light was already fading and I wanted to arrive back before evening surgery.

There was just one client waiting, a little Yorkshire terrier that needed vaccination, and I took her owner, Jenny Kellaway, to the fourth consulting room. A quick check-up, and a jab was given. She would need the final injection in a month. Just as she was leaving, Jenny said, 'She's got a bit of dandruff. I've been using my own anti-dandruff shampoo. That shouldn't cause problems, should it?'

Feeling weary after all the driving and a hectic day, and badly needing a bath and a drink and something to eat, I replied, 'No, that should be fine. We'll check that next month at the next vaccination.'

And so ended my second working day. I went back home and soaked in the bath for half an hour, listening to Tchaikovsky's violin concerto, which I had bought to celebrate my new-found wealth along with a record player to play it on. A record library has to start somewhere and I had started with this, which I had first heard one summer at Lesley and Brian's in Leicestershire, and which seemed to me to be the height of sophistication.

A knock on the door revealed Keith, looking for a drinking companion. For the second night running we walked to the local. He had no intention, he said, of going anywhere near my car until I'd had it thoroughly disinfected. And if *he* felt like that, he said, imagine what the girls thought.

I suddenly felt enormously tired and after only a pint left Keith in the company of the barmaid, and walked back to my new home. My first duty weekend was coming up and it filled me with dread. Anything at night was by definition emergency work, and the chances were they would be things I had never dealt with before. It's an apprenticeship that all farm vets have to go through, and is stressful. I fell asleep dreaming of difficult calvings, lambings and prolapsed uteruses, and awkward customers like Jed Dickens.

## *Chapter Three*

I had no need to worry about the boots. It was still the honeymoon period and a trip down to the local fishing shop soon produced a new pair of waders that went right up to the waist. They would really protect my trousers from unpleasant smells in the future. As for the calving apron, all it had needed was a good hose down. I threw the brown coat into the washing machine and it emerged smelling of nothing more terrible than Persil.

I had survived a whole week and was on my way to a farm on the southern tip of the practice. It was another lovely day and another boy's job. A herd of cows had recently been de-horned and one of them had developed an infection in the cavity under the horn, the sinuses. De-horning is definitely a man's job – one that even when I was really fit I never relished – but all this infection needed was a simple flushing of the cavity with dilute antiseptic.

'Dead simple,' was Alan's reply when I asked how this might best be done. 'Know what this is?' he asked, producing a metal object about six inches long. For once I did, and he knew it. It was a teat siphon. I had used one on my very first job, to drain milk from the swollen udder of Buttercup, the cow that had mastitis.

Alan had discovered another use for it. Instead of taking milk off, it could be used for siphoning disinfectant in.

'But make sure you look after it. They cost six pounds,' was Alan's parting shot. Six pounds was my weekly rent.

My route lay along a part of Kent I hadn't seen and, as I soon discovered, was quite untouched by the creeping hand of tourism. I doubted that much had changed for hundreds of years – except, of course, the quality of the roads, and the fact that I could listen to music as I drove along. Here in Kent, as well as the usual BBC programmes you could pick up the new pirate radio stations that were broadcasting pop music from boats in the English Channel. In that way they were avoiding British laws on advertising. Radio Luxembourg had been broadcasting to England for years, but now there seemed to be dozens. My favourite was Radio Caroline. Flicking the switches, the choice was between Tchaikovsky's fourth symphony on the Third Programme, as BBC Radio 3 was then called, and 'A Whiter Shade of Pale' on Caroline. I listened to Procul Harem's moody classic first, then switched over. Both bits of music fitted my contented mood in their different ways.

When I arrived, there was no sign of life, so I decided to wait until the Tchaikovsky had finished. Eventually a gnarled old farmhand made an appearance, with a cloth cap pulled so far down that his eyes were hardly visible. He had an old brown coat tied with baler twine covering most of his body and from his upper lip a hand-rolled cigarette bounced about as he talked, the ash blending with the white stubble that covered his chin. He escorted me to my patient, a young Friesian heifer. She was boxed up in a crate ready for her treatment. I glanced at my companion, who I later discovered was called Eddie. A tuneless whistle emanated from his tightly shut mouth. Surely he wasn't the only help I had? He must have been seventy at least.

'Are you going to be able to steady her?' I asked.

Eddie's mouth opened momentarily in astonishment. The cigarette, though, remained firmly stuck to his upper lip and bounced about as he replied.

'Mr Jenkins all-uz manages.'

The patient was starting to get agitated – leaping within the confines of the crate as I tried to get near. This old-timer wouldn't be much use with this animal. She was as wild as a hawk. It would take all my strength just to restrain her. I decided to see what I could do. My Leicestershire lessons in how to handle cows were about to be put into practice: I decided to try my old trick of grabbing her nose. It worked. She immediately became still. With my left hand I introduced the teat siphon into the hole where the base of the horn had been. The most difficult bit was syringing the antiseptic in. After some more struggling, I got half of it in – then disaster struck. With a great bucking of her head, the heifer made one last attempt to get away, the siphon slipped out of my hand and disappeared down the hole. All I could think of was Alan's last words. Six pounds. I went back to the car to see if a pair of forceps would enable me to retrieve it. No such luck – it had gone completely. I didn't think the presence of six inches of metal would do her any harm, as a cow's sinuses are so cavernous. Unfortunately, that also meant there was little chance of finding the siphon in all that space.

Eddie continued his tuneless whistle, with the cigarette bouncing about in time to the 'music'. If he had noticed the disappearance of the siphon, he didn't let on. I gave an injection of penicillin and set off back to base to face the bosses. A pair of boots and a teat siphon needing replacement within a few days of my starting. I could feel the dread build up as I neared the hospital. I couldn't not say anything. And the longer I put it off, the worse it would be.

Charles Harte was the other large animal vet on the practice. In fact he was made a partner shortly after I arrived, together with the other small animal vet, Peter Cooper. Charles was just loading up his car when I pulled into the drive. He was much nearer my age than either Frank or Alan, so I decided to broach the subject with him first.

'Any idea of the effect of a teat siphon finding itself in a cow's frontal sinus?'

His eyes nearly popped out of his head as I briefly related the sorry tale. He obviously saw that I was worried.

'I'll have a word,' he replied as we made our way to the hospital. There followed the first of many impromptu meetings in the X-ray room as I waited outside. Would I be sacked? The very least would be a docking of my salary.

Alan was first out. This morning his lapel was sporting a bright yellow daffodil, as cheery as his smile. I immediately relaxed.

'How did it happen?' I told him the story, embellishing the friskiness of the heifer a bit but with no need to describe Eddie – he knew him well.

'Wasn't Joe about?'

Apparently, Joe Anstay was a huge man more than capable of handling the heifer for me, but Eddie hadn't offered his services.

Suddenly Alan saw the funny side of things and began to laugh, but added that he would go to see the heifer himself next week.

'Although I don't know what we can do about it,' he added. 'I doubt whether she will come to much harm.'

Friday night and my first night-duty rota. I was on second call, with Charles on first call, so he had invited me round to dinner. Before I left, I thought I'd give Sally a call.

A flatmate who I didn't know answered the phone. Sally was out, she said. She didn't know when she'd be back.

'Who shall I say called?'

'David.'

'David who?'

'David Grant.'

'Does she have your number?'

Was it that long that I hadn't phoned?

Charles and his wife, Penny, lived in a pretty village about ten minutes' drive from the hospital. From the road, their cottage looked tiny, but once inside you realized that the house was in fact a whole row of cottages, with a large modern extension at the back, a wonderful open-plan kitchen and a dining area with huge sliding doors that opened on to the garden. This arrangement is commonplace now, but wasn't then.

We had just finished the first course when a farmer rang in to say that a ewe was having difficulty giving birth. It was on a farm in Charles's village, so we both went round and I watched as Charles expertly delivered twin lambs. It seemed so easy that I felt pangs of envy. I wanted to be as expert. There was something magical about delivering lambs and watching the intense concentration of the ewe as she licked the lamb and encouraged it to stand and get its first food. With twins it was even better, and there was jubilation all round, especially from the farmer, whose profit margins, already tight even before the vets' fees were improved by the arrival of twin lambs.

We were back within the hour for the second course, and Penny, obviously used to interrupted meals, had a rich beef casserole served up within minutes of our return. Charles was very keen to talk to me about my experience with foot and mouth, but Penny made it clear that this was not a conversation to be had over dinner. Charles was very proper and had a number of mannerisms, that when you first met him, were rather disconcerting. He had a slight military manner and was always slapping his thigh, especially when under pressure at work, which was often.

Penny was a very good cook and we ended the meal with not just one, but a choice of two desserts – profiteroles or Pavlova, with lashings of whipped cream. I was in heaven. I had reckoned that, living in Kent, I would be enjoying food similar to my mother's home cooking, but my mother was a housewife of the old school and her food was traditional English. Apple pie was about exotic as it got. And as for cream, she would never have thought of it. It was either custard or custard.

A very pleasant evening ended near to midnight without any further phone calls, apart from a small animal client who phoned just after eleven, just to find out hospital opening times. I got home just after midnight and fell asleep instantly. Maybe night duties weren't so bad after all.

I was dreaming. In the far distance there was a ringing. It got louder and louder. With a start, and with a feeling of dread in the pit of my stomach when I realized it was my phone, I staggered out of bed and answered. It was a woman's voice. For a moment I thought it was Sally. It was Penny.

'Sorry to wake you, David, but Charles is out on a milk fever on the marshes and a calving has come in.'

My heart skipped a beat. This was it. The farm was a small one, the owner apparently a businessman who kept milking cows as a hobby and for something for his son to do. I got directions hastily scribbled down and got dressed, my pulse racing. I glanced at the clock – five-thirty. I had had less than five hours' sleep and I set off on the twenty-mile trip through country lanes, dark, and at this hour completely deserted. I was praying all the way that I would be able to do it.

I found the farm without difficulty. It was pristine; white-painted picket fence, swept gravel drive, a Kentish oast house to one side, new farm buildings discreetly hidden behind an ancient barn. Rupert Charlton-Jones was anxiously waiting as I followed the stone mushrooms that edged the drive around to the farmyard. We were about the same age, but he had an upper-class voice that in the old days would have made me feel instantly inferior.

'She's our best cow,' were his first words as I arrived. Funny how often I was to hear that same phrase. 'I just hope nothing goes wrong.'

It wasn't that he didn't trust me any less than he would have trusted Alan or Charles, it was just that Rupert was a natural born worrier, even more of a worrier than me. Over the next few years I got to know Rupert well. Whenever he had a problem he called us out. He never waited until things had got out of hand.

His father was a barrister who had done very well for himself. Instead of a career in the City, Rupert had gone from one of England's most famous public schools to agricultural college. He was always very vague. But at least he had learned to call out the vet sooner rather than later. He would call you out at the drop of a hat. The trick was not to make it look too easy. Not because he would query the bill, but because he was so lacking in confidence he wanted reassurance that he was right to have called you out, as these emergency calls were as often as not in the middle of the night.

Rupert's father did not have much to do with the farm – he left it all to Rupert. It was quite a small set up, sixty to 100 acres all told, with a dozen or so cows, yet the milking parlour was the most modern in the area.

Even though it was only six in the morning, Rupert was

shaved and dressed in his usual outfit of beige cavalry twill trousers, checked shirt and tweed jacket. He provided me with a clean towel, a bar of soap and a bucket of piping hot water and I strode into the barn where my patient, Rosie, was waiting. As we walked in she gave a mighty heave and a groan, but there was no sign of a calf.

'She's been at it for nearly an hour,' Rupert said.

Rosie was a huge Friesian who had had her previous calf without problems. Rupert had been watching her all night once she showed signs of giving birth.

I put my hand in and immediately felt a large head and two legs. Remembering Alan's tutorial, I found the first joint of each leg and the next one up, to see if it was the carpus and elbow or the tarsus and hock – in other words, the front or back legs. I was puzzled. I was sure that it was the head and two front legs, so what was the problem? It was as if my thoughts communicated themselves directly to Rosie. Or more likely it was the presence of my arm inside her that stimulated her to give another almighty heave. The calf came out towards me. I didn't even have time to use the calving ropes. I just got hold of one of the legs and gave a tug. With a deep bellow, Rosie gave one final mighty push and the calf tumbled into me. I slipped back, holding it in my arms. The whole process must have taken less than five minutes, and within seconds Rosie was round licking her calf in that intense, instinctive way that I was going to see so often over the next year or so. But, for the moment, it was a first. I cleared the calf's airway and then let Rosie get on with it.

'It's a heifer,' announced Rupert as proudly as if he was announcing the birth of the heir to the throne. 'Marvellous! My God, that was quick. I've never seen a slicker performance than that!'

I'd done nothing. Just the presence of my arm had

persuaded Rosie to push really hard. However, I decided to save my modesty for another day. Rupert's praise was something I intended to enjoy to the full – as if, even then, I realized that future calvings wouldn't all be this easy. I cleaned up and left Rupert to fuss over his prize cow. It was six-thirty. Dawn was just breaking but with any luck I might just get another hour or so's sleep. But then, on the outskirts of town, I saw the welcoming neon of a transport cafe and suddenly felt hungry. Ten minutes later I was wolfing down a full breakfast with a huge mug of tea. I spotted a pay phone and couldn't resist the temptation to call Sally.

'It's me. I've just calved my first cow.'

A sleepy voice congratulated me, and suddenly I felt guilty at waking her up, and her flatmates too. I could have waited a couple of days more, when she would see plenty of me on my first full weekend duty. I got home just before eight. As I put the key in the lock, the phone began to ring. It was Charles.

'There's a milk fever on the next farm to Rupert Charlton-Jones'.'

He couldn't do it himself because he was due at another farm at nine. He said he'd tried to catch me before I'd left the area, but I'd already left, and this was years before mobile phones or bleepers.

'Rupert was full of praise,' he added. 'Don't let it go to your head. But well done.'

I had a quick shower and set off back the way I'd come – this time in daylight, and with the commuter traffic going against me into town.

My earlier tiredness had gone, helped, I suspect, by a burst of confidence that was as energizing as adrenaline. And, even better, milk fevers were something I had seen and knew how to handle.

Milk fever is a condition caused by very low calcium and occurs usually soon after calving. The cow goes down and can't get up, and will die without treatment. Fortunately, this is very simple – a bottle of calcium borogluconate injected slowly into the vein and there is often a near miraculous cure.

Farmers at that time were still reluctant to get into the realm of intravenous injections themselves. Good for business, but bad for sleep patterns, as most of these cases tended to occur in the early hours when the farmers were doing their rounds, checking on their stock.

I arrived to find the cow flat out and looking very unwell. The farmer, Harry Myers, had propped her up with bales of straw and was not only relieved to see the vet, but pleased that it was me.

'You the lad that calved Rupert's cow this morning?' I was to learn that news, good or bad, travels fast in the countryside.

For a moment he had me worried.

'Why? Nothing wrong, I hope?'

'No. No. Nothing like that. I just hope you can work miracles on this one,' and he gestured over to a Jersey in the far corner. She had a pained, anxious expression on her face and her breathing came in laboured gasps.

I checked her over and found her temperature to be lower than normal. She had not long calved and her udder was hard and full of milk.

'I'm pretty sure it's milk fever,' I said, and selected a needle. Using a rope, I put it round Tinkerbell's neck and tugged at it gently. This had the effect of raising the jugular vein. There it was! Even an inexperienced me couldn't miss it. The needle went in first time and I connected it up to the bottle of calcium via a long tube which was part of the kit I carried in the boot. The solution started to pour into Tinkerbell's system. Within minutes, Harry and I could see the difference. The agonized look went from her face and she started to breathe more easily. Next, a huge motion was passed. I was later to recognize this as one of the first signs of recovery. I soon learned that bowel stasis was one of the signs of milk fever, but I couldn't remember seeing that in my books. You could almost sense the cow's relief at getting the right treatment. I sat on a bale of straw while holding the bottle high above my head. Gravity ensured that the solution bubbled into the vein. Ten minutes later, she had had the whole bottle and we sat and waited a while. Then, as though she had been in a dream, she staggered to her feet and walked to her cubicle and started nonchalantly eating hay.

'Don't know what you call that there stuff in that bottle, but I call it dynamite,' said Harry. 'You'd better have a cup of tea!'

Feeling pretty pleased with myself, we made our way back to the great barn of a kitchen that was bigger than my entire flat, where Harry and his wife, Joan, immediately made me feel welcome. They didn't seem to mind that I was newly qualified. I had saved Tinkerbell and done a 'miraculous' calving on their neighbour's best cow. Without a doubt, I was 'in', and it felt good. A calving and milk fever within a few hours. Somehow it made the thought of the weekend duty when I would be number one less daunting – and, in any case, Sally would be down to keep me company. I was assured by Frank, with whom I would be on duty, that weekend duties weren't too bad usually. I would soon find out that it depended on what you meant by not too bad.

I picked up Sally just after seven-thirty. She was looking wonderful – white tights, a Biba minidress that did up at the front with a huge zip, and white knee-high leather boots. I just hoped she had brought something that wouldn't show the mud. I was determined to take her with me on at least one of my calls. We picked up some fish and chips. I had intended to make a nice romantic supper back at the flat, but somehow I hadn't had time. But it was good just seeing her there, having her make-up in the bathroom next to my razor. Because I was on call, we couldn't go out. So there was nothing much to do except watch TV and wait for the phone to ring. I was nervous, but nothing came in. Until well after one o'clock.

We'd been sleeping curled up together, but when the phone rang, Sally turned away and put the pillow over her head. It was Frank. There was a sick dog to see. He was at a farrowing, wouldn't be long, but the job sounded urgent – a German shepherd was in agony and the stomach was swollen. In under ten minutes I was at the hospital, where the client and the nurse were waiting. Sabre was desperately ill – I could see that right away. He had eaten his evening meal with no problems and gone to sleep at his normal time, but at about one o'clock the owner, a retired Brigadier, was woken by the sounds of the dog thrashing about and trying to be sick. As I walked in, the nurse on duty, Barbara, told me that the dog was getting worse by the minute. I had never seen the condition before, but Barbara, the senior practice nurse, said it looked to her like gastric tortion. Although I had never come across a case, I knew about it and knew it was beyond my surgical capabilities.

There was nothing for it; I would have to call in the boss. With some trepidation I looked at my watch. Two o'clock. Frank had just got home. But after I explained the situation, he said he was on his way. Not the slightest hint of annoyance. In the meantime, I gave Sabre a pain-killing shot and, together with Barbara, got a drip set up by the time Frank arrived in the operating theatre. Meanwhile, Brigadier Forbes set off home to await the outcome.

Sabre's stomach had swollen up and was as hard as a drum. For some unknown reason it had twisted on itself and then bloated. Barbara monitored the anaesthetic – only a quarter of the usual amount was required to get Sabre unconscious. When Frank and I had scrubbed up, we began. With a few deft cuts, Sabre's stomach was exposed and with a great whoosh the trapped air was let out with a large needle – the type I had been using for milk fever cases. A pungent smell filled the operating theatre. Next, the stomach was opened and the contents removed before we began to untwist it.

All was going to plan – then suddenly the shock was too much, and with a gasp Sabre breathed his last. We made frantic attempts to get him breathing again, but to no avail. So near and yet so far. Wearily we cleaned up and Frank went off to phone the Brigadier to break the sad news while I set off for home, collapsing into bed just before three-thirty. At least I didn't disturb Sally. My introduction to gastric torsion had been decidedly unpleasant and I slept in fits and starts – which was just as well because the phone rang just after six.

Two milk fevers had come in one after the other, at opposite ends of the practice. Murphy's Law. Frank had elected to go out to the nearest first, because he needed to be back for Saturday morning surgery as the small animal expert. My case was down on the marshes, near the coast.

I arrived at Richard Dell's farm just before seven and set off with him to get to the patient. The lovely weather of my first week had gone, and a chill bone-penetrating drizzle started. The wind, straight from the sea, whipped into our faces. It must have been at least a mile to where the cow lay and by the time I got there I was soaked and cold. The change of weather had taken me by surprise. From then on I always kept extra clothing in the back of the car. Right from the moment I arrived, Richard's face had told me that he was not pleased to see me. He had expected one of the partners. He was a 'gentleman farmer' – happy to take the profits and subsidies, but not so happy to get his hands dirty – he employed a farm manager to do that. I learned that both his farm manager and the cowman had 'flu and he was having to do the milking himself – starting at five in the morning. At the end of the session, Elsie, one of his best milkers, hadn't turned up and he had set off with his sheep-dog Bruce to find her. It hadn't taken long. She had gone down in the middle of a field near the railway line, and as we reached her she was obviously in a bad way.

It was a typical milk fever. I was now becoming an expert. She was sitting and every now and then made pathetic attempts to get up on her feet. As each attempt was unsuccessful, she let out a loud bellow and coughed. Her breathing was laboured and I decided to take her temperature.

'For God's sake man, give her the calcium,' was the exasperated comment from Richard as I listened to her chest while waiting for the thermometer to register.

I got the bottle out of the bag, hooked it up to the needle, and we waited as the solution went in. I had expected the same miracle as I'd seen with Tinkerbell at Harry Myers' place, but it didn't happen: no signs of relief, no easing of the breathing – in fact, no positive signs at all. Meanwhile Elsie continued to breathe in that desperate, laboured way that later I was to associate with a dying cow.

'Well,' I said as I packed up the equipment, 'I can't say

I like the look of her.'

Richard Dell was stony-faced.

'If there's no response in six hours,' I went on, 'call me and I'll have another look at her.'

As I uttered those words, Elsie gently keeled over and breathed no more. If looks could kill, I would have joined her: Richard's expression was now one of silent fury and the twenty-minute walk back was probably the most miserable time I can remember. It was in virtual silence and the drizzle had been exchanged for a relentless downpour. As I got into my car, Richard said, 'You can tell Mr Jenkins I'll be expecting compensation, or you'll be hearing from my solicitor.'

Two deaths in a matter of hours. And the day was only just beginning. I drove back with my jaws clenched so hard that when I got home my face hurt. I just had time to have a quick bath before going to morning surgery. Sally was still in bed. I made her a cup of tea but said that I didn't fancy breakfast. I told her I'd probably be back for lunch at about one.

Morning surgery was quiet until Frank, wearing a bright red-and-white polka dot bow tie, broke the spell. There was a difficult lambing, this time on the downland to the south-west of the practice, and I should get down there right away.

The main farmhouse was an old manor house built of pale grey stone that the rain seemed to have washed all colour out of. Only a line of wet washing hanging at the side hinted that this was not a rich man's house, but a working farm. The daffodils that ringed the pond in front of the house were looking totally bedraggled. Yet Manor Farm was going to become a favourite of mine, although I didn't know that just yet.

On some farms, I would find out, everything seemed to

go right, whatever. Looking back, I suppose it was a matter of confidence. If you knew that you were held in high esteem, it seemed to give that extra boost to succeed – though there had been nothing to give me confidence that morning. It was just luck that John Bolton, although from the other end of the economic scale to Rupert Charlton-Jones, was one of those people who didn't believe in taking chances. I soon found out that, particularly with sheep, there was a sense that nature would sort it out, so that many shepherds were inclined to leave the ewes too long before calling you out. Others had a go themselves first, often making life even more difficult when the vet was eventually called out. John Bolton would call as soon as there was a hint of trouble, which made his ewe a good introduction to lambing.

By the time I arrived, John had brought the ewe back from the downs in the back of his tractor and she was now ensconced in a makeshift pen of straw bales that would serve as the maternity ward. It was airy and warm inside the barn – a building that in its way was as lovely as the house, and these days would be sure to have a preservation order slapped on it. Over the last few days I'd suffered more than my fair share of bad farmyard smells, but this morning was different, and my nostrils were filled with the lovely smell of hay.

Even to somebody as inexperienced as me, it was obvious what the problem was. I could feel a head and one leg trying to pass out through the vagina. The other front leg was well and truly back. I pushed my hand in gently to try and retrieve it. This caused the ewe to push like mad, and the weight of the lamb against my hand on the pelvic brim was painful. 'Stop pushing,' might work with humans, but it has no effect at all on a sheep.

But she was already very tired, and after a few minutes

she gave up for a few seconds. I managed to hook the front leg with my forefinger and pull it through alongside the other leg. Then, with a little traction and four or five mighty heaves, the lamb shot out into the world. In a trice the mother was round urgently nibbling and cleaning her new-born with her tongue. She was oblivious to our presence as nature took over. It's surprising how one good thing makes you forget the bad, and I spent a couple of minutes watching as the lamb tottered to its feet and tried to find, very clumsily, its first food. John was obviously pleased with my efforts, doubly so as it was a ewe lamb and would add to the flock. Would I stay for a cup of tea? I certainly would.

The kitchen was even larger than the Myers' with, as far as I could see, no mod cons. At the far end was a range that I imagined had been there for at least a hundred years. It was still working and heated the whole room. Mrs Bolton opened one of the iron doors at the bottom of the range and brought out a tray of scones. Not cooked specially for me, she said, but for the Women's Institute. Out came more homemade WI produce, the best cherry jam I think I have ever had. As we sat around the kitchen table (itself big enough to play billiards on) I felt so comfortable and at home that I decided to own up to having just delivered my first lamb. They were both suitably amazed, although I did admit that it was a textbook case.

Suddenly a large grandfather clock in the corner boomed twice. Two o'clock! I looked at my watch, as if hoping that it would somehow tell a different story. I had told Sally I'd be back around one. That was an hour ago, and it would be a good forty minutes' drive back.

I could smell my lunch even before I walked through the door. Sally's speciality was chilli con carne and I always enjoyed it, but I'd never before eaten it cold. And coming on top of Mrs Bolton's delicious scones . . . Sally's expression reminded me of Richard Dell's earlier in the day.

'If I had known it was going to be like this, I would have brought a book with me,' she said.

'Look, Sal, I had no idea it was going to be like this. If I had I wouldn't have suggested you came.'

Perhaps if she experienced it herself then she would understand just how fascinating it is. I told her about the Boltons' ewe and how miraculous it had felt, helping to bring the lamb into the world. I had just swallowed my last sticky mouthful of congealed rice when, right on cue, the phone rang. A calving. The farm wasn't far. The cow was in a field and had gone down while trying to give birth.

'Why don't you come with me?' I said, hopefully. A sudden clap of thunder heralded the return of the rain with a vengeance.

'No thanks. I'd rather watch television.'

I hovered at the door, trying to think of something to say as she clattered about washing up our few plates.

'See you later, then.' Silence. 'About eight. We'll have a take-away. Chinese.'

Arriving at the farm was like going back in time. The farmhouse was about two miles from the road along an unmade-up track. It could have been used as a set for a film set in the 'Thirties. Bill Miller was a tenant farmer, struggling with a farm that was basically falling down. We set off along another ancient track with banks that towered a good fifteen feet above our heads, until we got to a meadow about a quarter of a mile away. Primrose, a huge Friesian, had been tying to produce a calf for several hours. Bill had tried to get her inside, but she had refused to get up, instead concentrating on huge pushes every few minutes. A nose and one leg had appeared and Bill could see that this was beyond his capabilities.

Primrose was lying on her side, becoming increasingly more tired. The rain pelted down as I made an examination. I could feel the head and one front leg – the other leg was back – just like the ewe earlier in the day. But this was on a different scale altogether. I tried to get at the other leg, but Primrose's immense strength as she pushed made this impossible. The pain was unbelievable as my arm was squashed between the calf's leg and Primrose's pelvis. I would have to stop her straining, not just hope she'd stop. I thought through my lectures on how to give an epidural anaesthetic. Trudging back to the car, I found a syringe, some needles and a bottle of local anaesthetic and slopped through the field again to the cow. Giving my first epidural didn't seem so difficult. I pumped the tail up and down and inserted the needle into the space at the hinge. It went in easily and I gave some local anaesthetic. While waiting for it to take effect, I examined the calf again. It was still alive, as I could feel it pull away when I grabbed hold of its presenting leg. Over the next ten minutes there was no let-up in the pushing, no relaxation which would allow me to hook the leg up. Meanwhile, the rain set in even more and I started to feel cold and intensely miserable.

'Anything I can do?' Bill asked. 'Do you think you should call for some help?'

He had seen it all before. I would not be the first newly qualified assistant that had been defeated by a calving. Calling in Frank had crossed my mind, as he lived just down the road. But the weather was atrocious and I didn't want to admit defeat, and drag the boss out without having a think first.

I knew that if she stopped straining I'd have a chance.

But why hadn't the anaesthetic worked? Suddenly it came to me. Blindingly obvious. Primrose was lying on one side, as cows often do. The anaesthetic wouldn't have spread to the upper part of the spine, which was why she was still pushing. I had also made things difficult for myself by not rolling her to the other side, so that I didn't have to contend with the weight of the calf lying against the leg I was trying to get at. Bill and I together managed to roll her so that she was leaning to the other side and I topped up the anaesthetic. Five minutes later it was delightfully simple. The leg was easy to reach with no straining. I got ropes on both legs, and another one behind the ears. With a few determined pulls on each leg by Bill, and with me gently providing traction on the head, the calf made its entrance into the world.

If only Sally could have been here, I thought. But then I remembered her white boots. Perhaps not. I heard myself sighing out loud. But even that thought couldn't bring me down. Cold, wet, extremely tired, nothing could take away the tremendous satisfaction that bringing a live creature into the world always brings. Primrose, too, was revitalized and struggled to her feet, turning to inspect her calf, licking it with huge sweeps of her tongue. The calf seemed none the worse for the ordeal – two hours of a difficult birth that, with hindsight, should have been sorted out in fifteen minutes or less. Bill picked up the calf and, with Primrose slowly walking behind, we went back to the farm buildings to get the two of them under shelter for the night. I resolved to write down every lambing and calving that I did, so that I could look back on my mistakes and avoid them. This had cost me a couple of hours and I'd be late for dinner.

Nearly an hour later, I arrived back with a Chinese take-away and for the second time in recent history was asked,

'What's that smell?'

I couldn't smell anything myself, but there was no doubt that I had the odour of cow lingering on me. I jumped into the bath while Sally dished up and soon I was feeling better. Sally had found a couple of candles in the cupboard. She was looking lovely and was telling me all about her latest client, a hamburger chain that wanted a new image. But somehow I couldn't take it in. Total exhaustion overcame me and I could feel my eyes going. All I wanted to do was sleep. Or at least go to bed. But whatever amorous intentions I might have had disappeared once my head hit the pillow. I was out like a light. Almost at once the phone rang.

'I don't believe it!' was all Sally said. With a groan I picked up the receiver, praying it wasn't another calving. Fit though I was, I could already feel the aches and pains of muscles unaccustomed to a different type of exercise. It was Frank's wife, Vivien. He had been busy with a succession of small animal emergencies and was on his way home from operating on another gastric torsion. He hadn't had the luxury of eating yet.

Would I mind helping a couple of policemen with an injured cat? They were waiting outside the surgery, having missed Frank by minutes. Wearily I dressed, leaving an already slumbering Sally, and decided to jog round to the hospital through the back alleys – virtually as quick as the car. It would help me to start getting fit for the season ahead, and maybe ease my stiff muscles.

Two enormous young policemen were standing beside their patrol car, a Hillman Imp – Hillman's answer to the Mini, which had become a design classic as soon as it was produced. It was so low and they were so tall that, exhausted as I was, I could see the funny side. They were both young; my age, I would say. They had been passing the hospital and seen a cat bowled over by a passing car. They had stopped and, when they realized it was still alive, although unconscious, they had put it inside the car while they phoned the duty vet for help.

'I think it's gone berserk, sir,' was the first thing that one of them said as I arrived. We shone a torch inside the car and the cat stared back at the light before furiously scratching at the upholstery. It had urinated and defecated on both front seats and maniacally attacked the lining of the doors. I could see a trickle of blood from the mouth, and this was spread liberally around the interior too. I cautiously opened the door, but the cat was ready. With amazing speed it shot through the very small gap that I had made between the door and the floor of the car and rushed out. Within seconds it sped across the car park on all fours – no broken leg evidently – scaled the wall at the end, then suddenly stopped and looked back to see if there was any pursuit. Needless to say, there wasn't. The cat then sat calmly on top of the wall licking his wounds and looking none the worse for his ordeal. The same could not be said for the Hillman Imp. With mounting dismay we inspected the damage and mess. It was quite impressive what a panicking tom cat could do in ten minutes or so. The smell was unbelievable.

'Well, if I see the cat around with its owner, I'll recommend castration!'

'Thanks,' one of the coppers replied. 'We've only just started the shift. We've got to drive around all night in this mess.'

They had my sympathy. But I still had another day and night to go on duty. At least they would sign off in the morning.

## *Chapter Four*

'I should have kept my mouth shut,' said a very tired-sounding Frank about an hour after I got back. 'You'll just have to believe me, David. It isn't usually as bad as this.'

This time Sally had not even woken up when the phone rang.

'I've got a milk fever and there's a hypomag just out of town I want you to do.'

Hypomagnesaemia, to give the disease its full name, occurs when heavily pregnant or milking cows go out to fresh pasture after a winter indoors and don't get enough magnesium in the diet. The effects can be dramatic, with the cow keeling over and convulsing. I had never seen the condition but had read all about it. With the adrenaline rushing again, and all thoughts of tiredness gone, I sped off. This was the biggest emergency I had yet tackled and if I didn't get the injection done in time, the cow would die.

Frank gave me directions and a quick potted summary of the treatment. I would need to get into a vein – any vein, but watch the feet if the cow was convulsing – and give the injection of magnesium slowly. I knew that giving the injection could cause the heart to stop. It was only eight miles or so to the farm and I was there in less than fifteen minutes. As I arrived, I could see the cow down in the field by a farmhouse, intermittently thrashing about and frothing at the mouth. Andrew, the herdsman, came over to the car with an anxious look on his face.

'You'd better be quick,' he said. 'She's gone right downhill in the last five minutes.'

The sight of the huge Friesian cow convulsing and shivering was terrible, and I tried to get into the jugular vein in the neck. This proved to be difficult and dangerous. Every time I tried to get the vein raised, she would shake violently and her great head would bash against me, with a force heavier than a boxer's swinging punchbag. Finally I leaned over her, put a small needle into the milk vein on her belly, hooked up the bottle of magnesium and let the solution run slowly in. Within minutes there was a response. First her breathing became less agitated, then the convulsions lessened and finally she lay relaxed, almost as if in a trance. I let the rest of the bottle empty into her and carefully removed the needle from the vein. Although the milk vein is big and easy to find, there is a danger of causing a big blood blister when you pull the needle out. I had been advised by Frank not to use it, unless all else failed. I stood with my finger on the vein for a couple of minutes and then had to jump out of the way as the cow lumbered shakily to her feet.

The herdsman's relief was enormous. 'Thank God you got here in time. She's our best cow!'

We went back into the farm cottage for a cup of tea and, as it turned out, a spot of breakfast. Andrew's wife, Carole, quickly rustled up some bacon and eggs, which I couldn't resist. In any case, I wasn't in any hurry to rush off, as I wanted to see if the recovery of my first hypomag was genuine. I still had difficulty in believing in my ability to cure sick animals! Although in some ways a curse, this self-doubt is something which has never left me. In other ways it's good, because you remain open to the possibility of always questioning your diagnosis. It is better to rethink earlier rather than later. Blue, as my patient was called, made a rapid recovery and not for the first time, then or subsequently, I marvelled at the extraordinarily rapid recovery that animals are capable of.

There was just time to get back to the flat before reporting to the hospital for my Sunday morning round. The routine was to see half a dozen cases in the morning that had been seen over the last day or so and needed repeat treatments. Theoretically, that would leave time on Sunday afternoon to just put your feet up and relax. That would be my last time over the weekend to spend any time with Sally. It was about nine o'clock when I opened the door into the flat and smelled coffee.

'I thought the least a hard-working vet deserved was breakfast,' she said, as she went over to the oven, opened the door and took out two plates of bacon and fried eggs.

'Oh, I've had some already,' I said – realizing, as the words left my mouth, that this was a mistake. A big mistake. Sally said nothing, but took my plate and scraped everything off into the bin, sat down at the table and ate her own breakfast in silence. I didn't know what to say. Suddenly I began to see things through her eyes, the first time I had done so since I had picked her up at the station. I was so worried about how I was going to cope with my new responsibilities that I hadn't really given a thought to anything else, least of all my girlfriend of nearly four years' standing.

'Look,' she said suddenly, halfway through her plate of bacon and eggs. 'There's no point my staying. I've hardly seen you all weekend and you can't even be bothered to wait so that we can at least have breakfast together!'

She got up, and I heard the clatter of her make-up being swept off the glass shelf in the bathroom.

'Don't worry,' she shouted from the bedroom. 'I know where the station is. You won't have to leave your precious phone.' Then she was gone. I couldn't even go after her. I was on call. I sat down and drank the cup of coffee she had poured me. Two hours out of London had seemed close compared with Leicestershire. But it wasn't really about geographical distances – the life of a vet is simply light years away from the life of a student vet, not to mention an executive in an advertising agency.

The trouble was I was hooked. Although my stress levels were going through the roof, I had to admit I was enjoying it. More than that, I was excited. Finally I was doing what I had been working towards half my life. How could I ever call myself a real vet if I didn't give my all? And that included learning everything there was to learn about farm practice.

For the first time, but not for the last, I realized that my newly acquired profession was going to take precedence. Over everything. Sally and I would have to talk. Perhaps I could phone her tonight when she had calmed down a bit. It wasn't as if I was on duty every weekend. I would just have to make sure that when she came down I was free, completely free to show her why I love my home county. Unfortunately, it would be three weeks before I had a complete weekend off and any possibility of mending fences would have to wait until then.

After a quick bath, I set off again for the hospital. There was a good three hours' work listed for me – mostly follow-up examinations and treatments. The sun was up and I left Frank to a busy emergency small animal session. I wondered what had made him specialize in small animals when he had achieved quite a lot of fame in his time as a cattle and sheep vet. Surely he must be envying me as I set out to enjoy a leisurely drive to the north coast to repeat some injections on some sick piglets.

These were so much better than the older ones I had vaccinated – it already seemed ages ago. The pigman simply picked them up and I jabbed each one with antibiotic. They were recovering from a severe bout of enteritis. Charles had taken a swab to isolate the bug and decide which antibiotic to use. Now, a few days later, they were on their third jab and looking as if they were going to make it, all thirty of them. There was quite a lot of money invested in those piglets and I suddenly thought of the responsibility I was taking on by becoming a farm vet, quite a different emotional load from dealing with people's pets.

I drove round the coast road – soon to be full of tourists, but in April virtually empty – and then turned into a side road which would take me across country to one of the biggest farms on the practice's books.

Jim Shearer farmed getting on for 400 cows and there was never a week when something wasn't needing treatment. This was my introduction to the farm. Today it would be just a couple of repeat injections for two cows with mastitis and from there to the outskirts of town to see a cow with a retained placenta. Nothing difficult, but nearly eighty miles' driving by the time I got home.

Tiredness and sadness in equal quantities hit me as I set foot in my empty flat. No lunch, no girlfriend – just a lingering smell of bacon. I slumped in the armchair and immediately dozed off, but within a few minutes there was a knock on the door and Keith appeared. Behind him were Angie and Julia.

'Fancy coming out for lunch? It's on me – I've been given a rise!' Keith had on an even more flamboyant shirt than usual, with a collar so high it looked as if it might strangle him. Somehow it put things in proportion and my spirits rose. I looked up the phone number of the pub and rang Frank to see if it would be all right to be on call from there. No problem.

'We'll have to go in two cars – I'm on call,' I said. With a giggle, the two girls said they would be going with Keith. Half an hour later I was tucking into a steak and ale pie while recounting the disaster the weekend had been so far. While the two girls went to the loo, Keith said, 'I think you're in with Angie.' A wave of misery engulfed me as suddenly as my spirits had lifted earlier.

'I don't know. It's a bit near to home, isn't it? Anyway, I'm hoping I can make it up with Sally. We're supposed to be going on holiday to Majorca in a couple of months.'

Keith sounded a bit pensive. I was pretty sure he had his eye on Julia and hoped the four of us could go out a few times while he got to know her better. I sipped my lemonade and lime and watched the girls come back all smiles. Apparently there was a party on at the house all afternoon and into the evening. Could we come? There would be at least twenty students, most of them girls. We stayed at the pub until closing time, two o'clock in those days. I kept checking with the barmaid, but there were no calls. As we left, I phoned in to the practice to say I was going back to the flat but that I would be at the Nightingales' telephone number.

'Good to see you're getting the hang of all this,' Frank said.

I should have enjoyed it, but I didn't. I just couldn't help reflecting on the irony of the weekend – when Sally was with me, I was never there. Now here I was with nothing to do, but no Sally. For an hour or so I watched the rugby on television, but by five o'clock the house was thumping with music, Manfred Mann, The Rolling Stones, so I put on a clean shirt and went to the party. I couldn't remember when I had last been anywhere where the women outnumbered the men like this.

In my years at college, there had been only six women out of about seventy students. Now it's quite different, and women represent seventy-five per cent of today's veterinary students. People wonder how women can cope with large animals, but they do, very well. The only problem is with reach. To get a purchase on a calf in its mother's womb, your arm sometimes goes in right up to the shoulder. But it's a problem men face, too. It's rarely a question of brute strength.

All those girls should have made me forget my troubles for an hour or two, but I couldn't help thinking of Sally. She'd never complained all those times I'd gone off to Leicestershire, and I'd never met a girl who not only shared my love of athletics, but enjoyed watching 'Match of the Day'. I couldn't blame her for walking out, not when I thought of what I'd put her through. I tried to look cheerful, but I didn't feel it. And it didn't help, of course, having to nurse a glass of lemonade while everyone else was making merry with beer and plonk. Fortunately, the festivities came to an end fairly early. The girls all started college the next day and had an early start. I went to bed and was asleep before my head hit the pillow.

On Monday morning at nine o'clock I reported for duty. Frank, who had worked even harder than me over the weekend, had been in since half past eight. He looked as relaxed as if he had spent a weekend at a health farm, although I noticed his bow tie – a startling shade of pink – was looking a little lopsided. I found it hard to believe that he could put so many hours in – the concept of the responsibilities of a boss had yet to percolate through to my juvenile mind.

'You up to castrating Ken Griffin's calves?' had been his rhetorical question as soon as I walked through the door. I had seen them on the list and had secretly prayed that I wouldn't get to do it. That was a prayer that I was frequently to make over the next few months, almost invariably to go unanswered.

Charles was out doing a tuberculin test already, Alan was down to do a load of pregnancy diagnoses on one of the big farms and the small animal vets had a huge list to get through. The trouble was I hadn't done many calf castrations. In fact I'd only done one, under Brian's supervision in Leicestershire about three years earlier. Once again I set out with a flush of adrenaline in my veins.

Ken Griffin was waiting for me. The calves were to be reared as bullocks and would be fattened up for the market by the time they were two years old. It was routine practice to castrate them at three months. Routine for everyone except me. It took three hours of fumbling, dropping the instruments and generally sweating over what would later be a simple, slick procedure. First I had to inject local anaesthetic and then do the operation. If Ken had any thoughts on my ineptitude he wasn't letting on. He kept up a patter of the local gossip, low prices of calves, and how rich vets were. It didn't feel right – I was sure things were going to go wrong as I packed up to go.

Ken's offer of a cup of tea had to be refused as I was due to have lunch with the partners. I had caught a glance of various entries in the day book with my name on them. With such a big practice, communications were all-important. The method in vogue was to write down important matters in the day book so that they could be addressed on a daily basis. But to me it looked like a meaningless code. 'DG to see FA' or 'AJ', followed by a list of more initials which meant nothing. I was shortly to find out what the list meant – the honeymoon was definitely over. It was time to lick me into shape.

Lunch was social and gossipy – talk of farmers whose names would become familiar to me but who at that stage meant nothing. Then up to the library and The Chat. Frank looked at the list. He was a stickler for detail. He had been through my small animal cases and noted all the incorrect drug doses that I had made – mostly silly things like too much vitamin B12 for a poodle ('That was a German shepherd dose, David'). But as I was always to find out later, he was a very fair man, never letting anything go but always correcting me in a kindly, direct way. He was quite pleased with the way the weekend duty had gone. Then it was Alan's turn.

'Do you remember seeing some calves at Jed Dickens's place?'

My blood ran cold. I remembered Jed Dickens right enough – who wouldn't? As miserable as sin. But calves? Then suddenly it came back.

'I saw them, but I didn't examine them. He asked me what I thought of them – four I think, just as I was leaving.'

'And what did you say?'

'Well, they seemed as fit as fiddles. Why, what's happened?'

'Two of them have died of the scours.'

'I'm sorry – I didn't think he meant me to examine them.'

A wave of nausea suddenly came over me. Alan's usual twinkle had been replaced by a seriousness I had never seen before. 'Fortunately, the other two are responding to treatment.'

I already knew that scours was the name that farmers used for diarrhoea, but some differences in language were less easy to fathom.

Alan explained that for some farmers, especially cussed ones like Jed Dickens, 'What do you think?' meant 'What's wrong with them?' He didn't want to see me on the farm again.

Nor did Richard Dell, although Alan had better news on this one. He had done a post-mortem at the abattoir. The cow had aspirated a lot of stomach contents into the lungs, something which could happen with a bad case of milk fever when they were really down. No wonder she hadn't responded to the calcium injection.

'I told him she would have died whatever we had tried to do for her. He seems to have calmed down. But he says you should have told him she was likely to die.'

Easy to say, but the diagnosis of imminent death itself is never easy – as I was to find quite often in the future.

Alan then broke into a grin.

'Still, it's not all bad news,' he said, producing a teat siphon.

'Where did you get that?' I couldn't have been more surprised if he had held up a diamond ring.

'Joe Anstey found it in his heifer's feed bowl. He was a bit puzzled as to how it got there.'

The heifer must have shaken it out finally. 'How is she?' I asked, fearing the worst.

'She's made a full recovery, and Joe's keen to meet you. According to Eddie, you really know how to handle frisky heifers. And apparently she got better almost immediately!'

I heaved a sigh of relief. With that, Frank produced a stethoscope, as if it were a rabbit produced by a conjuror.

'You left it at Harry Myers's place!' And then, for a

follow-up trick, he held up three calving ropes, all washed and neatly rolled up.

'And these at Rupert Charlton-Jones's.'

I felt that I'd survived the inquisition. But the telling-off had been fair and reasonable and without rancour. It had the effect of making me more and more determined to master this large animal practice game and to try to be less absent-minded. The trouble was, it seemed to be a Grant family trait and came out in me especially at times of stress. I had an adrenaline rush on an almost daily basis at present. However, I was finding that that was usually a good thing because it tended to bring out the best in me. There seemed to be no possibility of a more relaxing time. It was a busy time of year, and everything was so new.

Next morning proved the point. When I arrived at the hospital, Alan was on the phone, another daffodil in his buttonhole. He put his hand over the mouthpiece. 'Could you get on over to Wally Watson's place? There are some cows to de-horn.'

I had woken up with a slight feeling of dread, and now I remembered why.

'I know,' I muttered. 'Forty of them.' I had seen the entry in the job book and had just prayed it wouldn't be mine. But I should have known. De-horning was another boy's job.

He motioned to me to get a cup of coffee for both of us, then when I came back he went through the various ways that I could do the job.

'Take some embryotomy wire, shears, saws and lots of bailer twine. I take it you're au fait with the local anaesthetic techniques?'

I nodded. It was simple enough and I had done lots of it in Leicestershire. With the cow restrained in a pen, you had to feel for a ridge in the skull and then inject the local into the cornual nerve, which was the one that supplied the horns. My heart had sunk at the thought of the sheer physical effort. My body still hadn't recovered from the weekend's calvings. There were few more demanding jobs I could do. Alan knew what I was thinking.

'Well, you're in training – this will be good for the heart and upper body strength!' And as he passed he gave me a playful punch – though no punch when you're not expecting it, particularly from a former rugby player packing about fourteen stone, can be called playful. 'Anyway, you've got some help. There's a third-year student come to see practice with us and he looks pretty fit too. Called Bob. And if you finish in good time, there's a nice pub, the William the Fourth, or King Billy as the locals call it, in the next village. They do a nice spot of lunch.'

It turned out Bob was from Kent too, and the captain of his college rugby team.

'Ever done any de-horning?' I asked him as soon as we'd introduced ourselves. 'No,' he replied. 'This will be my first time.'

I was just about to say, 'Me too', then thought better of it.

Wally Watson, whose farm it was, was nowhere to be seen, but he had arranged for three tough farm workers to assist with the job and they had already set up two stocks to restrain the cows. All the men were in their thirties, stocky and red-faced from being out in all weathers. We soon had a system going: I did the anaesthetic on the two cows in the stocks, waited a few minutes for it to take effect, then Bob would tie bailer twine round the base of the horns and the really hard work could begin. We took turns, as it was very tiring work. It quickly turned into a macho competition to see who could stand the pace better. We had decided to use the embryotomy wire. Using special handles, you simply had to put the wire round the horns and saw away. The effect was like cutting cheese, except that the wire against the horn created heat and the whole horn would smoke. But the heat generated also had the advantage of sealing off any small blood vessels. The whole thing took only a few minutes. By Bob and me taking it in turns, I reckoned to get ten minutes' rest between cows. Alan was right: it was very good training – but I would have hated to have to do it on my own. A few hours passed and, before we realized it, the last few cows were being brought up. I let Bob do the last few anaesthetics and we were just finishing when Wally himself arrived.

'Well, I'm impressed,' he said. 'You've done well. I wasn't expecting you to be done this soon.'

This was too much for Robbo, one of the stockmen.

'That one's a sprinter and that one's captain of a rugby team, that's why, Guv.'

I looked at Bob. He was red-faced and sweating, and I suspected I looked much the same. Frankly, neither of us looked as if we were capable of running for a bus. Although I reckoned I had lasted the pace better, my heart was beating at somewhere near 160 a minute and my arms and shoulders ached. And I suddenly remembered it was only six weeks to the county athletics championships and I hadn't done any serious training yet. Still, all in all, my heart and lungs were in good shape.

'Drinks on you,' I said, as we put the equipment back into the Anglia.

'You're on,' laughed Bob, wiping his dripping brow, and we left the three stockmen and their boss clearing up. For him it would be a profitable morning's work, because there was a bit of fighting going on amongst the cows and an absence of horns would calm things down considerably and increase milk yields.

Bob and I headed off to the pub, both happy with a job well done.

'I'll let you into a secret. That was my first batch of de-horning!'

Bob laughed. 'I wondered why you got so much better at it as you went on!'

It was true though – it was surprising how quickly the skills came when you had to do the same procedure forty times.

The local brew was Shepherd Neame's, which went down a treat with shepherd's pie. Sitting down in a delightful country pub with a good pint of beer and hot food after so much physical exercise was marvellous. It was nearly as good as winning the 100 metres. An hour passed by agreeably and Bob and I chatted about the college – we were near enough in age to have several friends in common. I was tempted to have that second pint, but sensibly declined Bob's offer, perhaps because the phone was ringing and, in that telepathic way that vets develop, I felt sure it would be for me.

Alan had guessed correctly that I would take his advice on lunch.

'How's it going?' he asked, and was surprised when I told him we were finished – although with a bit of poetic licence I said we'd not long arrived.

'Perfect, that's worked out fine. There's a ewe with garget just down the road.'

'Garget? Not sure I'm familiar with – er – garget.' My mind flashed through the indexes of all the books I had ever read, or was supposed to have read.

Alan laughed. 'It's the local farmers' term for mastitis in sheep, and I know you're familiar with that. There's red garget when it's acute and blue garget when it turns gangrenous. Fortunately, it sounds like a straightforward case. The ewe's been suckling a big lamb and is suddenly refusing to feed her lamb and is off her food. Finish off your lunch and I'll phone Tom Hoskins and say you'll be there in half an hour.

And with that he was gone, without offering to give his opinion on how to treat the case. He probably reckoned that with a third-year student in the team, between us we would come up with a satisfactory treatment.

When I got back to the table, I decided to use the professor technique and asked Bob what he could tell me about mastitis in the ewe.

'Well,' he began, 'quite a lot. But as we've only got half an hour . . .' and with that he rummaged about in his rucksack and produced *Merck's Veterinary Manual*. Reading aloud, he went through the basics of ovine mastitis in ten minutes and we left the pub brimming with enthusiasm and confidence.

Tom Hoskins was matter of fact about his ewe. 'She's got garget and I reckon if you don't give her the needle she'll be dead in a day.'

Like many farmers I was to meet, he was a great believer in 'the needle', and also 'Dr Green' – the benefits of turning animals out to grass in the fresh air.

There was no doubt about his diagnosis. The ewe was listless and easily caught. I took her temperature – 107 degrees Fahrenheit. No wonder she looked so seedy! Four degrees above normal. One of her udders was hot and painful and the milk was watery and unhealthy looking. Bob had already drawn up a syringe full of the recommended antibiotic and I proceeded to inject it into the vein.

'With a bit of luck we're in time,' I told Tom. 'We'll know in a day or so. I'll leave you a couple of doses to give her over the next day or two.' And with that we moved to set off. Tom motioned to the barn.

'Before you go, take a look at another one while you're here.'

I was shocked by what I saw. A ewe had been trying to give birth all morning and was now lying down exhausted.

'I've had a go myself. She's past helping, I reckon. I was going to send her to the knackers.'

All you could see was the lamb's head protruding from the ewe's rear end. Every now and then she would give a half-hearted heave to try and rid herself of her lamb – a lamb which was obviously dead. I dared not ask how long this had been going on. Bob and I exchanged glances but said nothing. With a well scrubbed and lubricated hand, I made an internal examination. The front legs were well back and hadn't passed over the rim of the pelvis. Even the weak pushes of the mother were very painful, as my hand was trapped between the lamb and the pelvis. That was obviously the problem – not enough room with all the pushing and not enough lubrication. Bob had read my mind and passed me some soap flakes, and with lots of warm water I tried again. It was no good – the lamb was simply too big and had dried out.

I then had an idea – or maybe I dredged it up from one of my textbooks. Why not rotate the lamb upside down? Then I could push down on its stomach to make room for the legs to be pulled through the birth canal. A few minutes later it worked like a dream. Both legs came through and with a couple of gentle tugs the dead lamb came into the world. Its mother tried gamely to stand, but failed. She still managed to move round and began to lick her lamb. A quick examination to see if there was another one in there – but no. The old farmer showed no signs of being pleased by my efforts – I might have saved the life of the ewe, but he had lost a lamb. He just busied himself making a rough stockade of straw bales where the ewe could spend the night in reasonable shelter. I gave her a jab of penicillin and left a couple of doses to be given over the next few days.

As we left, I could see the ewe trying to get to her feet and find her lamb. It seemed a very cruel world.

'The problem is,' Bob said as we were driving along, 'sheep are not worth that much. And hard-headed farmers like Tom Hoskins don't like to call the vet in for a lambing unless they reckon there's a good chance of a live lamb.'

Bob had already done a season of lambing as a student, although he hadn't experienced anything quite as bad as what we had just seen. We continued the journey back to the hospital in silence.

'Fancy a beer tonight?' I asked. 'I live in a house with ten students – all women!'

If I'd told him he'd won £1000 on a premium bond he couldn't have been more delighted.

'You're on!'

## *Chapter Five*

It turned out to be quite a night. Phil, Mrs Nightingale's pilot son, had turned up looking very suntanned – he had been in Australia on a three-week trip. Keith and I turned up with Bob. After the introductions, Phil introduced Chantal, a Swiss girl studying English at a language school in the town, who would be staying at the house for three months. It looked as though they were already an item. To say she was beautiful was a complete understatement.

Bob couldn't take his eyes off her. She was from Zurich, she told us in the sing-song accent, so typical of her mother tongue – German. Her English was already very good and she could speak French and Italian too. Up until then I hadn't met anyone from Switzerland, and my preconceptions of the Swiss as being quiet and reserved were soon dispelled. She had a suntan to match Phil's – ruefully I had to admit they looked like a film star couple – and long dark hair down to her waist, with a figure to match.

She caught me looking at her and flashed a cheeky smile, then looked adoringly at Phil, who was talking about the joys of flying VC 10s to Australia. I wasn't even going to compete.

Anyway, I still had a girlfriend. With a sudden pang of anguish I realized that maybe I didn't – the situation still hadn't been resolved. Since the disastrous weekend, I hadn't phoned and had been swept along by the calvings and lambings and all the other exciting things which kept me from thinking.

Angie slipped her hand in mine. It felt warm and comforting rather than romantic.

'Want another drink?'

'Why not? But it's on me – I'm about to be paid.'

I'd phone Sally tomorrow morning before work. I had the weekend off – perhaps I could spend it in London.

Meanwhile, Phil had gone to the loo and Bob was busy chatting to Chantal about skiing – it turned out that she was expert at that too. Being Swiss, she had practically been born on skis. In the time it took Phil to go to the loo and back, Bob had made a date.

'When's your next trip, Phil?' I asked casually.

'The States next Monday, then to South Africa for a week.'

I grinned at Bob behind Phil's back. Bob wasn't due back at college for another two weeks. He would have his chance. But not yet. Phil left with Chantal soon after and, as they climbed into his latest model TR4, all shiny red paintwork and sparkling chrome, Bob was looking decidedly glum.

'Never mind, me old mate,' I told him, leaning in to make sure he heard me above the vroom-vroom of the engine, 'in just a couple of years you'll have a clapped-out Anglia and loads of free time like me!'

Meanwhile it seemed to be accepted that Angie was with me, and I didn't exactly fight against it. As the evening wore on, it seemed more and more an attractive proposition. Keith, meanwhile, was making headway with Yvonne – who everyone called Von. Julia had rejected his advances in favour of her long-term on-off boyfriend from Newcastle. Bob was obviously love struck, and couldn't get off the subject of the Swiss glamourpuss.

I was half drunk when I rang Sally at eleven-thirty. An annoyed voice told me that there was no point in talking about it as she was seeing someone else. She needed space.

A trial separation.

The words hit me like a body blow. 'Trial' really meant 'final', and I knew it. I could hardly blame her – I had thought of nothing but work for months and she couldn't see how she could be happy with me so wrapped up in the country way of life. I crashed out hearing the sounds of a distant party in my ears, like the roar of the waves in a seashell when you're a kid. I ignored a knock at the door and slept fitfully.

The next day I didn't have time to feel sorry for myself. I was out on the road soon after arriving for morning surgery. I was to go to the only convent on the practice books – way out in the wilds near to the north coast.

'You'll find it interesting!' Alan said. 'And if they like you, you'll get a bottle of home-made wine. Mind you, it's completely undrinkable, but, as I am sure your mother told you, David, it's the thought that counts.'

I already knew Alan was a bon viveur. I, on the other hand, just about knew the difference between red and white, dry and sweet. My area of expertise was beer. Alan was the sort of person who talked about vintages. He even had a cellar – and I don't mean somewhere he kept the coal.

It took about an hour to get to the convent, which consisted of a huge building, very old, which when you looked at it closely had been added to and added to over the years, a beautiful chapel to one side and a small self-sufficient farm which you reached round the back. As the massive wooden doors swung open, I was ushered in by a nun who introduced herself as Sister Maria Assumpta. She had a sweet round face that could have been anything from forty to seventy. She wore a large grey cloak with a hood. Round the waist was a white belt made out of cloth. Walking into the farmyard was like walking back 500 years. We were knee deep in straw, and a few Jersey cows meandered contentedly about chewing the cud. The buildings could hardly have changed in centuries – the only modern thing was electricity in the barns. Here and there I could see nuns, all in cloaks, quietly going about their business. I immediately caught the atmosphere of peace and tranquillity. This was a place I felt drawn to, and I knew at once that I'd be first in the queue whenever they needed a vet.

'Sister Teresa will help you,' my guide said, introducing me to another nun. 'She looks after the calves. One of them is having difficulty with breathing.'

We walked into a barn where four of five calves were being kept in neat pens. Sister Teresa had a soft gentle voice and explained how one of the calves had been ill for a few days – first with scours and then with a fever.

I looked at the calf. She was about two months old and was breathing rapidly, with the anxious look that all very sick animals seem to have. I took her temperature – 105 degrees – a fever sure enough, and little doubt as to what the problem was. I listened to the lungs. Each breath made a harsh sawing sound. She had pneumonia.

'Are the others all right?' was my first question. If it was viral pneumonia it could spread to the rest of the calves.

'They seem to be,' said Sister Teresa, letting her hood drop and showing her worried face. With a start I realized that she was about my age, and beautiful. I stared without thinking and she blushed.

'I'm sorry,' I said. 'It's just that I had this idea that nuns couldn't be young.' I found myself blushing too and a sadness engulfed me.

'How long have you been here?' I asked

'Nearly two years – after I got the call.' She went on to explain in the softest of southern Irish accents that she had led a normal life until the strong vocation had come to her almost as a flash of light. I wanted to know more and to talk about her life before she arrived at the convent. I couldn't stop looking at her and realized that I was being stupid.

'We'll have our work cut out to save your calf,' I said, tearing myself back to business. 'I'll go back to the car and get some antibiotic and syringes. Can you inject the calf yourself?'

The answer was 'probably', if I would show her.

We walked in silence across the medieval yard to where the Anglia waited. Alan had told me that the most effective antibiotic in these cases was chloramphenicol – a drug that I had thought was more or less reserved for serious human infections. But I was to find it very much in vogue in farm practice, particularly in situations like this. I found myself chatting to this young nun – who turned out to be a marvellous listener. After I had injected the calf and shown her how to do it, I told her about my vocation, which was to learn my profession and see as much as I could, and how that was interfering with relationships because all I could think about was the next day's cases and how I might cope. I wondered about her life before becoming a nun, but didn't dare to ask. I assumed she must have had boyfriends – had she suffered as I was suffering now? As I left, I said I would like to see the calf in five days and asked if they had any routine work which could coincide with the visit. This would make it more economical.

Sister Teresa thought for a moment. 'Well, there are some calves that need debudding,' she said.

This was a simple procedure which removed the horn

buds at a young age so that the horns didn't grow. It was far less traumatic than what Bob and I had been through a few days before.

'Well, I'll see you then,' I said. With a lovely dimpled smile, Sister Teresa said goodbye, adding that she would pray for me.

I staggered out into the real world, surprised by my reaction and feeling rather stupid. In the first village I came to, I had to slow down and wait while a troop of large white ducks waddled slowly across the road to the village pond. Not a care in the world, I mused. They weren't even concerned about the traffic. Although in this out-of-the-way place traffic was not a major part of anybody's life, duck or human. Watching their progress, I spotted a red telephone box in the shade of a huge horse-chestnut that was already heavy with its white candelabra. I decided to phone in.

Frank answered. 'David, thank goodness you rang. There's an urgent lambing at Jonathan Rowe's place. It's on the way back – about twenty minutes away. A lamb is stuck by its head. It sounds as if the legs are back.' He went on without stopping. 'Get plenty of soap flakes and warm water and see if you can turn the lamb upside down. You'll find it easier to get the legs up.'

Just the conclusion I had reached with that poor dead lamb yesterday.

'If you can't manage it in fifteen minutes, get Jonathan to bring the ewe in. Alan or I will do a caesarean.'

He gave brief instructions on how to find the farm and with that he was gone, back to the hectic world of a small animal hospital – a million miles away from where I was standing, leaving me no time to describe my heroics of yesterday and feeling slightly disappointed that I wasn't the first to think of that particular way of dealing with a difficult lambing.

I arrived at the farm in exactly twenty minutes – years of experience in Frank's case extended into precise estimates of journey times between farms. Jonathan Rowe was pleased to see me. He and his wife Eve were of a new breed of farmers, the beginning, I suppose, of the green generation that we now take for granted. He had been working for one of the big biscuit companies in marketing, and had just chucked everything up. A bit like that old TV series *The Good Life*, with Richard Briers and Felicity Kendal, but bigger. His attitude couldn't have contrasted more markedly from the one I encountered yesterday. There was the ewe with a lamb's head protruding, and still alive! With the confidence born of one previous case and a two-minute seminar from Frank, I asked for some soap flakes and warm water. Jonathan had tried to deliver the lamb himself, but quickly gave up and decided to 'call in the experts'. I smiled ruefully to myself. But at this rate I would soon have dozens of lambings under my belt. The lamb was breathing and every now and then blinked in the unaccustomed light. With plenty of lubrication, I turned her upside down and a few minutes later pulled the legs through. The lamb seemed quite small and came out easily. I searched inside.

'There's another one!' The lamb's twin followed a minute later. Both were ewe lambs, much to Jonathan's delight – he was building up a flock.

I turned to the firstborn who was weakly and not trying to stand. 'We'd better take her inside,' I said, 'and give her some attention.' The mother was meanwhile licking the second lamb, who was already struggling to her feet.

Inside the farmhouse, Eve gathered up some towels in front of the Aga in the kitchen. I was introduced as 'Mr

Grant, who has just performed a miracle!' We set to rubbing the lamb down to stimulate the breathing and Jonathan gave it a few drops of brandy. He had spent childhood holidays with an uncle on a hill farm in Wales and his uncle had always sworn by it for sickly lambs. Jonathan had a wealth of country lore that he loved to talk about and which I found fascinating.

'Well, it's in the lap of the gods now,' I said. 'Only time will tell if she'll make it. I'll pop in when I'm passing, if I may, to see how things went.'

While Eve continued to fuss round the lamb, Jonathan and I had coffee and I felt the glow that difficult births always seemed to give when the outcome was successful. Outside, the mother was already giving milk to the other lamb.

'Try and get her to accept her lamb as soon as possible,' I said. 'The lamb will need the first milk because she'll get protection against disease from her mother.' Jonathan nodded his agreement.

'I'll smear this one with the afterbirth when she's a bit stronger,' he said. This was an old trick to persuade the ewe to accept the lamb. Bonding occurs immediately after birth and might not occur at all if the mother doesn't smell the natural odours of birth.

'I'll be on my way then. Thanks for the coffee.'

'Thank *you*!' they both said in unison. I had made two new friends and grateful clients. I drove down the straight Roman road which led from this part of the county into town on a high – more resolved than ever to stay here and get as much experience under my belt as I could. All other aspects of my life would have to be put on a hold. The pain of separation somehow felt more bearable.

I checked in just before one in the afternoon. The

practice was quiet – in fact no one was about. All the vets had disappeared for lunch, so I decided to go back home. It was a warm spring day. A crab apple tree in the garden was laden down with blossom and Mrs Nightingale's tulips were making what she called 'a good show'. There was a terraced area just below my window, with a wooden bench where I could stretch out and, as long as I left my window open, I could hear the phone ring. It was the first time since I had arrived that it had been warm enough to sit outside. Just to feel the heat of the sun on my face was wonderful. I closed my eyes and listened to the buzz of bees and the miraculous songs of the garden blackbirds. This was the life. The afternoon list hadn't seemed too bad. There was the almost inevitable list of 'DG see FA' re a whole host of things, although two on the list had slightly worried me:

'DG see FA re Jenny Kellaway' and 'DG see AJ re Ken Griffin'.

I was puzzling over these names when Julia wandered out and asked if I'd like a cup of coffee. It was just an excuse really, because I could see that she wanted to talk. Soon, out it all came.

It was the usual story, commitment – or rather lack of it. She and a fellow student teacher, Neil, had been going out for the whole of their time in college and Julia wanted to make it permanent – get engaged. Neil, it had turned out, wasn't so keen. As I looked at the vision of loveliness before me, I thought he must be mad. She had the kind of skin that is called milky, not a blemish on it. The only make-up she wore was on her eyes, and there wasn't much of that left – just a sultry smokiness where her mascara had run. She had obviously been crying. Her hair was a rich dark brown, thick and lustrous, and in the spring sunlight glowed like burnished copper. Unusually for someone with her colouring, she had pale blue eyes.

I nodded and looked as sympathetic as I could. But the devil in me was already planning how to capitalize on her vulnerable state. Unfortunately, I said, I had to go back to work, but how about a drink tonight? I explained that over the last few weeks I had got to know some lovely out-of-the-way country pubs. Julia agreed and my spirits lifted. All too soon it was time to go back and face the music – whatever that was.

Alan was first off. Ken Griffin's calves had gone down with wound infections after I had castrated them – due to my having dropped the instruments and not resterilizing them. In the patient way I was already becoming familiar with, he gave me a brief seminar on the subject and a few practical tips on how to do the job better. It all made sense. In fact only about half the calves had infections: my technique had clearly improved as I went on. You had to be ready for the occasional kick if there was any residual feeling – rather like the dentist. It was better to give the anaesthetic in batches of five and then wait, rather than trying to rush the job. A case of that old English adage; more haste, less speed. Anyway, I was to go back to the farm that afternoon and drain any abscesses and supply antibiotics.

'Now,' said Frank, peering over the top of his glasses which, as usual, had slipped down and had practically fallen off the bridge of his nose. 'Jenny Kellaway. Remember her?' I looked blank. 'Yorkshire terrier with dandruff,' he went on. Although the name rang no bells, dandruff did, and after looking at my scrawled notes I dimly remembered. Yes, a pretty woman, red-haired, in her early forties and something about her using her own shampoo and my saying it would be all right.

'Well, I've just had her GP on the phone.' His eyebrows did the little jiggle they always did when he was about to pull a veterinary rabbit out of the hat. A not inappropriate description as it turned out. 'It seems the whole family has gone down with a rash, and he reckons it's Cheyletiella.'

'Cheyletiella?' In repeating the word, I switched on some circuit in my brain and, in that amazing way we humans have of digging out information that you don't even know you know, I heard myself saying, 'But that's a rabbit parasite, isn't it?'

'Correct,' said Frank. 'But also seen in dogs and cats. They have their own species.' The glasses were now in his hand, and I knew I was in for one of his impromptu seminars.

It turned out Frank had recently given a talk to the local GP clinical group on skin diseases you could pick up from your pets. Cheyletiella, a tiny mite just visible to the eye but normally only diagnosed with the aid of a microscope, had recently been recognized as an important cause of rashes in people who owned pets – particularly if the pet had dandruff. This was usually the only sign in the pet – something which most owners (and, as I now knew, some vets!) failed to take seriously.

'I've arranged for her to bring in the dog this afternoon. Should be here now – you'd better have a look with me to see if the GP is right.'

With that, he put his white coat on and dashed downstairs. Although he must have been the wrong side of forty (which in those days made him seem practically a pensioner to me), he was not unlike a puppy, always bounding with energy. He did everything at breakneck speed. I followed somewhat sheepishly in his footsteps, catching sight of an anxious Jenny Kellaway in the waiting room. Although it's impossible to diagnose everything correctly first time, you always feel a bit of a failure when you miss something. But to see the results of your failures – a whole family consulting their doctor – was truly humbling. I said nothing as Frank swung into action.

The striking thing was the copious dandruff that fell off the dog. Within seconds the table was covered in it. Frank moved the lamp over the dandruff and produced a small magnifying glass. 'There they are!' he exclaimed, and passed me the magnifying glass. I looked and at first could see nothing. Then, eerily, I could see that many of the apparent flakes of dandruff were alive and moving about.

'As you see, David, walking dandruff!' Frank then passed the magnifying glass to Jenny and while she was Oh-ing and Well-I-Never-ing, he got a small reel of Scotch tape and stuck it on the back of the wriggling dog. As soon as he had done this he transferred the tape to a microscope slide and peered down the microscope.

'Ha! What did I tell you? Cheyletiella!'

There, like something from a science fiction fantasy film, were these spider-like mites whose vicious little claws had been responsible for the rash that had afflicted the whole of the Kellaway family. As if she had read my thoughts, Jenny lifted up her blouse at the side and theory became reality as a blotchy, terribly inflamed rash revealed itself. I was horrified and looked up at her, expecting a diatribe based on my ignorance and incompetence.

But she was all smiles, and appeared nearly as excited as Frank, who called in Barbara to have a look too. Pretty soon everyone in the building had looked at this amazing sight of minute white mites shuffling aimlessly across the table.

'Thank goodness we got to the bottom of it!' Frank, by

now smiling and looking extremely pleased, went on to reassure her that she could expect to have got rid of the problem within a week or so once we had cured the dog – and that would be a simple matter of three weekly baths in a medicated shampoo which we also used for Sarcoptic mange.

'A very unusual case, David. And only just described in the literature. Hardly surprising you didn't pick it up straight away.'

Jenny smiled at me. 'There, you see, don't look so worried. It wasn't your fault.'

I could have kissed her – so generous of spirit considering that she had been to the GP several times before he had made the diagnosis – having eventually enquired whether there had been any dandruffy animals at home.

'My doctor told me that you gave a talk on this a few weeks ago, otherwise he wouldn't have thought of it,' said Jenny.

Frank smiled, took off his glasses and polished them on the pocket handkerchief that was always in the top breast pocket of his suit.

'Yes – a real bit of luck!'

And so what could have been a public relations disaster ended with a happy owner and pet, and a young vet who would never make that mistake again.

At Ken Griffin's farm later that afternoon, things weren't as bad as I had expected. About half the calves had varying degrees of infection where they had been operated on and one or two had abscesses which needed lancing.

Ken didn't seem too worried and, once they had been injected with penicillin, I felt relieved that it was nothing more serious. Ken was certainly a very easy-going farmer and we would be friends from then on. I was learning to be grateful for those clients who showed a bit of tolerance to my lack of experience. They didn't know it, but later, as the experience came, and I was to find it to be a very fast and steep learning curve, I would really put myself out for them.

Even at this early stage, I was beginning to relish being a part of the farming community with most of my waking hours. And a good part of the time I was supposed to be asleep was being taken up with their animals and the battle to keep them healthy.

As I drove back, idly planning where to take Julia, I was thinking how lucky I'd been. There had been a few sticky moments today and thank goodness everything had been resolved, otherwise the evening with Julia would have been plagued by my own worries, which later would have had me tossing about in bed. I was finding out fast that things didn't always go right, and when they didn't, I was well and truly wrapped up trying to put it right. It was definitely a case of highs and lows. However, tonight promised to be a high.

I decided on a casual look, a fine wool, white polo neck jumper which was all the rage, blue Levi jeans that Sally had bought for me from a shop in Soho that imported them from France, and a pair of elastic-sided Chelsea boots. Keith caught sight of me as I arrived in the house freshly showered and ready to go out.

'Well,' he said with a glint in his eye. 'You're looking a bit tasty, my old son. Who's the lucky lady? Angie?'

I felt a bit sheepish. Had I been leading Angie on? I didn't think so. 'No, Julia,' I said. 'We're just going for a drink.'

'You sly little devil!' he smirked, though there was no mistaking the jealousy in his voice. 'There'll be hell to pay when Neil finds out!'

Just then, Julia came out, looking just fantastic in a

black dress that my mother would not have approved of, though Keith clearly did. We climbed into the battered old Anglia, which I had given a thorough spring cleaning back at the hospital car park, and set off. The day's fine weather had continued into a warm spring evening and the hedge-rows were loud with birdsong as we trundled along the country lanes. I was already acquiring a photographic memory for the innumerable little roads that criss-crossed the country. Now I showed off as I took Julia on a cross-country route that avoided anything that resembled a main road or town. There's something extremely liberating about driving down the hilly tree-lined lanes at night. For a start there is no danger of bumping into anything coming the other way – the headlights see to that. I turned on the radio and recognized the third movement of Tchaikovsky's third symphony. It matched my mood perfectly – but not Julia's, and she immediately began to twiddle with the knobs until she found Radio Caroline, a typical mournful offering from Leonard Cohen that ended, 'That's no way to say goodbye.' Soon she was crying – and not only because it mirrored her situation, but apparently because Neil had bought her the LP. I just wished I'd not gone near the radio at all.

The next song was not much better. Herman's Hermits singing 'No Milk Today, My Baby's Gone Away'. Fortunately, no song in those days lasted more than a couple of minutes and soon she was cheerfully singing along to 'Lola', a strange song about a transvestite, by The Kinks.

The Plough Inn was so remote that we were the only ones there. The old couple who ran it had a log fire going and we settled down with our drinks, basking in the warmth and snugness. On the walls there were fading sepia photo-graphs of ploughing competitions and horses. The faces looking down from the plain black passe-partout frames didn't look that different from the faces of the farmers I met now, though the old leather ploughing harnesses that decorated the beams had long since ceased to have any practical use. Suddenly I heard a car pull up outside. Julia took no notice, but I was terrified in case it was Keith who after all had told me about the Plough in the first place. He was the last person I wanted to walk through that door. I certainly hadn't told him where I was going.

But I breathed a sigh of relief as two young men went into the public bar, clearly locals, farm workers who didn't even look into what passed for the saloon bar. However, the romantic evening I had spent the afternoon anticipating wasn't going quite to plan. I had hoped that the charm of a country pub – not to mention the charms of a country vet – would have dimmed this damsel-in-distress's memories of the dastardly Neil, and that the white knight, yours truly, would be justly rewarded in the time-honoured way. Not a bit of it. Neil dominated the conversation and even a hint of criticism from me at his behaviour had Julia jumping to his defence. I began to realize I was on a losing wicket. Julia was convinced that he would come round. She just needed to be tough, hence the split. He was being given time to think things through. I had to somehow change the subject. As she spoke, I had been trying to work out where she was from – somewhere up north – Middlesborough perhaps, not quite a Geordie. We began to talk about accents.

'I've only ever been out with Northerners,' she said. 'I love the Geordie accent!'

'Well,' I said, 'I'm half Geordie.'

She looked at me in disbelief.

'You don't sound it, and anyway, I thought you said you came from round here.'

'My father's family come from Alnwick, the ancient

capital of Northumbria just north of Newcastle,' I told her. 'I've been up there on holiday,' I carried on rather lamely, and then, with a flash of inspiration told her that my football team was Newcastle United. 'They're called the Magpies,' I added by way of proof, and I tentatively put an arm around her shoulder.

'I know. Neil comes from Newcastle,' she said. 'Though he supports Sunderland.'

Sunderland and Newcastle were the football equivalents of the two sides of the Romeo and Juliet tragedy, the Montagues and the Capulets.

It was another Grant own goal.

Julia began to shed a few tears quietly. Time to get another drink in. It was obviously going to be a long haul. Remembering Keith's grinning face as we left earlier that evening, it occurred to me that he obviously knew more about things than I did and that I needed to talk to him to plan my campaign. Just as Julia was convinced all Neil needed was time to come round, I was equally convinced that time could very well play into my hands. All I had to do was sit tight and be there for her. Solid. Dependable. After all, a shoulder to cry on can very quickly turn into something a little more passionate.

I suggested we went back to the house for a coffee, and Julia nodded. We walked out into a clear, starry sky and there was a bit of a chill in the air. This time I didn't go near the car radio but, instead, talked about my night duties and how exciting but also sometimes exhausting it was to clamber out of bed and face the farm emergencies. As we passed by Jonathan Rowe's place I told her about the upside-down lamb and what a thrill it was to get her out alive.

'I might pop in tomorrow and take a look at how she's

getting on,' I said. 'I still don't know if she has made it.'

I was also due back at the convent to check on the calf with pneumonia. As I chattered on, Julia stayed silent, lost in her own private world. As we neared home, she suddenly sat up with a start.

'That's Neil's car!'

Sure enough, outside the house was a car with someone in the driving seat. This didn't seem the moment for a dramatic confrontation, so I carried on past, dropped Julia off about a hundred yards up the road and then drove off round the block, Keith's words ringing in my ears. When I came back there was no trace of the car, so I wearily crept into my empty and lonely flat. A wave of misery engulfed me and I was tempted to pick up the phone and call London. But what was the use? Sally had told me in no uncertain terms that she was seeing someone else anyway. I curled up in bed and tried to sleep.

## *Chapter Six*

The next day was sunny and warm and I didn't have to do morning surgery. There were a couple of calls, including the return visit to the convent. I stopped the car outside the high gates, rang the bell for admittance, and as the gates swung open I felt my spirits lifting. Just the thought of seeing Sister Teresa again was enough.

There were five calves to debud and I carried the portable machine that we used to do the job, plus the local anaesthetic syringes and needles. In the courtyard there were several nuns in robes and hoods. One of them detached herself and greeted me.

'Good morning to you, Mr Grant. It's a grand day, is it not? But let me take you to the calves.' With that, Sister Maria Assumpta let her hood drop to reveal her kind, somewhere-in-her-sixties face.

'Where's Sister Teresa?' I asked as casually as I could manage, as we went round the back of the main convent buildings to the barn. 'I thought she was in charge of the calves.'

'She is in prayer.'

Digesting this piece of news, I set about injecting each calf with local anaesthetic which would make the procedure painless.

In prayer? Why today particularly? Looking at the wise, old, impassive face of Sister Maria Assumpta, I reckoned that I wouldn't get far with any cross-examination.

While waiting for the anaesthetic to take effect, I looked at my patient of five days earlier. There had been a great improvement. The calf was breathing easily and eating well.

'We are all so grateful,' said the kind old nun, and patted my hand. Could she sense my disappointment?

I plugged in the debudding machine and, using the hot end, burned out the cartilage that would develop into horns. It was very simple, easy and bloodless compared to the palaver that Bob and I had had to do with the adult cows.

As I was about to leave, the old nun shyly gave me a bottle wrapped in paper.

'Thank you, David Grant, and may God be with you,' she said.

This was my first-ever present from a client – the first of many.

'I'll open it tonight,' I told her.

'Well, now, there's no need to be doing that. Keep it for a rainy day.' But although the weather was still warm, inside myself I felt anything but sunny. Inside it was raining cats and dogs, just like that old Buddy Holly record, 'Raining In My Heart'. And this was surely one brew that Keith would never have tasted. I wanted to talk to him about Julia.

As we neared the Anglia, I caught sight of the most heavily pregnant cow I had ever seen. Sister Maria Assumpta followed my gaze. With a smile, she said, 'That is Ursula – she's in calf to a Charollais bull.'

Ursula was a Jersey cow and crossing them with the very large French breed seemed to be the fashion. Alan had warned me that some of the calves were very big as a result and difficult to get out. I looked at Ursula again. 'When is she due?'

'Next weekend,' came the reply. Like all the nuns in charge of the animals, she carried every conceivable detail in her head.

Next weekend. With a feeling of the inevitable, I remembered that I was the large animal vet on duty next weekend – it had come around very quickly. I bade her goodbye, thanked her again for the bottle of wine and sped off in the direction of Jonathan Rowe's farm to see whether the lamb had survived.

As I swung into the yard I was greeted with a cheery wave.

'How's the lamb doing?' I asked.

'Come and see. She's out in the field with her mother and sister.'

We walked in the sunshine to the far side of the field. There were about a hundred ewes and their lambs peacefully grazing. Groups of lambs were cavorting about without a care in the world.

'I've marked the lamb with a V – for victory!' said Jonathan.

And there, twenty yards away, stood the ewe with her twin lambs. On one of them I could see a large red V painted down the back.

'Try and catch her!'

I crept upon them and made a rush at the little lamb.

She took off, bucking and weaving through the lush spring grass, and I changed up into a full sprint – but I didn't have a chance, didn't get remotely near the lamb. In a matter of a week or so of her life, she could outrun me.

Jonathan was highly amused when I told him that I was defending the Kent sprint championships in just over a month's time.

'You'll have to get into training then!'

I agreed – in fact I had my spikes and tracksuit in the back of the car and I was trying to use my lunch hours running in the farmers' fields. I asked Jonathan if I could use an empty field to run in – looking at my watch, I reckoned I could still get back home for a quick shower before the afternoon round.

He laughed. Not the usual request from a farm vet. For the next forty minutes I raced flat out over roughly 200 yards with a quick walk back in between sprints. Jonathan looked on in amazement while resting on a gate.

'You're certainly moving!' he said. 'I reckon if you had those spikes on, you'd catch that lamb.'

I had been doing this for the best part of a week now and I was intending to do another session of sprint repetitions outside my flat when on call. Angie had volunteered to hold a stopwatch and listen out for the phone. I was coming up to five nights on duty and hoped to get some sessions in in spite of this. Frank was quite enthusiastic and didn't think it would conflict with my duties, although I sensed that Charles was less than keen – particularly if it involved having to keep phoning until he got hold of me.

The fitness seemed to be coming back quite quickly, although for a sprinter it was hardly ideal preparation. For a large animal vet, it was all that was possible.

Large animal vet. With a start I suddenly realized that that was me – how quickly I was adapting to it.

'Come and have a quick coffee before you go,' said Jonathan, interrupting my thoughts, 'and what about a spot of lunch while you're about it?'

Within minutes I was tucking in to a large ham sandwich washed down with delicious hot coffee. Life seemed to be a series of triumphs and disasters, with very little time to dwell on the disasters and disappointments. Every time I received a blow, something else turned up to restore my self-esteem. Finishing off my coffee, I decided that I hadn't sweated that much that a shower couldn't wait. Goodness knows I usually smelt far worse than this, and nobody except young women with nothing to do with the land had complained, so I phoned in to the practice to see if there was anything that needed doing in the immediate area.

Pauline, the secretary, picked up the phone. There was something I could do – though rather different from what I had been expecting. A budgie needed its beak and claws clipped.

'The owner, Mrs Peake, doesn't want to stress it by travelling in to the hospital,' Pauline explained. I agreed to do it – if only because it added to my burgeoning repertoire: budgies hadn't figured in my practice so far. I couldn't even remember seeing one at the vets where I had spent so many weekends when I was growing up in Rochester, and where I saw practice when I was a student. Oh well, I could vaguely remember my half dozen lectures on the subject of budgerigar diseases, so clipping claws shouldn't be a problem.

I arrived at Mrs Peake's house twenty minutes later. She could hardly fail to be impressed, I thought. I had arrived within half an hour of her phoning.

I knocked on the door and waited. I checked the address. 15 Osborne Crescent. It was right. I peered in the front window. I was about to give up when I saw a small angry-looking woman of about fifty peering at me from next door's front garden.

'And what do you think you're doing?' bellowed a deep, totally incongruous voice, given that its owner was barely five feet tall.

'I'm looking for Mrs Peake,' I replied. 'I'm the vet.'

There was a long silence, followed by an audible muttering under her breath.

'Hrrumph. Another young whippersnapper that doesn't know what he's doing.'

She walked up the next-door's short garden, opened the gate, closed it, opened the gate to what was clearly her own house and stopped in front of me, peering up as if I were a specimen at a zoo.

'I wanted an older man. Someone with experience!'

In spite of her size, Mrs Peake emanated energy and aggression.

'Well, now you're here, you'd better come in.'

In the corner of the kitchen there was a bird cage and inside was Pinky, Mrs Peake's budgie.

'He needs his beak and claws cut,' I was told, in a tone that suggested that this surgical feat was way beyond my capabilities.

Pinky sat on his perch impassively, contemplating this new and totally inexperienced budgie vet.

He had a twisted beak which had just started to interfere with his eating, and long nails which prevented him from perching properly. I searched in my black bag and came up with some clippers. Armed with these I set about the task of capturing my patient. This was easier said than done. Pinky had the experienced budgie knack of making himself very difficult to corner. He paced himself, never expending unnecessary energy. He waited until I made a grab, and then casually flew to the opposite corner of his cage. This was repeated at least a dozen times. Inexperienced budgies would by now be exhausted and submit, but not Pinky. He tried a different strategy. Now he began to screech and flutter maniacally about the cage, interrupted at frequent intervals by his owner's growl.

'Don't you hurt him. We never had this problem last time. He obviously doesn't like you.'

Ignoring the equally fearsome noise emanating from Pinky, I finally wedged him between the bars and his perch and eased him out. With a deft snip I had trimmed his beak nicely. Looking at his owner – hoping for some belated praise – I realized I had made a mistake. Her eyeballs were swivelling in disbelief and her mouth was pursed in an expression that reminded me of a sheep's bottom.

'Always do the claws first,' I was to hear from Frank later. Now I realized why. Pinky twisted his neck through a surprising angle and took a wedge out of my finger. I couldn't believe how painful a budgie bite was. Extracting my bleeding finger from his beak, I got him by the neck and proceeded to clip the claws. Just on the last one, he jumped, and I clipped it too short and made him bleed as well. There was a mixture of our blood all over my hand and the bird. It took another five minutes to clean up myself and Pinky before he went back into his cage. Sitting on his perch, he looked disturbingly shaky. I had heard of budgies dying after handling and for a moment that horrible thought crossed my mind.

I was vaguely aware of Mrs Peake's foghorn of a diatribe. 'Call yourself a vet! If you think I'm going to pay for that, you've got another thing coming.' She turned to Pinky. 'Oh, my poor darling. Never mind. We'll make sure it's Uncle Frank next time.' Pinky responded by snuggling up to her outstretched finger. His owner shot a malevolent glance at me.

'I think it's time you left.' As I got into my car, Mrs Peake banged at the window. I wound it down and she produced the clippers. As I drove away, I reflected upon the contrast between Mrs Peake's assessment of my professional capabilities and Jonathan's.

Evening surgery finished early – six on the dot – and I hurried home, determined to get another training session in. Angie volunteered to hold the stopwatch and we went to the local park. I measured out approximately two hundred yards and ran full pelt. The first run was just over twenty-two seconds. With two minutes rest I did the same run, each time trying not to go slower than the first. After eight runs I'd had enough and walked wearily to the car. The next training session would be when I was on duty, and Angie was quite keen to help. As we got into the car she said, 'Guess what? Julia's engaged!'

'That was quick,' I replied. 'What made him change his mind?'

'You, I think!' she said with a grin.

So she knew I had taken Julia out. Perhaps we could just be friends. I seemed to be as inept at romance as I was at budgies.

But it seemed that, not for the first time – or the last – the threat of competition had worked better than any ultimatum.

As we got back, Keith was at the door.

'Heard the latest?'

'Julia's engaged,' we replied simultaneously.

'Shall we go down the pub to celebrate?'

A couple of pints later I was ready for my bed. Two mini-sessions in one day. I would have to try to keep it up – but five night duties loomed.

The next day Frank had decided to keep me in the morning surgery and build up my small animal medicine knowledge. It made sense because, now I was fully operational on the night-time roster, I needed to be able to deal with small animals at night. The more I could cram in now, the better I would be able to deal with the emergency cases.

'Most of the cases at night aren't true emergencies, you'll find. Most of them are routine cases that have been going on a few days and the owners get really worried,' Frank advised me. And so I was let loose on the full complement of cases during a busy morning session. The great thing was I could ask Frank or Peter anything I liked and get an immediate answer. I was to become adept at slipping out on any pretext or, as in the very first case, just getting one of them to pop in and advise.

Mrs Andover was first in to consulting room four with her young whippet, Sam. A delightful dog, only six months old and already devoted to his owner, his problem was extreme itchiness.

I could see at once that his owner wasn't exaggerating when she said that he was keeping her awake at night with his constant scratching. I looked him over, and there were lots of little scabs but no sign of fleas. I had already learned that fleas were the most likely cause of itching in dogs and cats. Stalling for time, I asked lots of questions. How long had it been going on? Any other pets?

Just at that moment I saw Peter go past the open door. A sixth sense told him I needed help. He caught sight of the owner.

'How's things, Wendy? This your new pup?' I had already worked out that both Peter and Frank already knew most of the small animal clients by sight.

'He's got this nasty itch,' I said. 'I was just trying to get to the bottom of it.'

'Want me to have a look?'

Peter ran his experienced eye over the dog. He made

Sam scratch furiously just by rubbing his ears. The same effect was caused by tickling the dog's stomach. He rolled him over and looked at the rash on his chest.

'Very interesting. Mind if David and I have a discussion outside?' he said to Mrs Andover with a smile. No problem there – she was just grateful that we were taking such care.

Outside, Peter gave me the probable diagnosis.

'Looks like Sarcoptic mange,' he said. In the space of two minutes he gave me the run-down on the disease. Young dog, frantic scratching, ear scratch reflex, spots on the chest and also on the elbows.

'Ask her if she has a rash too – don't forget it can affect the owner.' I nodded – I didn't want to get caught out again like the dandruffy dog. 'See if you can find the mite with a skin scraping.'

Back in the consulting room with renewed confidence, I passed on Peter's thoughts. It wasn't too busy, so I went straight ahead and scraped a little skin on to the microscope slide and sped in to the new laboratory which the partners had had built. Minutes later I was gazing at my first Sarcoptes mite. I called the other two to come and have a look. Frank was particularly pleased. 'No doubt about the diagnosis, David. How are you going to treat it?'

'Quellada,' I replied. This shampoo was the standard treatment and the answer popped out of the recesses of my brain, information put there a year or so ago during the dermatology lectures.

Wendy Andover looked down the microscope and was horrified that it could have affected her – fortunately it hadn't. She went on her way armed with bottles of shampoo and warnings for the family not to cuddle Sam for the next few weeks. For me, seeing the mite, making an accurate diagnosis and knowing that I would cure the patient was the beginning of a love affair with skin diseases that would last the rest of my professional career, although I didn't yet know it. I was enjoying myself. I was meeting people and their pets with a variety of ailments and with a couple of very experienced colleagues on tap to advise at any time. Maybe small animal work was for me after all.

Miss Heskins was the last one in the waiting room. Her pure white hair was piled up on her head like meringue. I reckoned she must have been in her sixties, very sweet natured and incredibly grateful for everything we did. I took a shine to her instantly.

'It's Horace,' she said, indicating a large, obese tabby cat in the basket. 'He hasn't been eating and that is most unusual for him.' Looking at Horace, who must have weighed at least fifteen pounds, I could see her point.

I went through the examination procedure taught at college and couldn't find a lot wrong. A bit of a temperature and his third eyelids prominent. I seemed to remember one of our lecturers telling us that when the third eyelids came across it was sign of a sick cat, usually with a virus infection.

'I think he may have a viral infection,' I said. 'He'll need nursing and some antibiotics to prevent secondary infection.'

Looking at her worried face, 'Don't worry. If he gets worse I can always have another look,' I added. 'I'm on twenty-four hours duty for the next few days.'

As soon as I had said that, the thought flashed through my mind that I might have made a mistake. The little old lady grabbed my hand and tears welled up in her eyes.

'Oh, thank you, thank you – he's all I've got,' and she looked down with profound sadness at a decidedly seedy-looking Horace, already settled back in his basket and half asleep.

Alan bustled in just then.

'Morning, Miss Heskins. Our Mr Grant looking after you, is he?'

'Yes – he's told me not to worry. You're on duty, aren't you?' and she patted my hand. I thought I caught a glimpse of amusement in Alan's face, but he concealed it well. Afterwards he told me that Miss Heskins was a terrible worrier and well known for her late night phone calls.

'I'll tell Charles you've volunteered to take personal care of Horace,' he said with a grin. Charles was on first call tonight with me.

'Anyway, changing the subject, there's a couple of cleansings up near the coast to do before lunch. You might as well stay up there so that you can look at a couple of lame cows this afternoon on Roy Gibbons' place. Make sure you get the cows in a crate, by the way. His cows are big and a bit wild. Are you happy about restraining big cows to look at the feet?'

I nodded. I had had lots of practice in Leicestershire.

'If anything else comes in we'll phone you at Roy's, otherwise head on back and help in the evening surgery.'

I got into the Anglia and headed off towards the coast full of the joys of spring. Angie was going to time me outside the flat tonight while I did some sprints. She's so nice, I thought – but, try as I might, I couldn't see her as anything other than a friend. Just as well – I was far too busy. My thoughts strayed to Sally and her new man, but I quickly shut them out.

Alan had mentioned a good pub for lunch, and with an ample steak and kidney pie inside me and half a pint of the local bitter, I found Roy's farm just after two. Nestling in a little valley, I thought how nice it must be to live there. Maybe in years to come I would move from the city. Roy came to open the gate. A man in his early fifties, ruddy-faced, crinkly-eyed, I knew at once that he would be one of those farmers that I would get on with. While we got the first of his cows in, he told me he had bought the farm just after the war. He had been a bomber pilot and knew Kent very well and decided to settle here. Alan was right – he had some of the biggest cows I had ever seen – in all, about fifty Friesians. A couple of them were lame in their back legs. Getting them in to an examining crate was just the beginning. It took five attempts to get a rope round the back foot to hoist the leg up. It was a dangerous sport. I recognized from years ago the hunched-up position and head swaying from side to side that marked out the cow that was taking aim for a good kick. It was also back-breaking work trying to grab the foot while Roy hung on to the rope attached to the leg. Eventually I was able to clean out the foot, and using a hoof knife, pare away the horny part of the hoof to get at the root of the problem. A foul-smelling discharge welled up in the hoof.

'Foul in the foot,' I said to Roy. This archaic-sounding disease was caused by a germ which produced an abscess in the foot. I gave the cow a penicillin injection which would cure her and turned my attention to the other lame cow. Half an hour later I had diagnosed and treated both for the same condition. Roy and I were sweating buckets with all the effort. I took off my brown coat and started to cool down.

George, Roy's cowman, could be heard calling the cows in – it was just before milking time. We stood at the entrance to the milking parlour and looked back over the fields at the cows obediently trundling in. The lead cow was the biggest specimen I had ever seen. Roy caught my open-mouthed expression.

'That's Agnes. While you're here I'd like you to take a

look at her. She's a bit loose and has a cough.'

As if on cue, Agnes obligingly did a soft cough as she walked past us to be milked. I nipped back to the car for my stethoscope and by the time I was back she was contentedly eating her concentrates – or 'cake', as the farmers hereabout liked to call it. All the cows being milked were tucking in. I took Agnes's temperature – quite normal – and stood behind her watching the rhythmic rise and fall of her chest. There was no sign of any difficulty there. Just then she did another cough and the effort of it caused a large amount of very liquid faeces to shoot out. It hit me with an explosive impact just below the chin and quickly soaked my chest and my white shirt.

I looked round to see Roy sitting on the ground clutching his chest and looking even more red-faced than usual. For an instant it flashed through my mind that he had had a heart attack. And then I saw that he was doubled up with laughter, with tears running down his face. I looked down at myself and saw why. What a mess! Just then Katherine, his wife, popped in to see what was going on and soon the pair of them had started me off.

'You'll have to come in for a bath.' she said. 'And Roy will lend you a shirt.'

Half an hour later, newly clean and wearing a shirt far too big for me, I sat down to tea and listened to Roy's tales of pathfinder bombing during the war and how much the family enjoyed living on the farm. We were joined by Julie, their only daughter, just back from school. A lovely looking girl, but only seventeen. I tried not to stare. Long blonde hair and as neat and slim as a stalk of wheat. She smiled at me and was obviously used to male attention, taking it in her stride.

'I'm off upstairs to do my homework, Dad,' she said. Another smile; 'Nice to meet you.'

Her mother and father told me she hoped to study nursing in London.

After tea we went back to have another look at Agnes. I took a sample of her faeces, gave her an antibiotic injection and left two doses with Roy.

'I'll be back with your shirt at the end of the week.' I said. 'By then I'll have the lab results and we can see how she's doing.' Agnes lumbered out into the field followed by all the others. She stopped, turned round to look at me and let out a loud bellow.

'That's what she thinks of you!' said Roy, chuckling again at the memory of the state she had reduced me to earlier. We parted on the best of terms. This was one of those farms that I would look forward to visiting. I got back too late for the evening surgery and went into the house in search of Angie.

'So, ready to do some training?' she asked.

I handed her my stopwatch. Just then, Keith passed by and volunteered to stay by the phone and relay messages – the price being a pint afterwards. I quickly changed into my tracksuit, a very flashy affair, all purple, the University of London colours.

Outside I paced approximately 100 metres up the road. Angie stayed in earshot of the flat and at a signal I ran flat out towards her.

'Eleven seconds,' she called out as I shot past her. Looking at my watch, I walked back to the starting point and allowed two minutes rest. Then I sprinted again. Each time I tried to be as near as possible to eleven seconds. Twenty minutes later I had managed ten repetitions and knew that I wasn't capable of any more that session. The phone hadn't gone – I felt encouraged. A quick shower and I was starting to feel recovered.

I was just towelling my hair dry when I heard voices downstairs. Bob had turned up with Chantal, looking very pleased with himself, and we decided to go into town to the Olive Branch, one of the myriad of pubs we had to choose from. I looked up the phone number of the Olive Branch and phoned Charles. He was out at a calving. Penny, always easy-going and very nice, couldn't see any problem with me leaving the number of the pub in case I was needed.

'Enjoy yourself,' she added, 'but stick to orange juice!'

She was right, of course. It wouldn't do to turn up at a farm smelling of drink – although that didn't stop the farmers offering copious amounts after late night work. So Keith, Chantal, Angie and Bob piled into the car and we headed into town. The pub was unusually quiet, and after a drink or two the others were getting a bit restless. Keith suggested moving on to the bar of the Pilgrims Hotel.

'It's got a nice atmosphere,' he added by way of encouragement. He seemed to know the landlord of the Olive Branch and had a quick word with him, telling him that in the unlikely event of 'the vet' – indicating me – being needed, we would be at the following number. He had everything worked out.

Jack, the landlord, eyed me up. 'You a vet?' he asked.

'Yes, that's me,' I replied.

He shook his head. 'Blimey, I'm getting old!'

Arriving at the Pilgrims Hotel, I began to get an inkling about what was going on. Chantal and Bob were having an animated conversation – the gist of it being that Phil wasn't a serious rival as he was thinking about marrying his air hostess girlfriend. Angie snuggled up to me and explained my pint of orange juice to anyone who would listen, based on my preparation for the county championships. Keith, meanwhile, seemed a bit distracted and jumped up to get the next round in before I had even got halfway through my drink.

Then I saw why. Serving behind the bar was a beautiful blonde who put even Chantal in the shade, and with a cleavage that was rare in someone so slim. The ordering of the drinks took a long time while Keith went into his routine, and by the time they came I had finished the orange juice and was feeling a bit bloated.

'Who's that?' I asked. Keith got all defensive.

'Oh, she's new. She's from Liverpool.'

It transpired that Keith had spied her a week ago when he had decided to lunch at the Pilgrims and had been a daily visitor ever since. Judging by her frequent glances and smiles in our direction, he was on a good wicket. I suddenly felt a bit gloomy. Everybody was getting fixed up with these fantastic women. With a touch of guilt, I turned to Angie.

'I forgot to say thanks for helping me train.'

She blushed and said it had been fun, although I couldn't see how. Still, the evening was going pleasantly enough. I was interrupted in my thoughts by the blonde barmaid calling me. 'David.' How did she know my name?

'Telephone!'

It was Charles, and from the sound of it, not very pleased.

'Where the devil have you been? I've been ringing all over the place to try to find you.' He had lapsed in to the clipped sounds rather like a general, that you knew always meant that he was agitated. He made a rasping sound, another tell-tale sign that he was under pressure. And I could just see him slapping his thighs.

'Miss Heskins is waiting at the surgery. The cat has taken a turn for the worse and she insists on seeing you.' This was said with some satisfaction.

'I'll be there in five minutes,' I said, and told the others I'd see them back in my flat for coffee.

I quickly drove up to the hospital with that feeling in the pit of my stomach that I was beginning to feel whenever I was worried that my diagnosis might be wrong – a feeling that still surfaces from time to time.

As I arrived in the car park, Miss Heskins rushed over to meet me. She was beside herself with worry. From inside the basket a plaintive miaow emerged, as if to underline every aspect of her concern. We went into consulting room four – I had become accustomed to it and felt more comfortable there than in the larger rooms. Together we got Horace out. As we did, he let out a loud sneeze. He had developed a runny nose and eyes and looked the picture of discomfort. I took his temperature and said nothing. Miss Heskins started to shed a few tears.

'It's the end, isn't it?'

'No, no, not for one minute.' I replied, having listened to his lungs and found them to be clear. 'He's got cat flu.' I had seen a few cases of this and Horace was a classic case. 'He must have been just coming down with it when I saw him today. Now we can be sure of the diagnosis, we know what to do.'

I went through all the nursing procedures, keeping him warm, cleaning up the discharges, ointment for the eyes, a mixture of Vick and Vaseline for the bottom of the nose, and above all, tempting him to eat.

'He'll have lost his sense of smell,' I advised his owner, who was visibly brightening by the minute, 'so you might try something strong-smelling, such as sardines, and he'll need antibiotics for the next ten days.'

Tears welled up in her eyes as she thanked me. She gripped my right hand with both hers and for a minute I thought she was going to kiss me.

'Don't you worry,' I said. 'That's what we're here for. Any change, let us know.' And with that I headed back to the flat. I had spent the best part of an hour with Horace and his owner and was beginning to regret my offer of open house. When I got back it looked as though a party was in full flow. Some of the other students had materialized from nowhere, as had a couple of bottles of wine and beer. They had picked up one of the pirate stations on my battered old radio from student days and almost inevitably everyone was dancing to the Beatles – 'Back in the USSR'. Angie grabbed me as soon as I got through the door and for the next hour and a half I forgot that I was tired, on duty and in trouble with my colleague, soon to be one of the bosses. That would mean a trip to the X-ray room tomorrow, for sure.

# *Chapter Seven*

Considering I hadn't got to bed until two o'clock, having finally persuaded my guests to leave, I didn't feel too bad at nine the next morning.

Bob had crashed out in my flat without Chantal, who had left early, saying she was tired. He was a little worse for wear and had to face the trip back to London tomorrow morning to get back to college. I left him moaning about how rough he felt and drove round to the hospital. As usual, Frank was already in – he always got to work about an hour before everyone else. I told him about the night before and that Charles wasn't too happy, but he just laughed it off.

'How long did it take to find you?' he asked, and I replied that Miss Heskins had arrived only a minute before me. He seemed satisfied with that and asked how the training was going. Before I could answer, Charles arrived, looking very tired with bags under his eyes. He looked as bad as I should have felt.

'Tough night, Charles?' asked Frank, with the hint of a twinkle in his eye.

'I got phoned at two in the morning. Do you know Jamie Dobbin?'

Frank knew at once. He was a fourteen-year-old Jack Russell terrier that had been staggering on with heart failure for the last two months. Peter and Frank had tried every known drug to help the dog's heart, but it had been obvious for some time that the poor old thing was going downhill.

Jamie always coughed much worse at night, which had provoked several late-night phone calls over the last few weeks, and it had been Charles's turn last night. He had just advised complete rest and a check-up in the morning. After the twenty-minute phone call he had found it difficult to get back to sleep and then, just as he was finally dozing off, he had another call at four in the morning.

It was Miss Heskins. Charles turned to me and said, 'Did you tell her to contact us if there was any change in Horace's condition?' I nodded, dreading what would follow.

'She phoned to tell me that Horace's purr has changed, and would I let you know.'

Frank started to laugh and I couldn't resist saying, 'Thanks for letting me know!'

Charles finally saw the funny side too. In any case, in a week he was due for a two-week break and last night would soon be forgotten. I still had the weekend duty to look forward to, and was it my imagination or had Chantal suggested that she would love to see some out-of-the-way country pubs? Extreme tiredness had the tendency to bring on my forgetfulness.

Alan bustled in, a purple tulip in his buttonhole. 'Nice easy morning for you, David. A couple of cleansings at Don Burton's and he's got a couple of cows to wash out.'

This was another routine job that wasn't too popular. Cows commonly got a mild infection of the womb after calving, especially if a bit of the afterbirth was retained. To 'wash' them out you had to insert a long metal syringe through the cervix and irrigate with dilute antiseptic. This was usually followed up with a pessary left in the vagina.

'You'll need this!' and he passed me an instrument. 'You left it at Jim Shearer's last week.'

Frank shook his head, and with that patient matter-of-fact voice I was beginning to get used to, he went on, 'And while we're on the subject, why don't you get a single key ring for all your keys?' He produced the hospital keys which had been missing since yesterday. Over the last few mornings there had been a bit of a pantomime while I went round the hospital searching for my car keys.

'You should get to bed earlier, David,' added Charles. 'Was it a good night?' He knew I was living in a house with loads of students.

'Not bad,' I replied, 'But it seems everyone is getting fixed up except me.'

'Well, maybe you need a new image!' This was from Frank, and he tossed me a new set of car keys.

Outside in the car park was a gleaming new Anglia. Racing green.

'Mine?'

'Yes, of course. You'd better load up the boot before we change our minds.'

'Thanks!'

Without further ado, I transferred all the drugs and instruments into the boot and drove off, revelling in the smoothness and smell of a new car. Nice radio, too, and I tuned into the Third programme. It was Dvorak's New World Symphony. Apt in a way. I was thoroughly enjoying my new world. Sally and London life seemed light years away. The weather was warming up, soon it would be summer, with days off at the beach. It took nearly an hour to get to Don Burton's and I was able to listen to the whole symphony.

Don turned out to be a nice chap – although he couldn't disguise his dismay when he saw that it was the 'new 'un'. In his sixties, he had undoubtedly seen it all and remembered the first day that Alan had been to the farm as a newly qualified vet.

'More interested in rugby 'e were.' I thought it best not to mention my own sport. 'And one for the ladies.' Apparently Alan had caused a bit of a stir with the farmers' daughters, although he had ended up marrying a police-woman. I hadn't got round to getting the full story from him.

Don's farm was relatively small – he had about fifty milking cows – but he loved his work and his cows were his pride and joy. He watched anxiously as I removed the retained afterbirths. He was impressed by my mask and protective clothing and I could sense him relaxing as I got on with the washing-out of the other two cows. Visibly warmed up, he invited me for a cup of tea. His wife, Angela, produced some scones, jam and cream – straight from his cows – and time flew by as I tucked in. The farm had been in the Burton family for several generations, but Don and his wife hadn't had any children so he wasn't sure when to give up and what to do with the farm. He showed me round the gleaming milking parlour with its characteristic smell of cows, disinfectant and milk. In the distance his herd was grazing contentedly beneath some trees. It was a peaceful sight and I found myself envying his life style. He must have been reading my thoughts.

'It's quite a hard life, though. I'm usually up at four in the morning to get them in for milking and then again at four in the afternoon, 365 days a year.' He didn't have much by way of a holiday – a week in Yorkshire at his brother's. Even then he would worry that the relief milker wasn't doing the job properly. He had one farm worker who had been with him for years, but he didn't do the milking – Don preferred to do that himself. A huge cow spied us talking over the gate and lumbered over, followed quickly by the rest of the herd.

'That's Josephine,' said Don, 'Boss Cow and the best milk producer I've got.' She was obviously very heavily in calf.

'When's she due?' I asked.

'This weekend. I'm going to stay up most of the time. Can't afford anything to go wrong with her.'

By this time thirty or forty cows were standing staring at us. The odd one would pluck up courage and come up close, sniffing at us with its muzzle. Don affectionately stroked them – he obviously loved his cows. And they would stay with him, but rapidly shy off if I tried to touch them.

From here I could just see the coast.

'It must be great here in the summer,' I said.

'Yes, we sometimes go into the villages on the coast. There's some great fish restaurants. Come on back in and I'll jot some down for you.'

'What about pubs?' I said, with an eye for a few trips out with Chantal.

'Oh, there's some quiet out-of-the-way pubs only known to the locals.' He got out a map of the area and started to pick out a few. I wrote them down, with the map reference.

'Another scone?'

Both of them laughed when I accepted.

'You eat a lot but don't seem to put on a lot of weight!'

I explained about the training and the defence of the county sprint championship in a few weeks' time. Before I knew it, it was getting on for twelve. I thought about ringing in, but decided to get back and maybe start the afternoon rounds a bit early.

Full of tea and scones, and enjoying the smooth ride of a new car, I ambled back well within the speed limit. Just as well, because on one long stretch of virtually empty road I passed through a speed trap with a queue of dismayed drivers waiting to get a ticket. I looked at the speed gauge – thirty-five. No problem; the limit was forty. I made a mental note of that particular stretch. Alan had warned me that the local police were very hot on speed traps, and he knew where the majority were.

As I pulled into the hospital's car park, I was suddenly aware of a white-coated apparition waving arms frantically at me. It was Frank, red-faced and obviously furious.

'Hypomag at Jed Dickens's place. It's a mile from where you've just been. Why didn't you phone?' He handed me a bottle of magnesium and a giving set (just in case I'd left mine somewhere).

'Get there as quickly as you can, or you'll lose the cow!'

'But he won't have me on the farm!' I said.

'He'll have to. I've just anaesthetized a dog. Peter's operating and Alan and Charles are at the other end of the earth.'

Without further ado I shot out of the car park and headed back from where I'd come, only slowing down when I got to the road where the speed trap was. Suddenly, from a feeling of being on top of the world and full of the joys of spring, I was stressed with a dread feeling in the pit of my stomach, knowing that I was on a hiding to nothing with this particular farmer. Twenty minutes later, having made it in record time, I swung into his yard. There waiting for me was an even grimmer than usual Jed Dickens.

He didn't recognize me until I got out of the car, but as soon as I stepped out and went round to open the boot I thought he was going to collapse. He sagged against the gatepost he was leaning on, moaning, 'Oh, *no*! Oh, *no*!' And as if to emphasize the point, he banged his head against the post in frustration. Before he could get the inevitable questions out, I got in first.

'If it's an emergency, you've got to get the quickest help. All the other vets are either tied up or miles away. Where is she?'

'Well, I suppose you'll do. She needs some magnesium – and quick!' was all he would say, and he turned on his heel and strode towards one of the barns. The cow had gone down in a courtyard and was covered in muck. She was lying with her head tucked into her flank and breathing with great shivering breaths. At first sight she didn't look like a hypomag case at all. I endeavoured to get some history.

'When did she calve down?'

'Yesterday,' he replied with a gesture of extreme exasperation.

'She looks like a case of milk fever to me. I'm going to give her some calcium first. Did she have any convulsions when she first went down?'

'Yes, she were trembling all over. Don't you go giving me any of your young fella-my-lad nonsense. I tell you I've seen more cases of grass staggers than you've had 'ot dinners!'

Jed was getting all agitated now and beginning to look like a case of grass staggers himself. Meanwhile I had got into the jugular vein first time. I uttered a prayer of thanks to the Almighty, connected up the giving set and watched as the solution of calcium flowed into the vein.

'I'll give her this and some magnesium afterwards, just to be sure.' This was said more to shut him up, rather than from any thought that it was really necessary, although Alan was to point out later that low calcium levels were sometimes hand in hand with low magnesium. Jed just stood over both cow and me, not uttering a word. Having been kneeling down, I stood up myself and felt better that I was a good three inches taller than the farmer. By this time half the bottle was in and I could tell that it was having the right effect. I slowed the drip down by pinching the tube – I wanted to savour this triumph. Jed remained silent over the next ten minutes. The cow's whole demeanour changed dramatically in this time. From being dull and virtually comatose, she turned her head to look around. Her breathing became normal and she looked as if she was just resting. With the bottle finished, I hooked up the magnesium injection, but much slower this time. I had heard of cows dying while they were given the injection. I stood holding the bottle up as the solution went in and twenty minutes later took the needle out, satisfied that I had done all that I could. Still no word from the cow's owner. I elected to stay a while, keeping a check on her. Jed was obviously having trouble deciding what to say, and we stood in silence for a few minutes. Meanwhile, his cow looked brighter by the minute, lifting her tail and emptying her bowels and bladder. Looking around as if satisfied with her efforts, she lumbered to her feet and ambled back into the barn. She obviously didn't feel like venturing out, and I didn't blame her. A fierce shower had broken out. With a curse I remembered that I had left the driver's window open and I dashed back to shut it, getting soaked in the process. The seat on my side was wet and I would have an uncomfortable drive back.

'I told you she had grass staggers,' the old curmudgeon said through the window as I was setting off. 'Good job you listened to me.' I took this as praise, of a sort, and told him to ring the hospital if there were any further problems. At the next village I made sure to phone in. Frank came on the line.

'Did you manage to save her?'

'Yes, but I reckon she was a milk fever. She's back in the barn. Jed Dickens reckons it was hypomag, but it didn't fit with the symptoms.' I added, 'Sorry about not ringing in.'

'That's all right – you've obviously learned.'

This was one of the many good things about Frank that I was finding out. You always knew where you stood with him. He picked up on most mistakes immediately and never let them go. On the other hand, whatever misdemeanour had provoked his wrath was quickly forgotten about once it had been dealt with.

'There's nothing on the afternoon list at the moment. Come back and get some lunch and be in by three.'

With that he was gone, back to his world of high-powered small animal medicine and surgery. He was speaking at the BSAVA conference that year and was putting in even more hours than usual preparing the talk. Peter, meanwhile, had just had an article published on the examination of the nervous system in dogs, complete with photos of his Dalmatian. Postcards were pouring in from all over the world, requesting reprints of the article.

I was too busy learning about country practice to think about small animal practice – it would have to wait. I was beginning to realize that my learning curve was going to be steep and long.

I parked the car at home just in time to catch Keith coming out. He admired the car, saying that it was a better image than the last one. He looked full of the joys of spring. There was that added bounce in his step which always heralded a change for the better in his love life.

'How's the barmaid?' I asked.

He became a bit bashful and casual.

'Fine. As a matter of fact I'm meeting her tonight.'

'Come in for coffee later on, if you like. Chantal wants to see some country pubs so I'll probably be in later on after we've done a bit of exploring.'

For the second time in recent history his jaw dropped and a big grin spread over his face.

'Well, talk about a dark horse. You didn't waste much time. Right – might see you later then!' And he sped off, every inch the successful rep in his plush dark red Cortina, before I had a chance to say that it was Chantal's idea.

At three I was back at work. There was still nothing doing on the afternoon list, but Frank had plans for me.

The hospital was one of the first to have its own laboratory and that was very much down to Frank's drive and enthusiasm. So there was a good afternoon's work for a vet or nurse every day. Bugs from cows with mastitis were grown to find out which was the best antibiotic to use. There were blood samples to analyse, urine tests to do and samples of faeces to check for worms. This particular afternoon I was shown how to look for worms in the droppings of parakeets. In addition to being a small animal vet, Frank knew a great deal about birds and was often called in to sort out complicated problems which other vets couldn't handle. Parakeets were being kept by enthusiasts – sometimes in large numbers. They needed health checks and preventive treatment, including worming. I spent a couple of hours learning the concentration and flotation techniques required to demonstrate the eggs of parasitic worms. Every now and then Peter or Frank would summon me in to see an interesting case, so the afternoon flew by. Later, in the evening surgery, four of us were consulting, so that by half past six the day's work was just about done. Miss Heskins was the last client of the day. Horace had turned the corner and was making good progress. She had asked especially to see me.

I gave him a good look-over. Temperature normal, breathing easily, no sneezing, eating like a horse. He was fit and well.

'Well,' I said happily, 'I'm so pleased he's done so well. We can discharge him as fit and back to his normal and healthy self. No need to come back – unless you're worried, of course.'

That won't be long, I thought to myself.

Miss Heskins frowned.

'Now what was it? I've got a list somewhere,' and she fished out a large piece of paper with various items scrawled on it. 'Can you check his ears? He's been shaking his head lately.'

I examined the ears. There was hardly anything to see – except a little wax. I dispensed some wax remover.

'Could you look at his teeth? I'm sure he has a problem there.'

'Considering his age, they're pretty good actually. No need to do anything.'

'Could you cut his claws while I'm here?'

I picked up the nail clippers, at which point Horace tried to make a run for it.

'He hates having his nails done!' said Miss Heskins as an afterthought.

Ten minutes later, feeling hot and bothered, I had managed a manicure. Horace had got off the table twice, hidden under the cupboard once and wriggled free four or five times. By now it was getting on for seven and my thoughts were on something to eat and a trip to a pub near the coast, recommended by Don Burton.

Miss Heskins had other ideas. She studied her list and

with a smile said, 'Isn't it awful when you can't read your own writing!'

'Maybe it can wait until next time?' I suggested helpfully. 'I think he's had enough for one day.'

Just at that moment there was a knock on the door and Alan bustled in with that energetic, businesslike way that he always assumed when there was a rush on.

'David, there's a cow down, up at the coast. Excuse me, Miss Heskins, but we need this young chap right away.'

I opened my mouth to protest that I wasn't on duty and then shut it again when I saw the twinkle in Alan's eye. Gently leading Miss Heskins by the arm, he was enquiring whether the 'new chap' was looking after Horace well enough.

'Oh yes!' I heard her say. 'I couldn't ask for more. Well, I'd better be off. I'll just pay my bill, if that's all right.' This was one of her best traits. She always volunteered to pay the bill and always replied, 'That's very reasonable,' whatever the cost. I bade her goodnight with a thumbs-up thank-you to Alan. As I left I heard her say, 'Are you sure that's all it is? That's very reasonable.'

I shot round to the flat, jumped into the bath, changed into my only pair of flares, and ate in less than five minutes a dinner of baked beans on toast. No sooner than I had done the washing up than Chantal knocked on the door. As I looked at her – 'gaped' might have been the right word – I felt a twinge of guilt for Bob. She was looking fantastic with her olive skin and long black hair. Curiously, we were both dressed along the same lines. We both had flared jeans and tee-shirts. Even my boots were similar to hers. We both laughed as soon as we realized. Her boots were high heeled, lifting her to just a couple of inches less than me.

It was a nice evening, with soft, early summer light. I

flung a couple of sweaters into the back of the car and we headed north – I was going to follow up one of Don Burton's recommendations. It was a steep climb out of town and then it flattened out all the way to the north Kent coast. I followed the directions carefully and stopped every now and then to check the map. Chantal was bemused, but eventually, after going down a narrow one-way lane, I found a small village consisting of a dozen or so houses and a wooden-fronted pub. It was in an idyllic setting and looked as though it hadn't changed in hundreds of years.

I narrowly avoided bumping my head on a large wooden beam as I entered the small and cosy bar. There were a couple of farmhands drinking at the bar. Otherwise we had the place to ourselves. I ordered two pints of best bitter – Chantal wanted to experience real English ale – and we sat down in the corner. A game we had started in the car was to have a conversation in as many languages as we could. Chantal won hands down as she could speak four fluently, but I was surprised at how the schoolboy French and German flooded back. I had always enjoyed languages, and if I hadn't made it as a vet that's what I would have done. Every now and then I caught one of the farmhands looking over to us, but thought nothing of it. In the short time I had known Chantal I had got used to the admiring glances flashed in her direction. Having exhausted my entire foreign vocabulary, we decided to switch to English so that Chantal could practise.

'Why don't you get the next drinks in?' I said.

'Get them in?'

'Buy them,' I laughed. My colloquialisms were more common than I realized.

'Here's the money,' I added, handing her half a crown – enough for two pints of bitter in those days.

'Just say, "Two pints of bitter, please".'

Chantal trotted over to the bar and came out with it perfectly. This was the cue for one of the farmhands to join in the conversation.

''E's tetching you well.' And he added, 'You ain't from round here, is you?'

Chantal looked a bit helpless, while the farmhand turned to me.

'You're the new vet'n'ry! I thought I recognized you. You were at my boss's the other day – Don Burton.' I looked at him and tried to remember his name. Don had mentioned him. The name came back.

'Dave – isn't it?'

'Thas roight,' he replied, and he grinned to show a mouth with half the front teeth missing. Short and stocky, with biceps like Popeye and a ruddy face from being out in the fresh air all day. Probably in his late forties, his hair was still jet black and very curly, giving him a gypsy-like appearance.

'Can I buy you a drink?' I said. 'And your mate?'

'This is me Dad.' He indicated the older man to his left, and when he grinned I could see the resemblance – although the father had lost just about all his teeth. Dave explained that his Dad was retired but still liked to have a look at the 'beasts', as they called the cows, from time to time.

'We're keeping an eye on Josephine – she's due to calve down any time. This your young lady?' he said, with a nod at Chantal.

'No, just good friends,' I said with a smile.

'Well, if 'e can't make 'is mind up give us a call!' he said with a big wink.

Chantal had been struggling with the vocabulary and we retired back to our seats. I explained all about Josephine being the farmer's pride and joy – another new expression – and how she was due to give birth – calve down any day. I added that it might be me that had to do the delivery, as I was on duty for three nights starting tomorrow night.

Chantal was puzzled why she couldn't understand a word they were saying, because normally she could understand most people.

'They speak quickly and there's quite a few words that belong to the farming community. Most town people would have difficulty. Even I'm learning.'

I went on to explain about garget. Chantal listened and laughed when I told her that was one word that I doubted any English teacher was aware of.

After they had downed their pints, Dave and his dad departed with, 'Cheerio! Maybe see you later on.'

'I hope not. No offence.'

We were left on our own and the next hour flew by.

'Why don't you come to Switzerland?' Chantal asked me. 'You could learn German, ski and get a good job with one of the multinational companies. I've got a friend who works for Ciba-Geigy as a vet and he's earning lots of money.'

'Money's not that important to me right now,' I explained. 'I need lots of experience – I reckon about five years at least.'

Chantal seemed disappointed at my reluctance to even consider moving.

'But in a few weeks it will be time for me to go back – think about it.'

I was just too hooked on my present way of life to even think about leaving, and in any case, I just had to get experience – that couldn't be in Switzerland. If I wanted to work as a practising vet I would have to take their exams –

in German! I'd done German at school, but I'd have been hard pushed even to order a bratwurst. I looked at the exotic beauty at my side and then back morosely into my beer.

'Let's get back for coffee. Keith and his new girlfriend are invited round.'

As we left, the night was crystal clear. A new moon was out and the country lanes took on a silvery hue as we trundled slowly back to town. The trees made beautiful silhouettes against the sky and Chantal, sensing perhaps my sadness, snuggled up against me.

We arrived back at about ten-thirty and the only light on was Keith's. All the students had been away most of the week for half term. Although they were supposed to use the time for studying, most of them had gone back home. It was very quiet. Mrs Nightingale was in on her own and we popped in to say hello. We were soon joined by Keith and Jenny – the hotel barmaid. In her way, she was like Chantal – quite tall, nice figure, but instead of long glossy black hair hers was a striking natural blonde. Keith was hooked – no doubt about it. The pair of them were already discussing holiday options. Keith was due a week and was keen to go to Spain.

'Why don't you come with us?' said Jenny. Being from Liverpool, she made immediate friends with everybody. I looked at Keith, and to my surprise he didn't raise any objections.

'We'll have to wait and see,' I explained. 'I'm running in the county championships in a couple of weeks and I don't know how much competing I'll be doing after that.'

Keith went back to his room and brought back a pile of brochures. It's hard to imagine now just how glamorous somewhere like the Costa Brava or Torremolinos sounded to us. I had been to Germany on a school trip, and even that was quite unusual. Most people had never been abroad. Keith and Jenny certainly hadn't. I looked over at Chantal. Suddenly I felt profoundly tired. The long days and night duties were taking their toll and now I had three night duties to come on top of normal working days. From nine tomorrow morning until six on Monday evening I would be working and on call. I needed a good night's sleep to build up my resources. I kissed Chantal on the cheek, said, 'See you tomorrow?' and left them all discussing holidays. Chantal and Mrs Nightingale liked to stay up to beyond midnight chatting, but I just couldn't do it. I had that feeling that the weekend duty was going to be lively and I wanted to make sure I was prepared for it.

I could sense Keith's amazed amusement as I left, but in truth I wasn't ready for another relationship, especially if Chantal and I were to be separated in a few weeks' time. Being apart didn't seem to work for me. My head hit the pillow and I was instantly asleep.

## *Chapter Eight*

Friday started well with a quiet morning surgery. With a possibly heavy three nights to come, I didn't want to be rushed off my feet during the day, although there was no way of telling how things would turn out.

For the moment I was relying on beginner's luck – no doubt with more confidence and expertise I would take weekend duties in my stride and even get to enjoy them. I did three puppy vaccinations and saw Mrs Bell with Sophie, who had been my first-ever patient. Sophie's false pregnancy was on the wane and she had been brought in to be checked over prior to spaying. I listened to the heart and prodded around the tummy, making sure all the milk had gone.

'When would you like her to have the operation?'

'As soon as possible – I don't want her to have any more of those fantasy things you know.'

'It's a phantom pregnancy,' I corrected with a grin.

'Well, you know what I mean.' Mrs Bell began looking in her handbag for a tissue and then blew her nose loudly. She had a problem with anything to do with reproduction.

'Next week then.' I went to the operations book and checked with Peter as to the best day.

'Wednesday all right for you?'

Mrs Bell nodded.

'Quicker than for us humans isn't it?'

Which is undoubtedly true. 'And will you be doing the

operation? I'd really like that, Mr Grant. Sophie seems to have taken to you, haven't you, my darling?'

In spite of myself, I could feel the colour rising to my cheeks. I was getting little enough praise these days.

'That's very kind of you to say so, Mrs Bell, but it will be one of the small animal specialists – either Mr Archer or Mr Cooper. But you mustn't worry. Sophie will be fast asleep and won't know a thing about it.'

Shortly after ten I set out for Roy Gibbons' place to check over Agnes and to return Roy's shirt. I had been down to the launderette and ironed it as best I could, and made sure that this time my brown coat remained buttoned up.

Roy was still chuckling at the memory of the sight I made after the last visit. And Agnes was doing well too, no cough and back to normal with the rear end. I hadn't really been sure what was wrong with her, but four days of antibiotics seemed to have done the trick. Both the cows with the foul in the foot were walking normally, too. All in all, very satisfactory. I was invited in for elevenses. There on the table was my white shirt, neatly ironed and folded, and a pile of toast and scones. Half an hour later, and full to bursting, I remembered to phone in.

'All quiet,' I was told. 'There's nothing much doing here, either.' Alan suggested I could fit in half an hour's training and then come in before lunch to sort out who did what in the afternoon. Bidding farewell to the Gibbonses, I shot off home and changed into my tracksuit. Jogging into the local park to warm up, I did five flat-out one hundreds with five minutes' rest in between and then hurried back to the flat. All was still quiet. Too good to be true, I thought to myself.

There was a knock at the door. It was Chantal.

'Fancy a cup of tea?' I asked.

'Fancy?' The word was obviously new to her. I thought twice of going through all the meanings of the word and just rephrased my question.

'I mean would you like a tea – or coffee, of course.'

Chantal decided on tea. Although she didn't really like tea, she had decided that English coffee was even worse, consisting as it usually did of instant powder that bore no relationship to the coffee she was used to drinking in Europe.

'Aren't you working today?' She was pointedly looking at my tracksuit. A hint of reproach in her voice for not, perhaps, inviting her to spend the day with me.

I laughed. 'It's not what you think. I am working – I'm on standby and going back in an hour for the afternoon's list.'

'So, what are you doing tomorrow night? Would you like to go out?'

I groaned inwardly. Here was this amazing girl asking me out and I was on duty.

I explained that, although there might be nothing, the chances were high at this time of year that I'd get called out more than once. And that even if I wasn't called out, I would have to be near a phone. And the only entertainment I was likely to watch was *The Morecambe And Wise Show* on the box.

'Well, I could come and watch television with you – if you like.'

This was unbelievable. Then memories of that first duty weekend with Sally flooded back. 'But I warn you, you may find yourself watching it on your own. I may be out half the evening.' Was I sounding a bit negative? I was. I put on my broadest smile. 'But come anyway. You never know.'

Chantal was due to go out with her fellow overseas students later, otherwise I had a feeling she would be keen to come round that night as well. It was hard to explain how, when you were on duty, work took precedence – at least with me – over everything. Particularly social life. How could I explain it to her without giving the impression of trying to put her off? Maybe she would find out tomorrow, with two calvings expected.

The afternoon stayed quiet; some castrations and debuddings, a couple of cows with mastitis and some pregnancy diagnoses. This involved a rectal examination of the cow – inserting almost half my arm and then feeling for the womb through the rectal wall. With practice – and even I had to admit that it was slowly coming – you could feel enlargement of the womb and even feel the ovaries, part of which would swell, producing the hormone that was needed to sustain the pregnancy. It was something I wanted to become better and better at. In the old days it was done without wearing protective gloves, and you could always tell a large animal vet because one arm was permanently green from contact with the faeces. No amount of washing seemed to get rid of the colour, which came, of course, from the grass.

I was surprised to find myself on Bob Adams' farm in the first place. He was one of a few clients who had huge numbers of cows in milk – around 400 – and work on this farm could take a whole morning, or even a day sometimes, usually done by Alan or Charles. Bob, the farmer, was nowhere to be seen and I was helped by two stockmen. They were both about my age and had the typical build of many of the farm workers I had met, which made them seem as broad as they were tall. I could tell they were assessing me and no doubt would report back to their boss as to whether I was 'a good-un' or not.

All three cows were pregnant – they had been missed in Alan's last session – and the two cows with mastitis had the all-important needle. I washed up, put the waders into the boot and set off for base, stopping in the village to phone through. Still all quiet, I pottered along the straight Roman road that linked this part of the county with the town. As I drove along I counted the numbers of farms I already knew in this part, and I was already into double figures – time was flying by, as it always seemed to do in this job. It still does, even today. These late spring days were so pleasant. The air seemed so fresh, the flowers scented and the light had a warm glow to it, quite unlike the scorching days of summer. I hoped the weather would be like this in two weeks' time at Crystal Palace in London, where the county championships were being held. Next weekend I was due to go to a point-to-point with the Nightingales and a few of the students, and the following one was the championships. Not coming from a country background, I had little idea what a point-to-point was. But I had quite a lot to look forward to in the next two weeks, with two weekends on the trot completely off.

After evening surgery I had something to eat and put the television on. There was nothing much on. *Juke Box Jury* and a police drama afterwards. The black and white images had the effect of making me sleepy and I decided to read in bed. I was in the state of readiness for the phone to ring, which had already been ingrained into me and which normally meant two things: slightly fitful sleep whenever I was on duty and jumping whenever a phone rang, even when I was not on duty.

The alarm went off noisily and for a moment I didn't know where I was. I stopped it and looked at the time. It was seven-thirty in the morning and the reading light was still on. I had simply passed out with tiredness. But had the phone rung? I had been dead to the world and had slept for ten hours continuously.

I was on duty with Frank. Before I had a chance to ask him about the night calls, he just said, 'Nice quiet night, just a phone call from Miss Heskins to say that Horace was doing well.'

'Oh, what time was that?' I asked, expecting the worst.

'Just after nine, and it was peace and quiet after that.'

There was a quiet morning of farm calls, too, to the east of the practice. All were re-examinations, repeat treatments and check-ups, and should be easily finished by one. Frank suggested I clear the decks and he would stay in the hospital and do the morning surgery, so we should both be free to rest during the afternoon.

That was how it worked out. I arrived back at the hospital to find Frank climbing into his Rover on his way home for lunch.

'You might as well go straight home, David,' he said. 'There's nothing doing at the moment. Looks as though it's going to be quiet.'

I drifted into the house in search of Keith. He had gone to see Jenny, his new girlfriend at the hotel, and might be in later. I sat chatting to Mrs Nightingale.

'Chantal seems to be spending a lot of time with you,' she said with a twinkle in her eye. 'What does Angie think about that?'

I said there was nothing in it – yet – but that Chantal was going back to Switzerland soon anyway. There'd be no way she would want to spend a long time in England, as she was always going on about home. 'She's even suggesting that I find a job there.'

'Well, Angie's back on Sunday night – you'd better talk to her.'

Mrs Nightingale didn't like her girls getting upset. Many times she had spent hours talking to one or more of them, helping to sort out their problems, which were usually to do with boyfriends.

I sat idly stroking the family dog, Dusty, a ragbag mongrel who had for some strange reason (as far as the family were concerned) taken to me. He would bark at most people and refuse to be touched by anyone except a chosen few. Although only Jack Russell-sized, he could give you a nasty nip if you took any liberties. It had taken me just over a week to get round him once I had discovered his weakness for chocolate. Now as we talked he looked up expectantly, licking his lips.

'Quite extraordinary how that dog loves you!' said Mrs Nightingale. Although much loved by family and everyone else in the house, she was always called Mrs Nightingale. She filled me in about next weekend's excursion.

'It's just like going to the races,' she said, 'except it's for amateurs. You can still bet though. We'll take a picnic hamper and a few bottles of wine. You'll love it.'

I wandered out into the garden. The lawn needed cutting and I volunteered to do the job. The sun was up and I stripped to the waist and got on with it. An hour later the lawn was looking lovely. I opened the windows of my flat to let in the lovely smell of newly cut grass. A quick shower and change of clothes and I went back into the garden to sit and read. Keith and Jenny appeared, looking the idyllic couple. A twinge of jealousy briefly made a fleeting sensation in my chest, compounded when they told me they were off for a drive to the north coast and then for dinner in a nice restaurant that Keith had found in his travels.

Then came the inevitable question.

'Why don't you and Chantal come?' A further twinge.

'I'm on duty.' For the first time I felt the slightest resentment of the limitations forced on me. Everyone seemed to be out or going out and doing things and here I was, having to hang around waiting for the phone to ring. And the most frustrating part was that it obstinately refused to ring. My mind went back to the first weekend duty. Oh well – no point dwelling on it.

I was invited in to an early evening meal with the Nightingales. Phil had arrived home with Sue, his very glamorous air stewardess. They too were out to a restaurant. Another idyllic couple – they were obviously made for each other. Chantal seemed to be keeping a low profile.

I had told Frank where I was and he phoned me just after seven to say that a dog needed a shot of antibiotic after a dogfight. The duty nurse, Barbara, had had a look and didn't reckon the various wounds needed stitching. I walked round and gave the dog, a Jack Russell, a jab and some antibiotic pills. He had taken on a German shepherd and come off worst, not surprisingly.

On the way back I picked up a couple of bottles of beer from the Spotted Cow.

'Can't stop – I'm on duty,' I told Theo, the landlord.

This was becoming a refrain. As I walked out, the evening was warm – the first really warm evening of the year – and all about me people seemed to be going out. I was back at the flat in five minutes. Chantal was waiting for me.

## *Chapter Nine*

'Would you like a beer?' The bottles of Double Diamond I had picked up from the Spotted Cow had come from the cold shelf and were nicely chilled.

'Yes, I fancy one right now!' she replied. I smiled at Chantal's new word, went over to the cupboard where I kept the glasses and poured it for her in one of the beer mugs that had somehow found their way into my flat.

'You're learning fast,' I said, as I handed her the glass.

'Well, Mr Vet, is it quiet so far?' she said, sitting down on the sofa, her long legs unfolding, then folding again. It was all I could do not to stare.

'So far, nothing at all.' I joined her on the sofa, having already poured myself the second bottle of Double Diamond – not a patch on fresh, hand-drawn best bitter, but much better than lime and lemonade, which was all I seemed to drink these days.

Chantal had an uncanny knack of reading my thoughts. 'It's a pity we can't go out to another nice country pub. Can't we go and you leave the number?'

I thought back to the night I was called out by Miss Heskins.

'If we did, that would guarantee a call, and I don't think my boss would be very happy to have to ring round the pubs, particularly on a Saturday night.'

Chantal tucked her legs up under her and lay back on the sofa, as comfortable as a cat.

I put on a record I had just bought – the Albinoni concerto for strings and organ. It was beautiful and calming and I sat back and relaxed for the first time on night duty. With the lovely Chantal close beside me, and a cool beer, it was as good as going out. We listened in silence until it was time to turn the record over. Nearly half an hour had passed. Half an hour of peace and tranquillity. I was overcome by a tremendous sense of wellbeing.

'That's lovely, David. I have never heard it before.' Neither had I before I heard it in the record shop and asked the shop assistant what was playing. I bought it straight away. It brought my record collection up to three.

It later became famous in a TV commercial for wool, but this was long before then. Chantal leaned towards me, her eyelids slightly lowered, and I felt my heart pounding. Then this moment of perfect anticipation was broken by the shrill ringing of the telephone. We both nearly jumped out of our skins. With a groan, I went into the bedroom to answer it.

It was Frank's wife, Vivien.

'It's the convent, David. Apparently Ursula's having difficulty. They said you would know her.'

My heart pounded even more, though this time it was the adrenaline rush caused by knowing I had a big job on. It occurred to me that Vivien wouldn't know who Ursula was.

'Ursula's a Jersey cow in calf to a Charollais,' I explained.

I could hear Frank in the background.

'In case you didn't hear, that was Frank saying to give him a shout if you get stuck,' Vivien passed on.

It's the calf that will be stuck, I thought to myself.

'Thanks – tell him no news will be good news!'

I looked at my watch. It was nine-thirty. I went back into

the sitting room. Chantal was looking both cosy and sultry, if that's possible. I couldn't believe it. So near and yet so far.

'How long will you be?'

'Well, it will take forty-five minutes to get there and I could be working for an hour or two. There's no way I'll be back before one or two in the morning.'

She ran her fingers through her hair, twisted it and piled it up on top of her head, picked up a chopstick that was lying on the coffee table, and stuck it in. She looked absolutely beautiful.

'I'm sorry, but there's nothing I can do. I'll see you tomorrow.

Chantal said nothing but just continued to fiddle with her hair. She looked utterly crestfallen.

'Look,' I said. 'I'm really sorry, but it is my job and I did warn you there was a good chance that this would happen.' And I set out without further ado.

The drive took precisely forty-five minutes – I was starting to get a feel for the practice boundaries. I drove fast but within the limits. Saturday night was the favourite time for speed traps. I drove in silence, but with my heart still pounding. I had taken the precaution of checking my equipment: three calving ropes, lots of soap flakes, needles, syringes and local anaesthetic in case an epidural was needed. I found myself praying that I would get the calf out – appropriate, considering my destination.

It was a lovely golden evening and on the way towards the coast I found myself envying the cars filled with people who were making the trek back to town after the first really warm day of the year.

As the door of the convent swung open, I once again had the strong sensation of going back centuries in time. The only apparent nod towards the twentieth century was the odd electric light bulb shining now that night had just fallen. I trudged across the deep straw past one or two curious cows, following Sister Maria Assumpta. Another inkling of doubt crossed my mind. She was too frail to be of much help tonight. I was sure that the calf was big, which was the cause of the problem. I would need plenty of brute strength.

The good sister's stooped silhouette preceded me to the stable, where Ursula was doing her best to bring her calf into the world.

She was still standing, but every now and then would arch her back and furiously strain. There was no obvious sign of a calf.

'How long has she been in labour?' I asked.

'Just under two hours now.'

A steaming bucket of hot water, a soap and a towel were already neatly placed to the side of my patient. I stepped into the dark recesses of the stable and stripped off my shirt – I felt curiously a little shy in front of the old nun. Some vets liked to strip to the waist when doing calvings, but I had started the way I intended to carry on and put my calving apron on. This was made of rubber and went right up to my neck and down to my ankles. Plenty of protection against the mess that would surely envelop me over the next hour or so. I soaped my arm up and put it in towards where the calf should be. It was there all right! A huge calf coming out normally, but just too big for Ursula to push out on her own. I relaxed a little. At least there would be no need to struggle to get the head up or legs forward. I put in lots of soap flakes to get good lubrication and then set about putting the calving ropes on, one on each leg above the hoof. I double checked that they were both front feet. Next a rope behind the calf's ears and into the mouth. This would ensure that there would be no pressure on the neck and windpipe. We needed an extra nun.

'Any chance of any help?' I asked.

The sister nodded and five minutes later came back with another oldish nun. I restrained an impulse to ask for some younger, fitter ones. We began to help Ursula with her labour. As she pushed, I took the main force on the head rope while the two nuns tugged away on the legs. After ten minutes we were getting nowhere. I checked the presentation of the calf again. It hadn't moved an inch. More lubrication and a request for more help. Two more nuns arrived. In the dark it was hard to see anything but their hooded shapes. I wondered if this time one of them was Sister Teresa. But no. As Ursula strained, we all pulled, but again there was little headway. I felt the leg ropes as they pulled and reckoned I could pull harder myself.

'Stop and rest, everybody, while I have a think,' I said.

We had been at it for half an hour and I was beginning to get the dread feeling of failure. What were my options? Persevere with a bit more force or call in Frank, who would either succeed or fail – in which case a caesarean would be needed. I looked at my watch. Eleven-thirty. Frank would be turning in. I gave myself until midnight to calve her or call for help.

'Two more nuns please!'

This set the others into a paroxysm of giggles and they set off to haul another pair out of bed. Ten minutes later the latest two joined us, looking bleary-eyed. Still no Sister Teresa. But I didn't have time to worry about the reasons behind her absence. I now had six nuns who I reckoned to be about as effective as two average farm workers. Remembering Alan's mini-seminar of a month or so ago – it seemed like years – I gave the team a quick teach-in on the mechanics of labour.

'I'm going to call the left leg pullers team A and the right leg team B. Don't do any tugging. Just keep up a steady pressure when I ask you to.'

Coinciding with Ursula's next heave, I applied hard pressure on the head rope.

'Team A, pull.' And then at the next heave, 'Team A, relax. Team B, pull!'

As nuns, they were used to obeying without question, and that applied as much to me as to their Mother Superior.

At last I could feel the calf edging along the birth passage. It was very hard work for me, having to do the bulk of the pulling, because it would be the force along the head and neck which would finally deliver the calf. I took a breather and looked at the scene behind me. It was quite surreal. A semi-circle of nuns arranged around me, holding on to ropes like tug-of-war teams, to a backdrop of a straw-bedecked stable which had undoubtedly not changed in centuries.

'How long has she been in labour now?' I asked Sister Maria Assumpta, who was looking a bit shaky herself.

'It will be just over three hours, I think.'

'Well, I'm hoping we can get the calf out quite quickly now – so everybody get ready for some really hard work! But just to warn you, I haven't felt the calf move at all – it may be dead.' As I said this, one of the younger ones crossed herself. The mood took on a more sombre note as we started pulling again. I put in an extra load of soap flakes.

Suddenly, with one desperate push and a deep groan, Ursula shifted the calf past its shoulders. One more pull from me, with the nuns just keeping the pressure up, and out it slithered. In an instant I was at the mouth, clearing the fluid so that he could breathe. A sudden flick of the head amazed me. He was alive.

'He's alive!' I shouted.

'Praise be to God,' came the reply in unison, and I could feel an intense euphoria from my two teams – they hadn't dared to hope that the calf would be born alive – or had they prayed? They weren't letting on as we busily helped Ursula clean him up. She seemed none the worse for her ordeal, showing the instinctive care of all cows with their recently born calves. I looked at my watch – ten minutes past midnight. I felt a profound tiredness and was stiff about the shoulders. But also on a high. I retired to the adjacent stable, washed myself, and got my apron off and my shirt on. There was a chill about the air now and I started to shiver. Time to get home and into a warm but, I thought ruefully, empty bed. I packed up my things and had one last look at Ursula and her newborn. She looked happy enough, as did the two teams, who were now heading for their beds. I wondered if they would have trouble sleeping after all the excitement. As I walked through the great doors leading to my car and a very different outside world, Sister Maria Assumpta came with me.

'Many grateful thanks.' she said, and passed me two bottles of convent wine.

I got in at about half past one – taking it very easy on the way back. I was desperate for a good night's sleep and was relieved to find the whole house in darkness. I left the car out in the road for fear of waking people and crept into my flat. It was, as I expected, empty. I threw my clothes in a heap and got into bed. At first, sleep wouldn't come, but eventually I crashed out and heard nothing until the dread ringing of the telephone woke me. Cursing, I picked up the receiver. It was Frank.

'Morning, David! Thought you might be sleeping in.'

I looked at my watch – five to nine.

'No,' I lied, 'I'll be in straight away.' I would have to leave breakfast until later.

'Don't rush in.'

Now that was music to my ears. 'It's all quiet here. So, tell me, how did you get on with Ursula? A positive outcome, I gather from the good sisters.'

I told him about the night's adventures. 'They seemed quite pleased – I got two bottles of their brew.'

'Well, like I said,' Frank chuckled, 'it's lethal stuff. If I were you I'd leave it in the boot of the car and use it as antiseptic.'

He gave me the morning's list, which was over in the direction of the convent. All routine cases.

'You might as well pop in and see how Ursula's doing,' Frank suggested. 'And while you're about it, pick up your calving apron. They've been on the phone already. You left it in the stable!'

I groaned.

'Maybe you need a holiday, David,' Frank said. Another chuckle. He was clearly in a good mood and I wasn't going to get the lecture I deserved about being more organized.

Although I had only been there a couple of months, by July the pressure would be off, and as I hadn't had a break of any kind since leaving college – and the foot and mouth outbreak had really taken it out of me – a holiday was not such a bad idea.

I muttered something about thinking about going to Spain, but Frank was already thinking about something else.

'We'll talk about it later. Look, once you've done the

morning list, phone Vivien and, if there's nothing doing, head on home and put your feet up.'

Frank was a great one for pacing himself, especially on duty weekends. He had a huge appetite for work, and never complained once about being called out, but he rested in between calls. Vivien would take the phone calls and, like thousands of vets' wives all over the country, she knew how to protect him from non-essential business.

I struggled out of bed in search of coffee. Immediately I felt better. These night duties always contained the most exciting part of my work – but it was a roller coaster of highs and lows. Always the low first: Can I do this? Why am I doing it? Worry and anxiety. Usually followed by the euphoria when something had gone well, and then the relief when the phone hadn't gone again and the batteries were fully charged. I mused on how different I felt first thing in the morning after proper sleep. The previous night's insoluble problems seemed trivial.

The weather seemed set fair for the whole weekend and already there was a steady stream of cars full with day trippers heading for the resorts on the coast. For a while I followed the traffic before taking a side road that would lead me to the convent. It was going to be warm. All I could hear was the buzzing of some insect or other and the singing of the birds.

Even the air around the convent seemed imbued with silence and peace. I rang the bell and after what seemed like an age the huge doors swung open and an old nun I didn't recognize beckoned me in. There was no sound from within. The nuns were at prayer. The cows had been let out into the fields. Only Ursula remained with her calf, who was up and feeding hungrily from his mother. She seemed quite oblivious to my presence, chewing contentedly on some hay and idly flicking the early season flies with her tail. The drama of the previous night might never have happened as far as she was concerned.

'No point in disturbing her,' I said. 'She looks fine!' I picked up my calving apron and washed it under the cold tap outside the stable.

'Sorry to disturb your Sunday morning.'

With a wave of the hand the old nun bade me goodbye. I wondered if they had vows of silence on Sundays.

A mile or so down the road, I spotted a grassy path running along a stream and decided that, as I had plenty of time, it was the perfect place to do a little running. Changing into my tracksuit, I pulled the car off the road. The track ran through hazel and beech woods and the air was heady with the smell of wild garlic. But what was magical was the ocean of bluebells. First I jogged, to warm myself up, then turned around and did some flat-out dashes, the only noise the squeaking of the springy grass, still wet from dew, the low gurgle of the stream and birdsong. After a dozen or so sprints, I sat a while, drinking in the view. Through a gap in the trees I could just make out the glitter of the sea some ten miles away.

The stiffness in my neck had subsided and I had hardly broken into a sweat, so I had hopes, fingers crossed, that I would be reasonably fit in a couple of weeks. Having had no time for racing was a bit of a worry, but it couldn't be helped. Work came first.

'Work always comes first,' I thought to myself with a sigh. But I couldn't see any way round the problem. I had to become competent at my job – in all its aspects – in order to give me the confidence to get on with the other things in my life. That might mean retiring from athletics altogether unless I could find a job giving me every weekend off. Such a job didn't exist in veterinary practice as far as I knew. Anyway, I was determined to spend as long as it took in this practice to feel confident. That meant a couple of years at least.

I spent the rest of the morning in routine tasks but enjoying the lack of pressure. The fine weather seemed to put everyone into a good humour. A couple of phone calls to the hospital had not produced any extra work, so I headed home to await any further calls.

It was the Bank Holiday weekend and most of the students in the house had gone back to their families. But they'd be back tomorrow. I was looking forward to seeing everyone, including Angie. I needed at least ten more training sessions before the championships and a stopwatch holder was very useful. In the meantime, there was Chantal. Sunday lunch in a country pub might be just the thing to make up for last night, as long as it wasn't too far out of town.

As I turned into my road, I was passed by a taxi and had a fleeting impression of a face that I recognized in the back.

Mrs Nightingale was in the garden, tying back the rambling rose that was so heavy with bud that it had flopped down over the driveway.

'You've just missed her,' she said.

'Missed her? Who? What do you mean?'

'Chantal. She's left. Apparently her mother isn't at all well, so she decided to shorten her stay. She waited until the last moment, hoping to see you. But she wanted to get the two o'clock Dover ferry, so that she can get virtually home by tonight.'

'When did she hear about her mother?'

'This morning.'

It was the usual seesaw, but this time the high had come

before the low. I turned to go in to my flat.

'She said you can always go to Switzerland. She told me to tell you that.'

I shrugged my shoulders.

'Look, if you see Keith, perhaps you could tell him I'm around and in need of a bit of company tonight.'

'I'll tell him,' said Mrs Nightingale with a sad smile.

I made myself a cup of tea in the flat, which now suddenly felt very empty. The sofa still bore the dents of where Chantal had curled up. I thought about plumping the cushions, but didn't. Her half empty glass of flat beer was still on the coffee table.

Sunday afternoon. While the rest of the world was out enjoying the early summer sunshine, I was stuck here with only the TV for company. And there was nothing on, apart from an old war film.

It's a funny thing, I thought. A quarter of a century after Hiroshima and still there is an almost daily diet of it on the box. It was something that my German school exchange visitor, Klaus, had commented on eight years before. Nothing had changed.

I sat down on the sofa, swung my legs over and lay out at full stretch. The thought of spending the afternoon with Chantal had obliterated any feelings of tiredness, but now it hit me. I hadn't realized how tired I was, until I woke with a start nearly two hours later. I was woken by the far-off ringing of a phone. But not mine, just Mrs Nightingale's next door. But like a mother with a new baby, I was so tuned in that the sound of any phone ringing had me on red alert. I jumped into the shower to freshen myself up. If this weekend was going to follow the pattern so far, I might be in for it later.

The household was slowly returning to its usual bustle

and buzz. I wandered in next door to see who was around. Julia and Neil had turned up and were chatting to Mrs Nightingale in the garden. Phil and his air hostess girlfriend were in the living room and I heard about their latest travels. Phil had been to the States twice and Sue to the Far East. Now they were both off for ten days and were staying at home. If he had heard about my interest in Chantal, he didn't say anything. There was no sign of Angie. Mrs Nightingale rustled up some scones and tea. Back in the safety of my 'family', my mood lightened and they were all highly amused by my account of the delivery of Ursula.

I was just at the bit where I was explaining about the two teams of nuns when Keith walked in. He got the wrong end of the stick entirely and suddenly burst out laughing.

'It's not that funny,' I said.

'Sorry, mate. But I thought Ursula was some German bird you were chatting up!'

'She's a Jersey cow. And already spoken for by a Charollais bull.'

I had to say no to the pub crawl, which had become the standard Sunday evening activity in the household. The usual reason.

'And anyway,' I added, 'I'm supposed to be in training. But if you tell me where you'll be about half-nine, I'll see if I can join you for half an hour.'

It was a toss-up between the Spotted Cow or the Masons Arms. The Spotted Cow won because it had a garden. I went back to my flat a lot happier than I had left it earlier. Now I was hungry. I couldn't bear the thought of cooking. The choice of take-aways was limited. Chinese or fish and chips. I took the phone off the hook, nipped out for ten minutes and came back with a set meal for one from the local Chinese and devoured it in minutes. A quick clean-up and rest again. These weekend duties really took over your life. How I wished I could have some kind of walkie-talkie so that I wasn't stuck in for long periods. It was particularly irksome being on my own. Did other vets find it so difficult? Everyone else in this practice had wives to keep them company. But there was no denying it. Weekend duty left you either knackered or lonely. As there were still no calls by nine o'clock, I decided to phone Frank.

Vivien answered the phone.

'Is Frank there?' I asked.

'I'm sorry – but he's out on a call,' she said.

'I see. Do you know where he's gone and when he's likely to be back? It's David here,' I added.

I had to hold the phone away from my ear, the sound of her laugh was so loud.

'I'm sorry, David. I didn't recognize your voice. I'll just go and get him.'

Frank came to the phone chuckling. He was immediately available to colleagues.

'And what can I do for you, young man?'

'I was wondering if you'd mind if I went down the local for an hour.'

Frank said it was no problem, but not to turn it into a pub crawl.

In spite of the warm day, the evening air was chilly and I put on a thick sweater and walked down to the Spotted Cow. I had become a regular after a busy day, so as soon as I walked in the door, Theo the landlord was pulling my customary pint, and before I could argue, Keith was paying for it. There was a whole crowd and everybody was in a good mood, having had some time off. I sipped my beer and caught Angie's eye. We got talking and I told her about Chantal and that it was all very innocent, although privately

I wondered what would have happened if she had stayed longer.

'The problem is – I'm just too wrapped up in work and also a bit low after Sally to even think about another relationship.'

Angie smiled. 'Well, if you're worried about me, don't be. We'll just be friends. A deal?'

'A deal.'

And I gave her a hug.

'Hello, hello, hello, what's going on here then?' Keith said, in a John Cleese, Monty Python, take-off.

'Shut up and I'll buy you a beer. It's my round. In fact, I'll buy everyone a round, seeing as my duty weekend is nearly finished and we've got next weekend to look forward to!'

I had five pounds in my pocket and had plenty of change even after buying a dozen people a drink. In fact I had earmarked the fiver for taking Chantal out for a meal, so it wasn't wasted.

Keith and Jenny came over and soon the talk turned to Spain. It would be at the beginning of August. Mrs Nightingale's daughter knew some people in Torremolinos and could recommend a place to stay. As we talked, several of the others said they would be interested too. It seemed more and more a good idea.

'Phone, David.' Theo's voice rang out over the hubbub.

My pulse immediately doubled. What would it be? I went around to where the bar lifted up and cupped my left hand to my ear to hear above the noise. It was Vivien. Her voice was changed from the bantering tone earlier.

'Afraid I've got a nasty job for you, David. Frank's gone out to put a dog down, Jamie Dobbin or something like that, and he's got to pick up Barbara to help him. He'll be gone for at least an hour. But there's a problem at Don Burton's. He says he's got a cow with its calf bed out. Does that mean a prolapsed uterus?'

My heart sank.

'Yes, it does mean a prolapsed uterus. Could you phone him, please, and tell him I'm on my way?'

My mouth had gone completely dry.

I turned to a bemused Theo and asked him to tell the others that I'd see them tomorrow. 'I won't be back tonight until the early hours. And that's if I'm lucky!'

I dashed up the road as though it was the final of the county 200 metres and jumped into my car with my heart racing. It would take me half an hour to get there and I would have to think it through on the way.

Prolapsed uterus had figured prominently in my finals examinations six months earlier, both in the written and – because I didn't do too good a job there – in the oral. This was the occasion when my friend Dai had told me to put the book down and join him for a beer. I had just got to an interesting point where the advice was to siphon in two gallons of warm water to make sure the uterus was completely back in its normal position – rather like filling a glove up with water – when Dai decided a drink was more important than revision. So because of Dai's fondness for a pint, I didn't progress to the next page, which would have tied up all the loose ends as far as treatment was concerned. The next afternoon, when the question came up as I had anticipated, I got as far as siphoning in the water.

'And what next?' said the examiner.

For some reason, fatigue, exam nerves, thinking along too complicated lines, and last, but not least, not having read it in the book, I couldn't see what he was getting at. The frown on my forehead got more and more deeply etched while he pressed me on the point. Eventually he gave up.

'What about siphon it out again, perhaps?' Of course. Logical, even if I hadn't actually read it or done it.

I find driving a car surprisingly relaxing. You have to concentrate so hard with one part of your brain that it seems to free up the part that just thinks. And as I drove across the Kentish Weald I went through the required procedure in my head. In a prolapsed uterus, the womb, which is like a bag that holds the baby calf, literally turns itself inside out and descends into the birth canal and beyond. I would need an epidural anaesthetic to deaden the area, preferably a couple of farmhands to help, lots of warm water and soap. I seemed to remember the book saying that it wasn't too difficult getting the womb back if it hadn't been out too long and if the anaesthetic worked.

I swung into Don Burton's place and he came out of his house straight away to meet me. If he was worried that it was me and not one of the partners, he wasn't showing it.

'It's Josephine,' he said. It would be, I thought to myself. 'Charles is on the phone.'

This surprised me. I went in and picked up the receiver.

'Vivien's just phoned me – just to say I'm around if you need a hand.'

Then Charles went into a mini-seminar which could have come straight out of the textbook. But there was one bit not found in there.

'Get a two-pound bag of sugar and sprinkle it over the uterus once you've cleaned it all up. It helps to shrink it.'

'What about siphoning in a couple of gallons of water?'

'I don't usually bother. It's unlikely to come out again once you've got it back. Don't forget to give her the oxytocin.'

This was the drug that would make the womb contract down. I rang off, telling him that if I hadn't rung back within the hour it was good news, and he wouldn't have to come out. I got the distinct impression that he was itching to come and do it. But now I was here I was determined to do it myself, partly because of the silly mistake I had made in the finals. But also, now I was sure of the theory, why shouldn't I be able to put it into practice?

I quickly changed into my waders and calving apron and walked to the barn, where Josephine was tied up. Dave and his Dad were waiting, having been summoned from the pub. My first sight of a real prolapsed uterus was quite a shock. The whole of the womb had inverted itself and was now hanging inside out from the back end. It was virtually touching the floor of the barn where she was tethered. This was the first bit of luck I was to experience in this, my first case, because it was supposed to be easier to replace a prolapsed uterus in a cow that was standing. The second was the fact that the womb had not come into contact with any straw or dirt, and was therefore very clean. The third was the presence of three willing helpers – imagine trying to sort this out on some lonely farm with just the farmer to help.

I turned my attention to the helpers.

'I need three buckets of warm water, a bag of sugar, soap, a towel and a clean sheet – now!'

I surprised myself by the matter-of-fact orders. It reminded me of my time in north Wales during the foot and mouth epidemic, when on infected farms I had been put in charge of a squad of soldiers. They expected to be told what to do and obeyed instantly without question. Three buckets of warm water and a sheet appeared within minutes.

'Why the sugar?' Don asked me.

'You'll see! Lift the womb on to the sheet and support its weight while I give an injection.'

Dave and his Dad did as asked while I proceeded to give the all-important epidural injection. This was all the easier with Josephine standing up. Pumping the tail up and down, I found the space between the tail bones where I needed to give an injection of 10cc of local anaesthetic straight into the spinal column. In it went and I started to gently clean up the womb. Five minutes later I was gratified to find that Josephine's tail was completely limp. Now, theoretically, at least, it would be a lot easier to replace the womb, and also I wouldn't have to worry about her defecating all over it (and me). Next, the sugar was sprinkled liberally over the womb. Was it my imagination, or did it seem to shrink a little?

Starting from the edges, I started to push it back while everyone else took the weight, which was considerable. At first I seemed to make absolutely no progress at all and, although I said nothing, I began to feel the beginnings of despair. But gradually I did have the sense that there was less to put back. I persevered and looked up at Dave. He was whistling what sounded suspiciously like 'Land Of Hope And Glory'.

'Shut up, Dave. I'm trying to concentrate!'

I was surprised by my rudeness – something I was almost incapable of in the normal way of things. I could allow nothing to break my concentration. Don grinned at me by way of encouragement.

'Lift up a bit more.'

This made it all much easier and suddenly it became very easy and I returned the whole of the womb from whence it had come. With the whole of my arm inserted, it felt almost normal – I was almost sure that it had all gone back. I gave the cow an injection of oxytocin, the hormone which makes the womb contract after birth. Another injection, this time of antibiotic, and I was done.

'That was the easiest I've ever seen,' said Don. 'Time for a drink.'

His relief was palpable and we filed into the kitchen. I sat down before I realized that I still had the calving apron on. I wearily removed it and cleaned up in the kitchen sink.

'Just a beer for me,' I said, looking at the tumbler-sized whisky glasses that Dave and his old dad were sipping.

'Sorry I was short with you,' I said to Dave. 'I haven't done many of those and they ain't easy.'

He just laughed, but I sensed a new measure of respect from all involved.

The phone rang. It was twelve-thirty. As if by intuition, I knew who it was.

'If it's Charles, tell him to go to bed and I'll buy him a beer sometime for offering to help.'

The message was relayed and I finished my beer. It was like nectar, and I don't know whether it was the beer on an empty stomach or just simple euphoria but I felt that this weekend marked a turning point. I had a newly found confidence and appetite for the work. A quick check-up before leaving and there was Josephine silently munching hay while her calf was sucking for all its worth, having been deprived of her sustenance for a few hours.

I drove home slowly, only wondering at the contrast between the contented, happy person now and the anxious, adrenaline-flushed one of two hours earlier. I had cracked my worst anxieties. It was time for a battery-charging holiday soon. My head hit the pillow and I was out. It didn't occur to me that I might get another call – and I didn't.

## *Chapter Ten*

'So, you got it back all right then.'

This was less a question, more a summing up of the blow-by-blow account I had just given Charles of The Apprentice Vet and The Case Of The Prolapsed Uterus. He had quizzed me rapidly in the clipped, almost army officer manner that he always had about him when he was trying to do ten things at once, slapping his pockets as if he was checking if his wallet was still there. The first few times he did this, I found myself checking my own pockets, but I soon realized that there were no pickpockets about, it was just another of his mannerisms, something he did quite unconsciously whenever he felt under pressure.

It would have been a busy Monday morning under normal circumstances, but, to make matters worse, we were minus Alan, who was taking a well-earned holiday in the sun. There was a big tuberculin test to do, which would occupy Charles all day. A simple enough job but one I couldn't do, as I still hadn't got the LVI certificate – which stood for Licensed Veterinary Inspector. It would allow me to do my fair share of Ministry work, but it was only issued after new vets had been in practice for six months. Ministry work consisted mainly of tuberculin testing, blood sampling for brucellosis and some export certificates for pet owners who were emigrating.

Together we scanned the visits list. Fortunately it all seemed to be in roughly the same geographical area – to the south. There were the usual lame cows, some with mastitis, a cleansing or two.

'Paddy Dixon's got a sick pig. High temperature and a rash. Better check if he's had them vaccinated against erysipelas. Sick dog, too. Have a look. See what you can do. And while you're up in that neck of the woods, Mr Sarabini's dog needs its booster.'

The name Sarabini was familiar to me. 'Anything to do with the Italian restaurant in Church Walk?' I asked.

Charles frowned. 'The very same,' and, so saying, he flicked through the small animal records.

'Thought so. Name of Nero. A very difficult customer. You want to watch him – he bites.'

'Gee, thanks,' I said.

Just then, Frank, who had been half listening to the conversation while opening the post, butted in.

'Nero? I thought we banned him from the surgery.'

'Sarabini reckons he's better at home – anyway, it's only one injection, he won't need much pulling about.'

They were obviously winding me up.

Dogs seemed to be on the agenda that morning, as Frank announced that Jamie Dobbin had died during the night.

'Do you know,' he went on, 'the call came at getting on for ten o'clock. I picked up Barbara and then drove half an hour to where they live – only to be informed that my services were not required.'

'Why on earth not?' I asked.

'Because it seems that about ten minutes before my arrival the patient kicked the bucket on his own. There was a note pinned on the door saying not to knock as Jamie Dobbin has passed away, that consequently the vet wasn't needed and, as it was late, the grieving owners had gone to bed!'

Frank was particularly incensed because not a penny of the bill for his treatment to date had been paid, and there was a good chance that now that it wouldn't be paid at all. I was about to quip, 'The joys of being a boss', when I thought better of it. The number of 'DG see FA re:' had been declining of late and I wanted to keep it that way.

Neither Charles nor I were going to participate in the morning surgery as we were down to two. We left Frank and Peter with a full waiting room. They were going to have to work intensively for the rest of the morning. The small animal work seemed to be particularly busy. At this rate they would need another vet to help with that side of the practice.

As I sped southwards, the car seemed barely to touch the ground. No more weekend duties for three weeks. A social weekend to look forward to, and then the Kent Championships. A shiver of anticipation tinged with anxiety flooded through me. Would I be fit enough? I would soon know.

Mr Sarabini's dog was first on the list. Might as well get it over with. Nero's owner had a large house on the outskirts of a village about eight miles into the Kent heartland. The front door had an elaborate bell which you had to pull – a little notice thoughtfully advised you of the fact. Far away somewhere in the bowels of the house I heard it jangle. A horrendous barking and snarling immediately broke out. It got unbelievably louder and louder and culminated with a shuddering crash as the beast or whatever it was collided with the door. For one dreadful moment I thought that the door would burst open and I would be done for. A distant shouting in Italian calmed the dog and I heard the rattle of a choke chain being put on.

No mistake about the address then.

'Oo is it?' came a heavily accented male voice.

'The vet – er, I've come to inject Nero. But, don't worry. If it's inconvenient I'll come another time.'

'No – is all right.' The door opened a little, to reveal a balding, slightly corpulent Mr Sarabini and the biggest Boxer dog I had ever set eyes on. I swear it was the size of a Great Dane, though, I soon realized, without that breed's pleasant temperament. It was standing on a doormat marked WELCOME. This monster strained at the leash snarling, baring its non-too-white teeth at me (the word 'fangs' flashed through my head) while glancing at its owner from time to time as if awaiting the order to finish me off.

It was stalemate. To move towards the dog would have been madness, so I stayed where I was.

'Just a moment,' the Italian said. 'I take 'im to the kitchen. Don't go away,' he added, as if reading my mind. He disappeared into the recesses of his house, returning a few minutes later.

'Sorry about that,' he grinned, extending his hand ''E not mean it. Come in, please.'

Mr Sarabini motioned me to follow him into the sitting room. It had slowly dawned on me that Frank and Charles had not been winding me up at all. Far from it.

'When you are ready, tell me and I will bring him in and hold him.'

I was feeling distinctly nervous. 'Perhaps it might be better,' I said, clearing an extremely dry throat, 'if you introduce us first – let him get used to me before I try to do anything, er, nasty.' The psychology lectures had not been entirely wasted after all.

'A-good thinking!' and off he went, back to the kitchen.

A minute later Nero came in on the lead. I sat perfectly still while he sniffed me and slobbered all over my jacket.

He gave a warning bark and then seemed satisfied, retreating under the table. All I could see were two eyes which never took themselves off me. An occasional low growl reminded me, as if I needed reminding, that he was still about, and to watch it.

'My bag, please, Mr Sarabini. Perhaps you could pass it to me.' I smiled and used as nonchalant a tone of voice as I could muster.

I quietly opened it and extracted the syringe needle and vaccine. Why hadn't I made up the solution beforehand? A bit late now for wishes, I realized. A prayer suddenly seemed far more appropriate. As I made up the solution, I made the mistake of crossing my legs. As far as Nero was concerned, this was the canine equivalent of throwing down the gauntlet and he leapt out from under the table, snarling and growling. His owner stood between the two of us, talking all the while to the dog, saying that I was 'all right'. He was beginning to lose patience as he was due at his restaurant in twenty minutes.

'I grab him – you inject wherever you like!' he whispered hoarsely, like a gangster in an Edward G Robinson film. And with that, he grabbed hold of the dog's collar. As quickly as I could, I crept up from behind and stuck the needle in the dog's backside and pushed the plunger in. It is impossible to describe the noise that followed. It was unearthly and loud enough to permanently damage my ear drums. Nero meanwhile leapt away from his owner's grasp and for the second time in the space of half an hour I thought I was done for, but he elected to retreat under the table again.

'Is done?' asked his owner

'Yes, is done, thank God. I think I'll just pack up and go.' It was only then that I noticed the needle was missing.

We searched the carpet to no avail. Then a horrible thought occurred to me.

'I wonder, Mr Sarabini, if you could just check and see if the needle is still in him?'

Mr Sarabini went over to the still howling dog and there, firmly embedded in Nero's backside, was the green hub of a twenty-one gauge needle. Now what? This was turning into a bit of a disaster. A visit I hoped would last five minutes had already taken half an hour and I had a list as long as my arm. Mr Sarabini tried to retrieve the needle, but Nero was having none of it. As far as he was concerned, no one was going anywhere near his back end again – probably for ever.

They say necessity is the mother of invention. In my case it was unadulterated fear. Anyway, I suddenly had a brainwave.

'Tell him you're going for a walk and get his lead on. Then I'll start to leave. As he comes out from under the table to see me off, drop a towel over the back end and use it to brush the needle out. And don't, whatever you do, let go of that lead!'

The hairs on the back of my neck had been standing up for the last five minutes. Heath Robinson or not, the plan worked well and Nero took out his aggression on the towel, ripping it and shaking it with awesome power. The hairs stood up even more. Then the door bell rang. Nero forgot me for an instant, slipped the lead and hurled himself against the front door. Mr Sarabini grabbed the dog, dragging him back into the kitchen, and closed the door. It was a policeman.

'Sorry to worry you, sir. There's been a report of a disturbance. Some sort of screaming.'

'It's the vet giving my dog his booster.' said Nero's

owner. I nodded in agreement. 'And that's the last one he's having!'

'If you don't believe us, you're welcome to inspect the dog,' I said. 'Here's my bag,' and I displayed the drugs and equipment that I carried around with me on house calls.

The policeman listened to the cacophony of sound emanating from the kitchen and couldn't help laughing. We turned to leave together.

'This is one house that'll never get burgled,' I quipped as we crunched down the drive.

'I can't understand it,' said Mr Sarabini. ''E's never like this with anyone else – just the vet!' And he added, 'Look, I'm really sorry. Whenever you want a nice meal – come to my restaurant, on the 'ouse, as you say.'

'And Nero stays at home?'

'Sure. Nero, he stays at home.'

'In which case, I would be delighted.'

I drove away, making a note in the pricing docket that home visits as far as Nero Sarabini was concerned were out. Some other way would have to be found to deal with him. A poisoned dart, perhaps. I would leave that to the small animal experts. Suddenly the perils of the farmyard seemed positively peaceful. Then I remembered. Another dog. Paddy Dixon's. I seemed to remember an alert collie, ears cocked, in a basket in front of the Aga. But first there were his sick pigs.

I stopped in a lay-by close to the farm and got my *Merck's Veterinary Manual* out. I had got into the habit of keeping it in the car and reading about every condition that I saw. Seeing a condition and then reading up about it made the facts stick permanently in my brain. There was a good section on erysipelas. The two things to look out for were high temperatures and a skin rash. Sometimes this rash took the form of diamond-shaped red spots all over the body. There was a chronic form which caused arthritis.

With the knowledge fresh in my brain, I drove to Paddy's farm wondering if Charles's spot diagnosis would turn out to be correct.

Paddy greeted me like a prodigal son. 'Are you fit?' he asked.

'Yes. Why?' I asked with a hint of suspicion in my voice. But Paddy was just being polite. He definitely wasn't in the mood for winding me up, although it was the infamous Gladys's litter which was unwell, and, remembering what she had done to my boots on the previous occasion, I approached with caution. The majority of her litter of piglets were thriving – all ten of them – and were now in a pen on their own. I reckoned they must have been getting on for 50 kilos in weight. But several were obviously ill. Instead of the normal curiosity, the 'what's-going-on-here-attitude' that typifies pigs, they were lying around in a dejected, listless way.

'Gladys not showing any signs?' I asked.

He shook his head. 'This started yesterday with that one over there looking a bit sleepy. Now this one has a rash all over the sides.'

I looked at her first. She let out a squeal as soon as we went near her, which provoked Gladys in the next pen. She hadn't forgotten whose piglets these were. The temperature on the thermometer shot up to 108 degrees in seconds. I turned the pig over and there, clustered on her side, were diamond-shaped red spots. I looked at them closely to make sure I would remember their precise appearance next time I came across a case like this. I took the temperatures of several of the other pigs in the pen. All had a fever to a varying degree.

I turned back to Paddy. 'Looks like erysipelas,' I said giving him a potted summary of the text I had read twenty minutes earlier.

'I'll give them all shots of penicillin and if I'm right we should see a big improvement by tomorrow, although I'm a bit worried about this one,' I said, pointing to the runt of the litter. I had learned not to be too optimistic about the outcome of my treatments – better to be cautious, especially early on. I waded amongst the sick pigs giving each a syringe full of penicillin.

When I had finished the injections we went inside for a big mug of tea and some toast. It reminded me of my first visit.

'How are those piglets I delivered?'

'Great. All twelve have survived and she's doing 'em really well.'

Paddy was relying on all his young pigs to bring in some cash over the next few months when they were 'finished' – or at the final selling weight. Any losses would be a financial disaster.

'I think we should start a vaccination programme for the others,' I suggested. I couldn't insist. Vaccinations cost money. But there weren't any financial short cuts, as I was beginning to find out. With luck, we had caught the others in time, but prevention is better – and cheaper – than cure.

I was just loading my things into the boot of the Anglia when Eileen appeared.

'Did anyone mention Joker to you?'

Ah yes, the collie. We went into the living room, where he was lying asleep in his basket.

'He wouldn't eat yesterday and he's completely knocked out. Not like him at all,' said Paddy, stroking the dog's flank.

'How old is he?' I asked

'Just a young 'un. Three. We got him off a neighbour. I was thinking of rearing some sheep and training him up, but he's turned into a right house dog. Never leaves the wife's side. Can't be bothered even with me.' I laughed. I had already seen plenty of farm collies and they all seemed to latch on to one person as their favourite.

'He's worse than ever this morning,' Eileen added, trying to keep the worry out of her voice.

We got the dog out of his basket and he could hardly stand. I took his temperature – it didn't register on the thermometer and the dog felt cold in spite of being in a warm room. There was blood on the thermometer. I looked inside his mouth – he was as white as a sheet.

There could be no beating about the bush.

'I'm afraid he's dreadfully ill – can I use your phone?'

I dialled the hospital and Pauline answered within three rings, as she always did.

'Is Frank or Peter around? I need some advice. It's urgent.'

'Peter's just finishing an operation. Hang on a minute.' After less than a minute, Peter came on the line.

I gave a summary of Joker's symptoms. There was a pause while he thought. I could practically hear the cogs clicking over. Even though he spent all his time in the hospital, he still knew many of the farmers from night calls.

'I seem to remember that Paddy had a problem with rats a while back,' he said. 'Ask him if he's been using any rat poison.'

As I passed this on, Paddy's expression said it all. He turned to his wife rather than me. 'Well, you know what he's like, Eileen, always got his nose into everything.'

I turned back to the phone. 'Seems like it's a possibility,

Peter. Warfarin?' This was a common rat poison which interfered with the blood clotting mechanisms, causing internal bleeding.

'Exactly,' came the reply. 'We've got to get him in right away – if he's as bad as you say he is, he may need blood. At the very least a drip.'

I turned to the distraught couple.

'Can you bring him to the hospital?'

Eileen burst into tears.

'The car's in the garage having a new clutch and service. It won't be ready until this afternoon.'

I put the receiver to my ear again. 'I'll have to bring him in, Peter. Expect me in forty minutes, and can you ask Pauline to let the remainder of my list know that I'll be delayed?'

Without further ado, I wrapped the sick dog in a large blanket and put him on the back seat of the car. I left in a rush, telling the Dixons that I'd be back in an hour when I resumed my rounds, to let them know how things were going. As I drove out of the farmyard I could see Paddy in the rear view mirror, trying to console his distraught wife.

It took half an hour to get the dog to the hospital. I parked and carried him straight in to the prep room, where Peter was just finishing off the morning's minor operations. Frank was still busy in the consulting room. Barbara, the senior practice nurse, and Jackie, a new addition to the small animal team, had got a drip set up and were warming-up the saline solution. The practice was one of the few in the country that regularly performed blood transfusions and luckily there was a bag available.

Peter looked over the dog. By now a lot of blood was coming from his back end.

'I think you're right about it being Warfarin,' was all he

said as the team got to work trying to save the dog. The veins were so collapsed from lack of blood pressure that Peter had to cut down to the vein in the front leg before inserting the Mitchell needle, a large bore needle used for intravenous infusions. The convenient, easy-to-use disposable, plastic catheters had yet to be invented. Much as I would have liked to follow the case, I had work to do. The back of the car needed a bit of a clean-up and once more there was a smell which would take a few days to shift.

I drove quickly down the Roman road out of town, regaining the tranquil countryside within minutes. I popped into Paddy's kitchen for a few minutes just to give an update. He was as white as a sheet and full of guilt for not calling the vet in sooner, and of course for allowing the inquisitive dog to come into contact with the poison in the first place.

'What do you think? Will he be all right?' he asked me.

'Look, I'm sorry, Paddy, but I just don't know.' This was simply the truth. I had never had to deal with a Warfarin poisoning before.

'What I do know is that he's got the best chance possible with Peter treating him, plus the fact that a bag of freshly taken blood was available. Fingers crossed. Peter will phone you before he goes home. He's also on duty tonight, so he'll keep an eye on him.'

Looking at the two of them, so worried about their dog, I couldn't help but reflect on the contrast between the usual matter-of-fact down-to-earth farmer and the average doting pet owner. Here, for once, I could see both sets of values. Joker wasn't a working kennelled dog, he was one of the family.

I pressed on and decided to go without lunch. By two o'clock I had finished the morning's rounds and phoned in for any other calls. There were just two – at opposite ends of the practice boundaries.

'Got your stitch-up kit on board?' There was a slight edge to Frank's voice, which suggested that if I hadn't, I would be for the high jump. It would mean I would have to make the unnecessary journey in to pick it up. Vets were supposed to update the boots of their cars daily, to make sure they never ran out of anything.

'Yep!' I was pleased to say. I had done a check on Sunday afternoon. 'Why – what have we got?' This time there was an edge to my voice. What did I need to stitch up?

'Joe Anstey has got a cow that's trodden on her teat. It will need stitching. Ever done one?'

'No.' I was getting better at telling the truth.

'Well, don't worry. It should be straightforward. Get him to restrain the cow and do a ring block round the base of the teat and then stitch up. Blast – I don't suppose you've got a teat siphon, have you?'

As a matter of fact I had, because I had decided to keep one in the car for any sinus jobs.

'OK. Put it in before you stitch up and leave it with Joe. Tell him to put it in at each milking. He'll need to sterilize it each time he uses it. Get the job done and phone in again. I might do the other call myself – I could do with a breath of fresh air.'

With that he rang off. I suspected that every now and then Frank hankered after the large animal vet's life, having done years of it before specializing in small animal work. Understandably, it was sun-filled days like today that tempted him, rather than middle of a winter night call-outs. I walked over to my car. Yes – it was a beautiful day and I had hardly noticed. For a moment I toyed with the idea of finding a clearing to lie down and relax for a while. But Joe

Anstey was waiting for me and I didn't want a repetition of last time, with only old Eddie to help me.

Ten minutes later I rolled into the Anstey's farmyard. It was eerily quiet – in the distance I could hear the rhythmic swoosh and click of the milking machine. I walked over to the milking parlour and went in. There was Eddie, busy finishing off the milking on the last four cows. My heart sank. As he saw me, I got a cheery wave as he pushed on a lever to let the cows amble out – all except one, which I quickly realized would be my patient. I could see blood dripping from one of her teats.

''Ow are you?' he said. I marvelled once again at his ability to talk with the hand-rolled cigarette still stuck to his upper lip. It looked as if it had gone out. Maybe it was the same one as before, I mused to myself. It had the same shape. Very thin, with an indentation in the middle. There didn't seem to be much tobacco in it. Maybe that was how he had survived the habit this long. I was about to ask where Joe was, when my question was answered.

'Guvnor'll be 'ere any minute.'

'That's the cow, I take it?' I said, pointing to the large Friesian standing in the parlour, still eating the rest of her allocated cake ration.

Eddie nodded. 'She's a bit of a wild 'un, she is. You'd do well to watch 'er.' There was a mischievous glint in his eyes, with obvious memories of my last visit.

'Wonderful!' I said to myself. Visions of getting a good kicking with less than two weeks to go the county championships came to my mind. That particular gloomy thought was put out of my mind by the appearance of 'the guvnor'. Joe Anstey was well over six foot and broad to go with it.

'Glad to meet you, Mr Grant,' he said, grabbing my

hand and virtually squeezing the life out of it. 'They tell me you can handle cows.'

'Well, I was rather hoping you would be able to help me with this one,' I said. 'She'll need her front leg tying up and someone to hold the tail up.'

The standard way to prevent cows from kicking was to get someone to hold the front leg up. This made kicking difficult, since the cow would then be balancing on two legs out of four. The other method was to push the tail up so that it was almost vertical. It wasn't painful for the cow and somehow made kicking very difficult. Ideally, I would have liked someone to hold her by the nose as well. The invention of convenient and effective sedative injections was a few years off, so manual techniques were the order of the day.

Joe proved himself to be a resourceful and experienced herdsman. He put a loop of rope round the front leg and hoisted the rope over the top of the milking cubicle. Having secured it, Eddie was given the job of holding on. Even I trusted him to do that. It needed very little strength as the rope was more or less a pulley. Joe pushed the tail up while I injected the local anaesthetic round the base of the teat. The needle I used was as fine as that I had experienced myself only a week or so before in the dentist's chair. All the paraphernalia was to protect me from the mighty lashing out that the cow would produce at the slightest prick. I had seen them lazily kick out at flies. It would be my face at the receiving end if I didn't take all the precautions. With five injections I finished a complete ring round the teat – the so-called ring block. Then it was a question of waiting five minutes, putting the siphon in and cleaning the teat up. The cow didn't move while I gently cleaned up the teat to reveal a nasty jagged wound.

Stitching-up proved to be a long job. It was partly due to my inexpert technique but mostly due to the cow constantly changing feet and shifting about, even though she couldn't feel anything. I was sure if Joe hadn't been holding the tail up she would have lashed out just for the hell of it. It took half an hour in all and ten stitches, and even Joe's massive frame was showing signs of fatigue by the end. Bright red in the face, and sweating, he was mightily relieved when I told him to let the tail go.

'Just a jab and she can be on her way. And I gather you're happy to give her an injection for the next three days?'

Joe nodded. I had forgotten Eddie, who had got quite stiff holding on to the leg. With a toothless grin, he produced a box of matches and tried to get his cigarette alight. After a few futile attempts he gave up and, reaching in his pocket, produced a wad of tobacco and set about hand-rolling a new one. It brought back memories of my grandfather, who had lost an arm in an industrial accident. With the aid of a cigarette rolling machine he was able to make a much better job of it than Eddie. The new version – looking much the same as the others – did light up, and the pungent smell of pouch tobacco filled the air.

'Well, she were tamed.' he said as we watched the cow wander out to join the rest of the herd. 'I thought we'd 'ave a lot more trouble than that!'

Joe seemed pleased as well. My reputation as a cow handler was secure. I was secretly pleased at my minor surgery and I wasn't going to let on that it was another first. Time for a cup of tea, and as I sat down a wave of weariness came over me, which wasn't helped by the thought of evening surgery looming. I looked at my watch – quarter to five. I had a brief sense of envy for all those 'normal' people in nine-to-five jobs. It would be half-six tonight if I was lucky. And then I looked at Joe, who was beaming away at the thought of a cow saved from the knacker's yard, and I thought that life wasn't too bad after all. What had I to complain about?

In the event, evening surgery was finished just after six. There was no pattern, no rhyme or reason. The morning had been hectic, the afternoon and evening quiet. Before leaving, I took a look at Joker. Barbara was with him and would be there all night. He was unconscious, but breathing steadily. His colour was slightly pinker than the deathly white of earlier. I simply had no idea whether he would make it or not. I suddenly felt exhausted. Perhaps I could get a full night's sleep.

Before heading home, I dropped in as usual at the Spotted Cow.

Theo caught my eye and was pouring a pint before I got to the bar. His son was helping out too, and we were introduced.

'Hi, Dave, meet the chip off the old block, my son, Tony.'

Theo was the only person who ever called me Dave. And it didn't surprise me when a few minutes later 'Tony' introduced himself to the others as Anthony.

I was getting to know the regulars. There was Jonathan, a consultant in neurology at the local hospital. He had been a Spitfire pilot during the war but rarely talked about either his work or his wartime experiences, unless he had had a few drinks. I did get out of him one time that he had ditched in the Channel after a dogfight during the Battle of Britain. Then, in his usual place in the corner, was Steve. He was a jazz clarinettist and liked to get out for a couple of pints whenever he wasn't working. His wife had just had a baby and he tried to get out while they were both sleeping. He had that drawn look of parents of newborn babies who were finding out that they could do with much less sleep than they had thought possible.

A quick drink threatened to turn into an evening. First Barbara and Jackie dropped in. Barbara didn't stay long, as she wanted to get back to Joker, but left Jackie with me. Joker didn't need both of them, she said. I felt I couldn't leave a newcomer on her own, even though we were already a jolly group. Then Keith and Jenny and Phil and Sue turned up. Anthony, who had come the other side of the bar, was soon deep in conversation with Jackie, talking about the pitfalls of working long and arduous shifts. He was a trainee chef. 'Who's that?' Keith asked as we were getting last orders, indicating Jackie.

'Our new nurse.'

'Been expanding the career options, eh, doing a bit of match making?'

'Well, I don't seem to be having much luck on my own account.'

Keith raised his eyebrows and looked pointedly at Angie.

'Just friends,' I said.

I suddenly felt totally wiped out, made my excuses and left.

By any standards it had been a heavy day. But as I pushed open the door to the flat, I caught sight of my track-suit and running shoes in a heap where I had left them the night before, and I was flooded with guilt. The defence of the championship was less than two weeks away. But, frankly, after a hard day rushing around the Kent countryside, all I wanted to do was crash. But in Angie I had a guardian angel – or tyrant from hell – depending on your point of view. She would hear my heavy step on the stairs, and no sooner had I slumped wearily in my battered old armchair trying to summon up the energy to get something to eat, than her beaming face would appear around the door, like the Cheshire Cat in *Alice In Wonderland*.

It was becoming a regular feature of my routine.

That night, all I really wanted to do was to sleep for twelve hours.

'No, Angie,' I groaned when she stood at my door wagging her finger in her don't-forget-I'm-a-teacher way.

'Not now. You have no idea what kind of a day I've had. I just can't face it.'

'Yes you can. You've got to. And you know it. Come on – just half an hour and then perhaps I can tempt you to some fish and chips.'

I hauled myself out of the chair and got into my tracksuit, picking up the stopwatch as we left. Angie was right, I would have to do another eight or nine sessions of training to give myself a chance.

Warming up by jogging round the park brought a surprising amount of life into me, and I paced out 150 metres to be run flat out. It felt surprisingly good, and in the end I managed ten of them. I dropped off Angie at the local fish and chip shop, just a couple of hundred yards from the house, and jumped into a hot bath after I had put a couple of plates into the oven to warm. By the time she got back, the tiredness had dropped away and fish and chips never tasted better. However tired or gloomy I felt, Angie always seemed to laugh it out of me. I imagine the day-to-day life of most student teachers is much the same, but Angie had the knack of turning everything that happened to her into a story, an adventure. She was now on teaching practice and was loving it, in spite of the pressure, knowing you were being watched and judged at every moment. But I knew even then that she would make a marvellous teacher. With Angie you were never bored. Whatever went wrong in her life – and a lot did – she always managed to see the funny side. And when it was my turn to recount the day's adventures, my own stories always seemed funnier when Angie was around.

Now I could relax. I had a normal week to look forward to, with only two night duties and, at the weekend, the social high spot of the season, the local point-to-point that is so typical of English rural life. We had decided to make a day of it and take a picnic. Even Keith had agreed to come, and I was looking forward to seeing him dressed in something that wasn't hot off the rails in Carnaby Street.

As for Joker, Angie was as concerned as I was. I had been planning to go round and see for myself how he was getting on, and I asked if she'd like to come.

We walked the five minutes round to the hospital. There we found Barbara checking his pulse and making sure the drip was running. Every two hours he was turned to help the circulation and to prevent bed sores. Peter had just left – he wouldn't be getting his evening meal until nine-thirty. Joker had regained some consciousness. There was a desultory wave of his tail if you spoke to him. His colour was improving – at least to my untutored eye.

'I just hope he makes it,' I said.

'What do you mean, *hope*,' Barbara demanded. 'Of course he's going to make it! We're looking after him!'

She said this with such confidence that I found myself believing her. For some reason or other, I had always tended to be a pessimist, but this experienced nurse inspired confidence.

Barbara was a no-nonsense redhead, who always

reminded me of Lucille Ball in the Fifties American TV series, *I Love Lucy*. She was older than anybody else in the practice apart from Frank – in her mid-thirties I suppose – and always looked immaculate. The nurses' uniforms accentuated her tiny waist. Jackie, on the other hand, appeared to have no waist at all. In stature she was like Twiggy, the same size everywhere. Barbara's great strength as a veterinary nurse – apart from her unfailing good humour and her motherly way with distressed owners – was her encyclopaedic memory. Any disease or condition, and no matter how obscure, Barbara had seen it.

Joker was definitely improving. He lapped a little water when his head was supported and was obviously enjoying being stroked.

'Shouldn't we phone Paddy and Eileen – they looked frantic the last time I saw them,' I suggested to Barbara.

'No – it's too soon. Imagine how they'll feel if we raise their hopes and he goes downhill again!'

'Who's being negative now?' I laughed. She was right, of course, but it did look as though he would make it. We would have to wait and see, maybe another twenty-four hours. It was with an effort that I left Joker in the capable hands of his nurse, and also with a tinge of guilt as we walked home.

# *Chapter Eleven*

Tuesday morning. Another nice day. The sun was already high in the sky by the time I awoke and I was beset by a sense of guilt. June in Kent is, to my mind, the most glorious month of the year, but sometimes it doesn't seem to want to get going. The cricket season was in full swing and, although I didn't play myself, Charles played for his local village and I was looking forward to lazy days of lying around listening to the thump of leather on willow, desultory clapping and teas of lemonade and cucumber sandwiches. Dare I hope that we were going to have one of those rare spells of English sunshine lasting a few weeks? A quick shower, a hurried breakfast and I just made it for nine. Frank had already been in for an hour and had arranged all the morning calls.

Again I was to be spared morning surgery as we were a large animal vet short. I had already booked a repeat visit to Paddy Dixon, so while Frank was sorting the rest of the visits out I checked on Joker. He was still on a drip, but was now taking food for himself and had shifted position a couple of times. Peter was checking him over.

'I'm off to see Paddy and Eileen in a while – do you want me to relay any messages?' I asked.

'Tell them he's going to make it, but we'll need to keep him in for another couple of days,' he said, while expertly changing the needle in Joker's vein. 'It's been touch and go, though. Just as well you brought him in quickly.'

I was quite pleased to hear this, as it hadn't occurred to me that my role in the drama had been anything more than an extra.

I stroked the dog's head and he responded by shutting his eyes and pushing his head up, as dogs do. I was looking forward to passing on the good news. If the number of anxious phone calls that had been coming in all morning were anything to go by, the Dixons had had a tough time coping.

I wandered back in to find out what was in store. A couple of lambings, some calf castrations, a few pregnancy diagnoses and a vomiting dog. I frowned at that one.

'Can't they bring it in?' I asked Frank.

'I've tried, but they insist the dog won't travel in a car. Have a look, and they'll have to get in by hook or by crook if it's serious.'

Visions of another Nero came to mind. With no time to reflect, I checked the drugs and equipment in the car, climbed in and set off with a good feeling about the morning's work.

I swung into Paddy Dixon's yard forty minutes later. He came out before I had even got out of the car. His anxious face showed that he hadn't got through to the hospital. Eileen came to the door, her hands covered in flour.

'He's going to make it,' I said. She burst into tears and went back in.

'Thank God!' was all Paddy could say. 'We haven't slept a wink all night.'

'Mr Archer wants to keep him in for another day or two to be absolutely certain,' I said. 'How are the pigs doing?'

'The pigs?' I might as well have asked him the odds on England winning the Ashes, he was so distracted. 'Oh – they seem a lot better. They're virtually back to normal, in fact.'

We walked over to the pens where the sick pigs were. They were no longer sick. Injecting them needed plenty of pig nuts, which they ate ravenously. There were no longer any diamonds on the flanks. I was amazed at how rapid the response had been. It was as the books had told me. A rapid response to penicillin was typical with erysipelas.

'Right – reckon you can jab this lot for a couple more days?'

Paddy nodded.

'And if it's all right with you, we'll set up a vaccine programme for the rest. I'll find out exactly how much it will cost. Any chance of a mug of tea?'

As we went into the kitchen, Eileen, looking much more like her usual cheery self, was already pouring the water into the kettle.

'You two look as though you need brandy in that tea!' I said.

Paddy laughed, as he remembered making the same suggestion to me after I had performed Olympian feats getting out of his pig pens on my first-ever case as a qualified vet. It seemed like years ago, although it was only a few weeks. In that short time I had made quite a few friends, including the Dixons, and learned more than I could possibly have imagined. Now well on my way to being a fully fledged vet – at least on the farm animal side – I couldn't stay long. I was learning that time was precious too, and I never seemed to have enough of it.

I had my tea but then excused myself. 'Can't stay around, I'm afraid. I've got two lambings and a vomiting dog amongst other things,' and added, 'Oh, and Peter says he thinks it would be better it you didn't visit Joker in case he gets too excited and dislodges the needle in his vein. Just give the surgery a call to see how he's doing.'

I wrote down a note to talk to Frank about arranging some vaccinating next week and to get a costing. Then I was on my way to two lambings, both on neighbouring farms. The last of the lambings were coming in and I positively looked forward to them. It had surprised me how quickly my theoretical knowledge had expanded with a bit of practice on the real thing. Neither of the two lambings caused me any bother and I delighted myself and the farmers with two live lambs. Then on to the calf castrations, which I also did in double quick time. A far cry from my first fumbling efforts. I looked at my watch. Half twelve – time to have a look at the vomiting dog in a village on the outskirts of town. I might even get an hour's lunch.

I knocked on the door of the small cottage. A pathetic soft barking announced that a dog lived there, but not a healthy one from the sounds of things. The door opened to reveal a harassed looking woman in her late thirties holding a baby. As I entered, I got an inkling of the reasons why she looked so frazzled. In front of the television, which was on far too loud, were five children all under seven years. In a basket right in front of the box was my patient, a young Dalmatian bitch.

'What seems to be the problem?' I asked in time-honoured fashion. The answer was lost to the cacophony of sound emanating from the TV.

'Sean – turn that blasted thing off!'

When nothing happened, she pushed through the sprawl of bodies and pushed the 'Off' knob. Immediately a howl went up.

'Oh, Mum,' whined the eldest, 'we're watching it.'

'Perhaps we can examine her in the kitchen,' I suggested helpfully.

The dog was moved, the TV went back on and I

attempted to examine Olga. The noise levels went back up again, so that I could hardly think.

Mrs Turner either read my mind or the expression on my face and went back in to the lounge. She turned the noise down, but as soon as she walked back into the kitchen it was up again.

'You wait until your father gets back!' she bellowed in reply, but made no further attempt to lower the level of noise.

It took twenty minutes to get a reasonable history and when I looked at Olga there was nothing much I could see. She had been sick for two days and was very lethargic. Her temperature was up a bit, but apart from a tender tummy I had nothing much to go on. I made a snap diagnosis – gastritis, or inflammation of the stomach, and gave the dog an injection of antibiotic.

'Try her with a little food – but not until tomorrow, and then see if she's hungry.' But Mrs Turner wasn't listening. A fight had broken out between two toddlers over the ownership of some marbles.

'If she's still vomiting tomorrow,' I continued above the mayhem, 'you'll have to get her in.' My head was splitting with the noise of the TV and children combined.

'Bring her to evening surgery if your husband can't get time off,' was my last bit of advice.

I rolled back into town and realized that I would only get twenty minutes for lunch. I was beginning to dislike these small animal visits. Irascible, biting budgie owners, terrifying dogs and now futile attempts to make sense of a history and examination to the background of infant warfare. Three quarters of an hour of mayhem instead of ten minutes in the civilization of the hospital. Some of the practices in London, I was told, were giving up on house visits altogether. I could see why.

I was just downing a cheese sandwich, helped by half a pint of shandy, when the vision of chaos in the living room returned into sharp focus – and in particular the marbles strewn all over the floor. Olga couldn't have eaten one of them, could she? The thought began to dominate and spoilt my lunch. Now I would worry about it until tomorrow. I decided to broach the subject with Frank when I got back.

Frank was about to fix a broken leg and was preoccupied enough with how he was going to manage it. The patient, a German shepherd, had slipped out of his owner's house and been hit by a car. His elbow joint was broken. Frank was studying the X-ray as I went in to discuss Mrs Turner's dog.

'What's your advice on this one?' he asked me.

The elbow was well and truly smashed.

'Pins and screws?' I suggested vaguely. 'You're welcome to it. It looks almost beyond repair!'

I thought back to the college professors who did nothing but this kind of thing every day but I couldn't recall what the usual method of repair was for elbows.

'What can I do for you?' said Frank, coming straight to the point.

I explained about the Turners' dog and my worry about the marbles.

'Well, it's quite possible, I suppose. Young Dalmatian and kids playing with marbles. Did you check the pulse? What about the capillary refill? Did you check the scleral membrane of the eyes?'

All these questions came while he was making measurements with a ruler on the X-ray. He went on.

'Foreign body. You'd expect a lifeless dog, vomiting but nothing coming out the other end. A weak thready pulse and injected scleral membranes round the eye. You get that in pyos too, don't you? It's a sign that the dog is toxic. Should get a sluggish capillary refill, too. Well, if it is a marble, the dog will get worse. I wouldn't have given the antibiotic, though. That will mask the symptoms.'

I hadn't done the examination as well as I might have. I opened my mouth to tell him about the chaotic conditions that hampered my thinking – but decided not to.

'I'll put a note on the card to check for a foreign body and phone Mrs Turner to get the dog in tonight.'

Pauline came in, interrupting our conversation. 'A milk fever and a calving have just come in – and a personal letter for you.'

'Fan mail already?' Frank said with a grin. 'You'd better save it for later. Looks like you're in for a busy time!' With that, he went into the prep room to give his patient an anaesthetic for an operation that was going to occupy most of his afternoon. With the letter in my pocket I set off for my afternoon's work. The sun was up and it was a very pleasant seventy degrees. I'd do the milk fever first and then on to Rupert Charlton-Jones, ten minutes away, for the calving. With a bit of luck, the calf would be out naturally by the time I got there.

I had to suppress a grin an hour later when I got to Rupert's farm. I had arrived five minutes too late. Already the spindly-legged calf was on his feet, having found his mother's teat, and was tucking in to his first meal. Every now and then he would butt the udder as they all do – it stimulates milk let-down. He was too enthusiastic though, and would lose his balance and topple over after a particularly strong butt.

Rupert was all apologies. 'Sorry to waste your time,' he said, 'but it didn't look as though she was going to get on with the job.'

'That's OK – I had a milk fever just down the road anyway.'

'We're just about to have tea – you're welcome to join us.'

All the training was making me permanently hungry, and I didn't need a second invitation.

We took our boots off and went in to the farmhouse. Like everything else on the farm, it was immaculate. Passing through the farm kitchen, I was ushered into the lounge, which Rupert called the drawing room. It was huge, with great oak beams across the ceiling.

'Parts of the house are five hundred years old,' he said.

'And it needs lots of upkeep!'

This was said by an older woman, tall and elegant in a flowered silk dress that wouldn't have been out of place at a society wedding. She was carrying a silver tray piled high with scones, cream, jam and butter.

'Bring in the teapot, will you, darling?'

Rupert smiled a lop-sided smile and dashed out.

'Mr Grant. How do you do? I'm Rupert's mother, Helena. You've timed your visit very well. A proper tea is one of my little rituals. Rupert has learnt to indulge me. I'm afraid we couldn't do without it, could we, darling?' she added as her son returned, bearing the most ornate silver teapot I had ever seen.

Rupert grinned. 'Well, Father doesn't get in from London until eight-thirty and we normally eat dinner then. Tea keeps me going.'

Mrs Charlton-Jones smiled at her son. It was obvious that he was the apple of her eye. As we chatted, she turned out to be far less forbidding that I expected. She had originally trained as a violinist, but now spent all her time looking after the men in her life.

'We always listen to music around this time. I do hope you don't mind,' she apologized as she put on their latest acquisition, a violin concerto that, in spite of non-stop listening to the Third programme in the car, I failed to recognize. The elegance of the music perfectly matched the elegance of the surroundings. For a second – but only a second – I felt a twinge of guilt, thinking of Frank probably sweating over the dog's elbow at this precise moment.

'Mozart's violin concerto number five,' said Rupert's mother. 'Zukerman. I do love this one in particular.'

'Mother used to be able to play it,' said Rupert, 'before I came along and changed everything!'

'Nonsense, darling. I wouldn't have it any other way. Milk or lemon, Mr Grant? And I do hope you're happy with Indian. Milsoms failed to include my order for China in their delivery. When I remonstrated with young Mr Milsom he told me that we were lucky to have a delivery at all, that soon we would all be doing our shopping in supermarkets.'

I was in a different world. In an elegant five hundred-year-old house eating the most magnificent scones I had ever tasted, comfortably installed in a luxurious armchair and listening to beautiful, calming music. I suddenly envied Rupert his lifestyle. What on earth did he have to worry about?

As the concerto came to an end, Rupert broke into my daydreaming.

'Do you think we should give the cow some calcium? Do you think she might get milk fever?'

Back to the real world.

'Well, it won't be a bad idea if I take a look at her before leaving. Thanks so much for the tea,' I added, smiling at Rupert's mother.

'You're most welcome. Now you know our ritual. Tea's at four-thirty on the dot.'

'I would love to. How many records do you have?'

In answer, she led the way into the library, decked from ceiling to floor with books and records.

'Hundreds, if not thousands.'

'Another time I'll get your advice. I've just started my own collection.'

We were just about to get into a long conversation when the phone went. I jumped, instinctively knowing it was for me. I had been an hour away from the busy world and was about to be reminded of it. Could I get in to evening surgery as quickly as possible? Both Peter and Frank were still hard at it, getting the day's ops done, and the signs were of a busy session building up. After checking out the cow – she was fine, of course – I jumped into the car and shot off. It would only be half an hour into town.

As luck would have it, I got stuck behind the bus, also going into town. There was no way past it and the driver was determined to take it easy. I resigned myself to being late, following along at a sedate twenty-five miles an hour. I was lulled into thinking about Olga and the possible presence of a marble. She had the typical signs – Frank had described her to a tee. I should have checked those mucous membranes – I would, next time.

The bus had just pulled away from a bus stop – I had no reason to think it would stop. But it did. Suddenly. To exchange greetings with the driver of another bus coming the other way. It was the last thing I was expecting on a straight country road. In spite of hard braking, I hit the back of it at ten miles an hour, enough to bang my knee and make a dent on the dashboard and wreck the lights and radiator. There wasn't a scratch on the bus – but goodness knows how much damage to the car.

'Your fault, mate!' was all the bus driver said. 'It's the law.'

As there was no damage to his bus, he couldn't have cared less. We exchanged insurance details and he went on his way. To my temporary relief, the car was drivable and I limped back to base. As I arrived, Mrs Turner, five kids and a very sick-looking Olga were walking through the car park. She could only just walk, and by the time she got to the door she sat down and refused to go any further. I picked her up and carried her in. Frank had not long finished his operation and was looking in need of a rest.

'This is the dog I told you about,' I said, deciding to leave the news of the car until later.

I put Olga on the table in consulting room one while Frank cast an eye over her.

He went through the examination with me – all the signs were there. With a little sedation he could feel a lump in the intestines and, just to be sure, he took an X-ray. Although a marble wouldn't show up, its presence was strongly suggested by the copious build up of air behind where it was causing an obstruction. No doubt about it – she would need an operation, and pretty soon. First, because she was dehydrated she would need a drip. Frank looked at his watch.

'You and I can do this after evening surgery,' he said. 'The operation should be straightforward.'

I nodded my agreement – assisting in the operation would complete my education in foreign bodies.

It was only when Mrs Turner said she had to go if they weren't to miss the bus that I remembered to tell Frank about the car. He seemed more concerned about me than the Anglia, noticing for the first time my gashed knuckles.

'Just as well we haven't got rid of the old one,' he added, as he and Barbara set up the drip. 'You'll have to go back to that for a few weeks. Might as well transfer all your gear before you start consulting, just in case we get a calving in.'

Frank could always think of all contingencies even when doing half a dozen things at once.

Once more my spirits were down. I had failed to make the correct diagnosis in Olga's case, meaning she would have her operation a day later than necessary, making it more risky for her, and keeping Frank in until seven-thirty at least. He would have put in a twelve-hour day today. I felt another twinge of guilt when I compared the pleasant day I had had – up to the crash that is – sampling the good life. Still, he had taken the news about the car very calmly. I had expected a real dressing down.

A couple of hours later I was trimming the sutures in the skin in Olga's abdomen. The operation had only taken half an hour. Frank worked fast and with tremendous precision and concentration. The marble had been found almost immediately – where Frank said he expected to find it, at the junction between the large and small intestines.

'That's where things usually get stuck,' he said, as he squeezed it out through a small incision.

It was bigger than a traditional marble, more the size of the two-for-a-penny sweet we used to call gobstoppers when I was a kid. I wouldn't miss one of those again I told myself. But at least Olga would be fine and we didn't anticipate any complications.

It was a quarter to eight by the time I got home. Keith and Jenny were just going out to dinner, all dressed up.

'Where's your car?' Keith always had a knack of asking the most obvious question.

'I had an argument with the back of a bus. The car came off worse!'

Keith grinned.

'Not to worry, Champ. Angie's indoors, waiting for you with the stopwatch.' He and his girlfriend hopped into Keith's car, looking like film stars. For the first time I did catch a glimpse of the George Harrison in Keith, helped no doubt by Jenny's Patti Boyd silhouette.

I heaved a sigh. What I really wanted to do was drown my sorrows in several glasses of best Kentish bitter down at the pub. I must be mad, I thought, as I trudged into the flat to get changed into my tracksuit.

It wasn't until I was on my way in to the hospital the next day and felt the envelope in my pocket that I remembered the letter Pauline had handed me the day before. It was from the convent.

> Dear Mr Grant,
> We had a film to use up and we decided to take a photo of the calf you delivered. He is doing very well, as you can see.
>
> Many grateful thanks for what you have done – will do for us!
>
> God be with you.
>
> Yours sincerely,
>
> Sr. Maria Assumpta.
>
> PS He is four days old in the photo. He loved kissing his girl companion!

There was a photo of one of the nuns holding a huge calf nearly her size. I looked at it and marvelled that the birth had been natural – well, almost! My mood lifted immediately – getting appreciation for your efforts made up for the things that went wrong. I couldn't help thinking about the smashed car as I tucked the letter back into my pocket and went into the hospital. Frank and Jackie were checking Olga over as I walked in.

'Don't look so gloomy, David. She's doing well.' Jackie knew well enough that I was smarting a bit, having failed to make the diagnosis first time, and feeling a bit low having smashed up a new car. Frank, ever the teacher, told me to check her pulse, capillary refill and scleral membranes to monitor the improvement. It was quite remarkable what the operation and twelve hours of fluids had done for her. It was a double reminder for me of what was normal and what was abnormal. Olga already had all the signs of a healthy dog, although a bit of caution was still necessary. Tonight she'd be offered some chicken and, all being well, would go home. Though, as I remembered the blaring television and screaming kids, I wondered if, given the choice, Olga wouldn't have preferred to stay in the peace and tranquillity of the hospital kennels. I suspected she had eaten the marble out of boredom. The Dalmatian puppy the Turner children had no doubt fallen in love with had grown into a big dog that needed more exercise than I suspected the harassed Mrs Turner had time to organize.

I cast my eye over the morning farm calls and picked out an itinerary from the list – I was starting to become a seasoned pro. Frank nodded and grinned at my suggestions. I suspected he was pleased to see me progressing in confidence, but he didn't say anything as he hauled his white coat on and went into his consulting room.

The morning was taken up with routine things. I was learning rapidly that most illnesses were common and occurred time and time again. Many of them would get better whatever I did – small animal medicine seemed to be a series of minor ailments with the occasional life-threatening one, like Olga's marble or Joker's poison. The secret was to recognize the serious problem when it turned up, a total contrast to the farm side, where the majority of call-outs were potentially serious from the start – most farmers not bothering us with minor problems. It was taking quite a bit of getting used to.

Having only a couple of night duties that week to disturb my sleep pattern made a world of difference to my energy levels. That spring there was very rarely a night without a call – and on the farm side that would usually mean something fairly major and almost invariably late at night, or at some ungodly hour of the morning, or, if you were unlucky, both. But night duties were at least beginning to lose their terror for me. Now it was more my single man's sense of irritation at the disruption to my social life. As for farmers, they didn't have a social life. Most of them put in even more hours than Frank. But for the next few days at least, the dread words 'I'm on duty' were to have a rest.

The weekend had arrived on a positive note: both Olga and Joker had been given the all clear. When Paddy and Eileen arrived to collect Joker, his tail wagged so furiously it was hard not to laugh. Eileen could barely speak, she was so overcome with emotion, while Paddy stood in the background beaming. Nothing I could say would dislodge their conviction that Joker's dramatic recovery was all my doing.

And the whole Turner family had turned out to take Olga home, including Mr Turner, a genial man who, unlike his wife, had the children totally under control. There was an atmosphere of euphoria in the waiting room as the two families picked up their dogs. It must have been good for business, as the other clients saw it all. It certainly made me feel extraordinarily happy.

Phil and Sue were home for the weekend, Phil the poorer by several hundred pounds having bought an engagement ring for his now fiancée. Mrs Nightingale, who had been hoping for just such an eventuality for some time, had immediately organized an impromptu celebration evening meal – which would be infinitely better than anything I could prepare. The days of ready prepared TV dinners, not to mention microwaves, were way in the future. Fish fingers and frozen peas was as glamorous as the Grant cuisine got. A glance in my fridge would have revealed a bottle of beer, a few foil-wrapped wedges of Kraft Dairylea slices and precious little else.

It wasn't that I didn't like food or enjoy cooking, but in those days there were no short cuts, no oven-ready chips or frozen pizzas. Even pasta was a bit of a novelty. Mrs Nightingale was an inventive cook and my nostrils were regularly assailed by the delicious smells coming up from her kitchen. Tonight was no exception, and twelve of us sat down to a Hungarian goulash washed down with red wine – lots of. Phil's fiancée had just been to France and brought some lovely bottles back with her, and her entire duty-free allowance went that evening.

The engagement was naturally top of the agenda, but eventually talk turned to the next day's racing, the main point of which seemed to be betting. Keith surprised everyone by saying that, in his view, gambling was 'a mug's game'. He had always struck me as someone who was as well known in the local bookie's as he was in the local pub. But apparently an uncle had gambled his life's earnings away 'on the gee-gees' and left only debts when he died.

I had never had a bet in my life, not even on the Grand National, and knew absolutely nothing about how to do it. The mechanics were as vague to me as the ethics. Phil reckoned that the important thing was to have a limit and stick to it. He would start with a pound and be prepared to lose up to ten. I gulped. That was nearly half a week's wages for me.

'Anyway,' Phil went on, 'as far as the condition of the horses is concerned, we're in luck. We've got an in-house expert.'

All eyes turned to me. Expert?

He went on to explain that the punters, as the would-be gamblers were called, could have a look at the horses in the paddock before they were saddled up for the race, to check up on their condition. This sounded interesting. I had learned a lot about horses at college and reckoned on being able to recognize a healthy horse, and, of course, being an athlete might help in recognizing a supremely fit one.

The more Phil explained what happened, the more my confidence grew. And then there was the wine.

I leaned back in my chair and, with the wine glass in my hand, silenced the general hubbub.

'If it's as you say, Phil, then I don't see why I shouldn't pick the winners. With my background, I can't lose.'

Keith snorted. 'Catch me losing money on that game,' he scoffed. 'Ever heard the expression "fools rush in"?'

Only as my head hit the pillow an hour or so later did I wonder whether Keith might not be right after all. I might be a vet, but so far I hadn't any experience at all with horses – or, even more importantly, their owners, who were universally reckoned to be more difficult than farmers or pet owners. The practice rarely dealt with horses as there was an exclusively equestrian vet in the neighbouring town, who was very successful. What little we did was done by Alan. But at least tomorrow, I thought, as sleep came, I could indulge my fancy.

The day dawned wet and windy. The rain appeared to be relentless, hammering on the skylight that was let into the bathroom ceiling. Curses. I had been looking forward to this outing for weeks, and if it went on like this the point-to-point would be completely washed out. I tried to remember all those childhood sayings that my father had trotted out when we were on holiday. Rain before seven, dry by eleven. Was that it? My watch said seven.

I buried my head in the pillows and went back to that deep sleep that comes when you're really exhausted, until a loud knocking on the door woke me again. It was Keith, in cowboy boots and fringed shirt.

'Dear me,' he said, as I peered blearily towards the door. 'What's all this? I thought you'd be all togged up by now. The fillies are all saddled and champing at the bit. Where's that famous get up and go? If you don't get a move on, we'll all be got up and gone.'

I looked at the clock – it was half past nine. A shaft of sunlight flooded into the room as I opened the curtains. The weather had changed dramatically. I was showered and dressed in ten minutes and decided to forgo breakfast. Knowing Mrs Nightingale, the picnic would provide enough food for a week. Half an hour later our convoy of cars left for the hour's journey into the Weald of Kent. The old Anglia was given a day off and I sat in the back of Keith's car with Angie, with the ever-more-permanent Jenny in the front. Phil had left his TR4 behind and was driving Mrs Nightingale's old Hillman estate car, bursting with students. Keith said that it reminded him of Dr Who's Tardis. Karen, Mrs Nightingale's daughter with a car of her own, took up the rear. There were going to be sixteen of us in all, and strapped on top of the Nightingales' car were two massive wicker hampers, which I suspected were designed for laundry rather than food.

The downpour of early morning had cleaned the air and the countryside looked incredibly fresh. For once I wasn't driving and could wonder at the beauty around me without worrying about the road.

We arrived at the course just before half past eleven. There was already a queue of cars trundling along a muddy track to find parking spaces alongside the track. Everywhere the tailgates of estate cars were up and disgorging picnic baskets and Thermos flasks and fringed tartan rugs. Some people had even brought chairs and folding tables, and later we saw them laid with cloths and what looked like best china.

As for the race track itself, it was a simple oval course with about a dozen jumps set in a natural amphitheatre, so everyone could have a good view. On the far side I could make out dozens of loose boxes and horses. Around us, the crowd was growing by the minute. All ages and all classes were represented, from small boys wearing miniature versions of their fathers' cavalry twill trousers and hacking jackets to gnarled old men whose backs were as bent as shepherds' crooks, and old dowagers, fragile as bone china, perched on shooting sticks. There was a real sense of expectation and excitement. For an amateur race course, I was amazed at the scale of it. On the far side there was a beer marquee doing a roaring trade, and towards the finish bookies were setting up.

Mrs Nightingale had thought of everything and soon we were installed in our pitch with a waterproof ground covering, deck chairs and blankets. Not that we needed warmth, as the sun was well and truly out and the only hint of the recent deluge was the damp grass which, it turned out, had greater significance than just the risk of damp bottoms.

'The going is soft,' Phil pronounced, with the air of an expert. This meant nothing to me. He explained that the knowledgeable punters would know which horses did better in the soft conditions – part of the thing known as 'Form'. Although it was barely midday, we were soon munching away on large sandwiches washed down with red wine. Another couple of glasses and I felt my eyelids growing heavy and found myself nodding off. Even after a few weeks, my body was still getting used to working twice as many hours as it had been accustomed to and the lie-in this morning had made me feel even more tired.

Karen, who had been a keen pony club member until she left school, knew quite a bit about the county horse scene and had already been chatting with the local farmers, some of whom were going to be riding.

'There you are,' she said, flopping down beside me, a race programme in her hand. 'Have a look through that.'

I cast my eye over the runners for the first race. Names of horses and owners and riders – none of which meant anything. After a while I realized that also included was their form for the last three races – which should be some kind of help in picking a likely winner, I supposed. Except that it was information available to everybody.

The first race was due to start in an hour, so Phil, Sue (the fourth finger of her left hand always prominently displayed), myself and some of the others went down to the paddock to take a closer look at the horses. Keith resolutely stayed put – he was drinking a beer straight from the bottle, reclining like an ancient Roman, with Jenny snuggled up to him, basking in the pleasant warmth of the sun.

There's a lot of talk about systems in the racing world. I knew about systems from my grandfather, the only person in our family who showed any interest in horse racing. In the early 'Sixties he had acquired his first television set and every Saturday afternoon he would be glued to it, having invested a few quid on 'a dead cert'. He was a great believer in his system, which was to back the horse that looked the most frisky in the beginners' enclosure.

My system was going to be to look at the form book and check any recent winner. The first such that caught my eye was River Boy. He was frisky, right enough, trying to buck off his rider, who looked like Rupert Charlton-Jones. Unlike the professional jockeys I had seen on TV with my grandfather, this man was tall and had a definite 'horsey' look about him. I did a double take. Surely Rupert would have said something? After all, it was only a couple of days ago that we were taking tea and listening to Mozart – but a quick check in the programme told me it wasn't Rupert. But the horse did catch my eye. River Boy had been a winner, but had failed to finish his last two times out.

'Five bob on River Boy,' I said to Phil.

'Don't waste your money,' he retorted. 'Believe me, he won't like the soft ground.'

We ambled over to the tote and I was shown how to place a bet. I decided to put the money on for a straight win. The odds on River Boy were ten to one. So fifty shillings – two pounds fifty in today's money – for a bet of 25p – if the horse came in first. Phil put a pound on the favourite, Rough Justice, which was laid at two to one. When we got back, it was for another glass of wine and some cake. The world seemed just right, and I squeezed Angie's hand and got a kiss in return.

'Now, now, young man!' Mrs Nightingale warned. 'Just you mind you look after that girl.' It wasn't only that she felt responsible for the girls under her roof, she was genuinely fond of them and she could see what was developing. She had also seen how cut up I'd been about Chantal, only a week before. I shrugged my shoulders and was about to say something when a shout went up and the distant drumming of horses' hooves signalled the start of the first race.

They were to do two circuits, and as they thundered past us I thought I could see River Boy up amongst the leaders. The loudspeakers around the ground began to let us know who the front runners were and who was down, as hoofs were caught in the jumps. These were mainly built out of straw bales and never presented any real danger, as they might in a professional steeplechase. I ran over towards the finish line, caught up in the general excitement, especially as I could see that River Boy was up there with them. The sound of the crowd reached a crescendo as they neared the finish line, but I couldn't see how anybody could distinguish the horses as they flashed across the line. A minute later River Boy was confirmed as the winner. I went over to the tote to collect my winnings – two pounds and ten shillings.

'Beginner's luck!' muttered Keith as I swaggered back.

'Luck had nothing to do with it,' I boasted. 'Don't forget, you're talking to an expert. I could see it was good horse.' But I was trying not to laugh.

Beginner's luck or not, I was now the centre of attention. The wine was going down too well and I had to be encouraged to look at the horses for the second race. I followed the same plan. This time I liked the look of a big bay horse, Tiger Lily.

'Five bob on Tiger Lily,' I said. Again Phil scoffed. 'Now that *is* ridiculous. The odds are far too long. What do you think you know that these people don't?'

I shrugged.

This time I watched the race from the start, surrounded by half our party. They had agreed with Keith that my first win was a case of beginner's luck and had made their own choices.

Tiger Lily was slow to start but then just went for it. The collective expression on the faces of the others as I went to collect my winnings can only be described as awesome.

For the next race I chose a beautiful grey with a woman rider. The horse was called Jenny's Fancy.

'Come on Keith.' I said. 'You've got to put a few bob on that one.'

He wasn't to be swayed, though this time I noticed that Phil had stopped his know-all act and had followed suit – at eight to one, the horse looked a good bet.

Fifteen minutes later we were collecting our winnings after Jenny's Fancy romped away four lengths ahead of the field.

Looking back on that afternoon, it really was unbelievable. The same pattern followed for the next two races. I would pretend to look at a horse with a professional eye and then back one of them, based, frankly, on nothing much more professional than whim. With alarm I realized that I was attracting some interest, as one by one each horse came in a winner. For my initial five shillings I had now amassed the amazing sum of fourteen pounds – just over half a week's wages. Each winner was celebrated with a glass of wine, and I staggered up to the paddock for the last race of the afternoon. However, my 'system' did involve giving the horse the benefit of my professional eye. My confidence deserted me as I realized that I couldn't even get the horses into focus. However hard I tried, they all looked the same.

Honesty, I decided, was the best policy.

'They all look the same to me,' I declared.

They would have none of it. I was the Oracle. Even Keith had decided to put a pound on whatever I recommended. In desperation, I looked at the chalked-up names on the bookies' boards, and it seemed that Desert Spring was the punters' favourite.

'Desert Spring looks a good bet!' I said with more conviction than I felt. Almost immediately I found myself on my own as everyone made tracks for the tote. I went smartly in the other direction: all that wine had gone through me and I was desperate to find the loo. Five minutes later, greatly relieved, I returned, but was too late to place a bet as the race had already started. As I weaved my way back through the cheering crowds lining the course, I caught a glimpse of our party yelling at the tops of their voices, as the horses flew by on the first circuit. The fever had even engulfed Mrs Nightingale, who had been left in charge of the feast. As I flopped down at her feet and tried to pour myself a cup of black coffee, she stayed glued to her binoculars, whooping, 'Desert Spring's in the lead!'

I couldn't believe it. Surely I couldn't pick all six winners in my first-ever point-to-point? I tried to stand up, immediately felt dizzy and sat down again. The usual crescendo of yelling and shouting signified the finish, but when the horses came past I didn't recognize the one at the front, because I couldn't see it. 'Desert Spring?' I said to Mrs Nightingale. I hardly dared ask.

'Yes,' replied Mrs Nightingale. 'But he hasn't got a rider.'

I looked again as he started to slow down. Sure enough, he was riderless. Meanwhile, Mrs Nightingale was scanning the course with her binoculars.

'There he is.' she exclaimed and passed me the binoculars. At the far end of the course I could see a disconsolate rider walking back towards the finish. It was the Rupert Charlton-Jones look-alike.

As our group came back, I pretended to be asleep. Most people had lost money, or just broken even, except Phil, who was still quids in, having put five pounds on Jenny's Fancy which came in at eight to one.

Keith was a fiver down, having put two pounds and ten shillings each way on my last tip. Jenny was furious, not so much at Keith losing the money, but because he'd made the bet at all.

Slowly we packed up the picnic baskets. The party was over.

It had always been planned that Jenny would take over the driving on the way back, and perhaps it was because she was completely sober while the rest of us were at the other end of the scale, that she couldn't see the funny side. But all afternoon she had made it clear that she didn't approve of gambling and, as a result, the atmosphere in Keith's Cortina was decidedly cool as we queued to leave the ground.

To feel utterly responsible for this row was not a pleasant feeling, and to make amends I suggested that I take them out for dinner the following night, on my winnings.

'We can make a foursome of it, assuming Angie ever wakes up,' I added. Angie was already fast asleep on my shoulder.

Keith visibly brightened, but Jenny didn't move a muscle.

'Look, Jenny,' I said. 'Blame it on me. I've never had a bet in my life and I can't explain how I managed to pick five winners on the trot. It was only luck I didn't lose on the last one. And that was only due to my weak bladder.'

Even Jenny couldn't resist laughing at this and she soon regained her spirits. But I felt pretty certain that Keith wouldn't be backing any horses for a while, if ever.

The celebrations over Phil and Sue's engagement continued that evening and it turned out to be quite a night. It had been dancing right from the start to the music of the Beatles, Stones, The Who and Manfred Mann I could remember, dancing with Angie and agreeing we were just good friends.

I finally got to bed at half past three and slept until eleven, one of the best sleeps I had had since starting the job. The wine must have been good, too, as I had only the slightest of headaches.

## *Chapter Twelve*

The rest of the weekend went too quickly. It seemed strange, although, on reflection, not surprising, that the long working days made the week go slowly. This was particularly so when there were too many night duties. It seemed the weekend would never come. And when it did, more often than not I would spend half of it sleeping. Perhaps I wasn't yet tough enough. The other vets in the practice seemed always to have unlimited energy; I could honestly say I had never seen any of my colleagues look as wrecked as I regularly felt. Maybe it was trying to combine top class athletics with the demanding life of a vet in country practice. It was a problem I would need to address once the county championships were over.

It was something we discussed over dinner.

I had taken up the offer from Nero's owner and taken Keith, Jenny, and Angie for an Italian meal at his smart restaurant in Church Walk. We were ushered in and a table found for us, which was right beside the toilets. Every now and then the door clunked as someone went in or came out. Not a great start. But I needn't have worried, because while we were still looking at the menu, the owner himself came out like a good patron, making sure everyone was happy, and recognized me instantly.

Issuing rapid instructions to a harassed waiter, we suddenly found ourselves moved to a quiet table on a slightly raised area overlooking the rest of the restaurant.

From then on I experienced what it might be like to be a VIP, though I felt sorry for the group that came in immediately after us and watched through the corner of my eye as they were ushered to the table we had just vacated.

Keith was clearly impressed as we became the focus of the best the restaurant had to offer. Casa Sarabini was quite a different kettle of fish from the pubs Keith was used to frequenting in his work. Not a meat pie in sight. A glass of champagne on the house while we looked over the menu? Why not.

'I'm in the wrong profession.' Keith protested, as red roses appeared for the ladies.

The business of athletics had been preying on my mind for some time, but it was Angie who brought the subject up. She knew that next weekend was the all-important county championship, the start of the summer season, and made it clear that she was intending to come and support me.

'Look,' I said. 'Don't get me wrong. I'd love you to come, but I'm not really ready. I haven't had any racing practice and, to tell you the truth, I feel like giving the whole thing up. I just don't have time to train really hard and even if I do retain the title, I have hardly any weekends available for competition this summer.'

No one really knew what to say and quietly carried on eating. But it was as if the floodgates had opened. Although this was the first time I had put it into words, it had begun to dawn on me that throughout the next few months I would be on duty more or less every other weekend due to one or another of the vets being on holiday. The way it worked for 'normal' non-athlete vets was that you yourself would get a break of a couple of weeks to make up for it. But what good was that to me? Gloomily I sipped a glass of Valpolicella, looking for sympathy and a way out.

Angie had one.

'Go for it. Win this weekend but forget about the rest. Then at least you can defend it again next year. You might be in another job by then, with more time off for training and competition.'

I looked at her fondly – what a marvellous teacher she would be. She really knew how to motivate people.

'Do you reckon?'

Before she could answer, we were interrupted by Mr Sarabini.

'Everything all right?' he beamed.

'Couldn't be better.' said Keith. 'I trust David looks after your dog just as well!'

''E no like the vet, but 'ere is no problem.' And with that he disappeared behind the swing doors leading to the kitchen.

A worrying thought occurred to me – Nero? Not here, surely. There must be all kinds of rules and regulations.

A minute later my worst fears were confirmed as the huge dog was brought out on a lead. He was all sweetness and light, sitting in front of Jenny and Angie and lifting his paw to be shaken. My guests were entranced. Nero took a particular fancy to Keith, pushing his head up to be stroked and cuddling up to him. When he got to me, he allowed himself to be stroked and then suddenly stood up, all stiff, and his expression changed.

Immediately the hairs on the back of my neck stood up as he stood quite still and showed his complete set of perfectly yellow fangs.

'Erm, Mr Sarabini – I think he's recognized my smell.' I said, very softly, so as not to draw attention to myself. Nero stared at me and then, moving towards my chair, insolently cocked his leg.

His owner pulled him back and dragged him away – returning a minute later to apologize. But he needn't have worried. Angie, Keith and Jenny were in hysterics. I wasn't going to live this one down for some time to come.

At the end of the meal we all got a drink on the house and even Mr Sarabini saw the funny side of it. As we left, in good humour after a fabulous weekend and an excellent meal, I made a mental note to add on Nero's card that he should be seen on a rota basis and that I wasn't due for at least five years.

* * *

As soon as I got in on Monday, Alan, who was just back from holiday in the Greek Islands and looking very brown, sent me off to Roy Gibbons' farm. Apparently he had asked if I was available. Agnes had just collapsed in the yard this morning and it looked to Roy like a milk fever, though he wasn't convinced.

'Roy says you'll remember who Agnes is,' he added with a quizzical look. I decided not to elaborate.

'I just hope she responds to treatment,' I replied. 'She's the biggest cow I've ever seen.'

'You haven't lived long then,' replied Alan – quick as a flash. 'But seriously – if she's down in the yard there's bound to be a fair bit of muck around. It'll be a right messy business.'

He thought for a minute.

'Of course,' he said. 'It depends how right Roy is with the diagnosis. She might be a downer cow, especially if she's delivered a big calf. If it was a tight squeeze she may have damaged part of the sciatic nerve. Best if you can move her somewhere comfortable. An old vet taught me a trick – take a gate off the hinges and roll the cow on to it. Tie her down and get a tractor to move her to somewhere more suitable.'

Alan never ceased to amaze me. I bet if I'd asked him what part of the sciatic nerve was damaged in these cases he would have answered in a flash. But in case it was milk fever, I had to get there as soon as possible. I shot off to what was becoming one of my favourite farms. On the way I stopped for a moment to refresh my mind on downer cows. Out came the trusty *Merck Manual*.

All the relevant information had been compressed into just a page. Downer meant literally down, unable to get up. If this was the diagnosis, she would be bright, maybe even eating, but just unable to get back on her feet. Damage to the sciatic nerve was one of the possibilities, especially after delivery of a large calf. It was a wonder Ursula hadn't suffered from it.

I put the book away in the glove compartment and sped down the last mile before turning down a steep lane which led to the valley in which Roy Gibbons' farm nestled. As I turned into the yard, I saw Agnes right away, stuck in copious amounts of mud where the cows entered the farm from the fields. It was as slippery as ice and I had made a note to talk to Roy about moving the gate or some other idea, as it wouldn't do the cows' feet any good walking through such thick mud. The foul in the foot I had seen on my first visit could easily be transmitted there – quite apart from the danger of slipping.

Agnes had gone down in the middle of it and every now and then would make a feeble attempt to get up. It was obviously the back legs which were giving rise to her problems. She would stand up on her front legs but the back ones would buckle under and then slip away from under her. She would have to be moved.

Roy came out as I was studying his prize cow. He had none of his usual cheerfulness.

'We can't leave her there,' I said. 'She'll never get up in that mud, and more likely than not she'll do herself more mischief.' I squelched across to her, stepping as carefully as I could. The last thing I wanted was to slip. And it was treacherous. This provoked the fiercest attempt yet to get to her feet, but it only made things worse as she fell on to her side and floundered about. When she had calmed down, I examined her. Normal temperature and pulse. While waiting for the thermometer to register, I pushed my fist into the left side where the main stomach – the rumen – is situated. After a minute or so I felt a contraction, followed by a belch. So she was ruminating, one of the signs of a healthy cow. This made milk fever highly unlikely. In fact, apart from her hind leg problems, there seemed very little wrong. Roy told me she had delivered a very large calf the day before and seemed a bit weak on her pins. She had just slipped over this morning at this very spot. I told him I thought it wasn't milk fever at all, but sciatica, although vets don't actually use this term.

'Where can we move her to? We need somewhere dry, with deep straw.'

I looked over in the direction of the barn. I remembered it housed calves.

'What about in there?'

There was a large opening through which a tractor could drive.

'But how on earth are we going to move her?' said Roy, as George his cowman joined us.

'If the pair of you can get that gate off its hinges and bring it over here and get it under her, we're in business.

We'll need some ropes too, to tie her down. And we'll need a good tow rope.'

With a relieved grin, Roy nodded. Ten minutes later we rolled Agnes on to the gate and roped her to it. Gradually, using the tractor, Bill dragged the gate towards the barn with Roy and me holding the cow's head. It took twenty minutes to get to the barn with frequent stops and then we hosed poor old Agnes down with water to clean off all the mud. Roy came out of the house armed with virtually all the towels he could find and we dried her as much as possible. Finally we got her under cover and quickly built a stockade out of bales and bedded her down on very deep straw. I stuck a bucket of water under her nose and she drank greedily from it. We then propped her up as best we could and left her nibbling at some fine quality hay as we went in to clean up.

'Hard work!' I said. It was an understatement. I was sweating profusely and my boots were covered in mud. George and Roy were the same. While George set to work drying Agnes, Roy and I did the best we could under the pump in the yard. It took us five minutes to clean up before we dared go into the kitchen. Katherine had a huge teapot on the table, with the obligatory scones, butter and jam. Roy had brightened up now that his favourite cow was in the dry and warm, but I was quick to warn him that it might not turn out for the good.

'You'll have to keep turning her for the next day or so or things will get a lot worse. They can damage the muscles by lying in one spot all the time – especially a huge cow like Agnes. She might start turning herself, in which case well and good, but if she's not up within a week it starts to look bad.'

'A week?' Roy's troubled look returned. In addition to

being his favourite cow, she was his best milker.

‘’Fraid so.’ I took another scone, a bit guiltily, having just dashed Roy’s hopes. He had been expecting the cow to get up now she was on terra firma. I explained about the knuckling fetlocks and weak hindquarters – fairly conclusive evidence of nerve damage. ‘Though hopefully it’s only temporary,’ I added.

We went outside to have another look. George was grooming her as though she was about to enter the county show and she had drunk some more water. I checked her over again, but took some blood to check for calcium, magnesium and phosphorus. I was pretty sure my diagnosis of damage to the sciatic nerve was right, but I wasn’t going to leave any stone unturned. This was one of my best farms and the first farmer to ask for me. The phone went. Roy’s neighbour, Chris Oliver, just up the road, had a difficult calving. Could I get down there straight away? Pauline was pleased to catch me still at Roy’s.

‘I’ll look in on the way back,’ I said as I packed my boots and coat into the back of the car, ‘to see how she’s doing.’

‘Make it for lunch,’ said Katherine. ‘Say one o’clock. And ask Chris and Di to come as well – we haven’t seen them for a couple of weeks.’

‘Thanks,’ I replied. ‘I may even get a session of running in if the calving isn’t too difficult.’

‘For a man with your abilities, it should be a piece of cake. Chris isn’t the interfering type. Talking of which, how’s the training going? Or daren’t I ask?’

I made a face and admitted that I hadn’t done any training for nearly five days. As I said it, I realized just how close I was to losing the title.

I swung out of the yard to travel a mile up a country lane to Chris Oliver’s farm.

Not all farmers are friends with their neighbours, so Chris and his wife were lucky to have Roy and Katherine just down the road. They had been running the farm for only a couple of years, having inherited it after Chris's father had died. Although he had been brought up on the farm, Chris had never intended to make farming his life and had gone into the City. But when his dad died very suddenly from a heart attack, he had decided to make a go of it. His wife Diana had given up her job as a high-powered secretary to live the life of a farmer's wife, and seemed to be enjoying it, although I noticed with amusement that she picked her way through the muck-filled yard with the care of a townie as she took me to the cow. It was obvious the animal was in trouble – two legs were sticking out, and had been for an hour.

'You were quick!' Diana said. 'I've only just come off the phone.'

I explained that I was down at the Gibbonses. 'And before I forget, you and your husband are invited to lunch today.'

A couple of minutes later I found the cause of the problem. The calf's head was back. I just managed to grab its ear and pulled it round to get hold of the mouth and then, surprisingly easily, the head came into the right position. With three calving ropes in place, and Chris and Diana on the end of them, we hauled a live calf into the world in five minutes.

I suppose I had done a dozen calvings all told and they no longer had me so worried. 'Careful not to get too blasé.' I thought to myself.

'See you in a bit!' I called out, after cleaning up and getting back into the car. On the way over I had spotted a flat grass track that would do for half an hour's training. It was still only twelve-thirty. The thick early summer grass wasn't the ideal surface, but I got a reasonable speed up and was pleased that I hardly got into a sweat. Maybe I was fitter than I thought. I would find out on Saturday for sure.

Lunch was a jolly affair. In spite of their difference in age, the two farmers were very good friends, as were their wives. The Gibbons' lovely daughter Julie joined us – she was looking relaxed, happy and relieved, having just finished her A-levels. All being well, she'd be off to London to study nursing in the autumn.

Roy's wartime experiences had strengthened his faith, Katherine had told me on a previous visit, so it didn't surprise me when he said grace before we tucked in. It had been a family tradition ever since they had come to Kent. Roy had considered himself very fortunate to be alive after what he had been through.

We had a typical farm lunch: home-made vegetable soup, with crusty bread, ham, and local cheese with pickles. Apple pie and custard to finish. I had to tear myself away from the conversation, which had somehow got on to the subject of the Battle of Britain, to phone in and see what was on for the afternoon.

I was needed in the laboratory – the small animal vets were working flat out and I would be doing evening surgery and night duty. The contrast would be total – but I couldn't complain as the morning had been so fulfilling, with the added bonus of a convivial lunch with friends. Just before leaving, I went into the barn to see my patient. George was still with Agnes. She looked comfortable and had turned herself to her other side – a good sign, because it meant that George and Roy wouldn't have to do it. With Agnes's size, it would have been back-breaking work.

The job Frank had earmarked for me was doing

bacteriology tests on milk samples. Frank was an expert at this, as well having a postgraduate qualification in the subject, and with his guidance it hadn't taken long to get the hang of the basics. A sudden cloudburst from a blackened sky made an afternoon inside all the more acceptable – I could easily have been out in it. And thank goodness we had got Agnes under cover.

Alan arrived towards the end of the afternoon, looking wet and bedraggled as if to emphasize the point. He had been caught out in a field, looking at some lame sheep.

'Thanks for the tip on moving the cow,' I said. 'It worked a treat.'

He sniffed, too wet and miserable to care. Coming back to a hectic week after a fortnight's Mediterranean idyll wasn't easy. Still, it was his early night off and he disappeared, muttering that what he needed was a hot bath and a visit to an Italian restaurant. He and Helen had had enough of Greek food, he said, and they'd not had time to shop since they got back. I told him about Nero and Casa Sarabini, which forced a smile.

'Just where I was thinking of going,' he said. I suggested he keep well out of the hound's way. Alan might not have quite my smell, but it would be similar enough to set Nero's alarm system ringing.

The weather decimated evening surgery and I was home by six-fifteen. By prior arrangement with Charles, I did a session of running up and down outside the flat in the pouring rain. It seemed as though the bad weather was keeping everyone indoors and an evening on my own passed without any interruptions, giving me the perfect opportunity to catch up on some sleep: ten hours in bed. It was a pattern to be repeated all week. The practice suddenly went into the doldrums on all fronts. Quiet days in the hospital and nothing much on the farm animal side, apart from the Ministry work – blood testing for brucellosis and the tuberculin testing. It would be another six weeks before I could go out with the vet from the Ministry to be taught about testing for TB and get my licence. Then I would really start to earn my keep.

I anxiously scanned the weather forecasts each night, hoping against hope that Saturday would be warm and sunny, and found myself easing down on the training just in case of injury. After what I knew would be my last practice session on Friday night, I went for a drink with Angie.

'So. You coming tomorrow then, coach?'

A big grin said yes, and I would have a cheerleader.

It was obvious that Angie should come. Without her cracking the whip over the past few weeks I wouldn't have had a chance of retaining the title. I still wasn't at all confident, but I knew I was fit enough not to make a complete fool of myself. But there was still the question of Sally. Last year when I won the title, she was competing too – and only just missed taking the 100 metre hurdle title herself. Although she wasn't as committed to sport as I was, there was still the possibility she would be there. I suppose I still cherished a hope that she would be – and that somehow it would rekindle things. And perhaps my motives weren't all that honourable: if Sally did turn up, the sight of a gorgeous-looking girl on my arm wouldn't do any harm.

Through my dad, the local radio station at home had tracked me down, and that evening I had been subjected to a phone interview on my chances of retaining the sprint titles. I was cautious, not having raced since the previous season, but I didn't give much away just in case my main rival was listening. Sports psychology may not have been a precise science in those days, but instinctively I knew to play things down. Chris Bowen had come second for the last two years and was desperate to win. I knew he was thinking about retiring and wanted to go out a champion. We were quite good friends off the track, but deadly rivals on it.

Angie was very impressed that I was considered important enough to be interviewed on the radio.

I laughed. 'Not many people will be listening. But if I do win at least one of the titles, there will be lots of photographers from the local rags,' I warned her. ' "Local hero stuff", you know the kind of thing. *You* might end up famous if they include you, as my – er – coach,' I ended rather lamely. I so nearly said girlfriend, but just stopped myself. I sighed inwardly. Here was this lovely girl, but I just couldn't feel for her in that way. Maybe it would come. If it didn't, maybe I would regret it in years to come.

'Penny for your thoughts?' Angie squeezed my hand.

'Just wondering what tomorrow will bring,' I replied – with just a grain of truth.

# *Chapter Thirteen*

Surprisingly perhaps, I slept well, and by eight-thirty in the morning Angie and I were on our way to Crystal Palace, one of the most famous running tracks in the world, and the venue for the Kent County Championships. Soon I was on familiar roads I had driven up countless times as a student. The weather was superb and already there was a heat haze. Nobody, but nobody, was heading for London. Instead there was a steady stream of traffic heading for the coast, even at this early hour. I could imagine the traffic jams later on in the day.

Kent was looking its radiant best. We drove through the Medway towns past signposts to villages I knew so well from my childhood, when I had more or less lived on a bike in the school holidays.

'This is Charles Dickens land,' I told Angie as we passed a sign to Cobham. 'There's a fantastic pub he used to drink at in that village.'

'Maybe on the way back?'

I laughed. 'Maybe. But I've a feeling I will just about have enough energy to drive back and turn in – especially if there are heats and semi-finals to contend with.'

Even the grey sprawl of south London looked good in the summer sunshine and we were soon heading off down the South Circular road past the familiar suburbs: Hither Green, Lewisham, Catford, Dulwich and finally Crystal Palace. By ten I was parking at the National Stadium.

Angie had never been to an athletics meeting before and I installed her in the main stadium before going to the changing rooms and getting a programme. I looked at the entries. Most of the athletes I knew, and I got a sudden flash of butterfly tummy as I looked down the list. No sign of Sally.

The heats of the 100 metres were starting at twelve, so I had plenty of time to warm up and it looked as though there would be straight heats and a final in both the 100 and 200. I checked in at the organizers' desk, depositing the cups for the 100 and 200 that I had won last year in my final year at college. I had managed to get quite fit in spite of studying for finals, mainly because the lecture rooms were next to a playing field. I had won the 100 in 10.9 seconds and the 200 in 22 seconds. This had been enough to get me an AAA vest, running for the Amateur Athletic Association. Seeing practice in Leicestershire on Brian and Lesley's practice had curtailed the rest of the season though.

The main stand was starting to fill up and I caught sight of my Dad, pouring tea from a Thermos flask.

Angie and I walked over.

He gave me a playful punch in the stomach.

I introduced Angie as a friend who had helped train me up.

'Don't believe a word of it,' he laughed. 'Young rascal doesn't know the meaning of the word!'

To give him his due, my father did know what he was talking about. He had been a championship cyclist and Olympic triallist. The outbreak of war had put a stop to that as he had joined the Royal Navy in 1939. By the end of the war he was married, I had arrived, and he was never able to train properly again. He used to ride twenty-five mile time trials, and 10.9 sprints were nothing compared to the pain of spending just over an hour in the saddle.

At eleven o'clock I started to warm up. A jog round the track with some stretching and half-speed sprints. The sun was up and I was sweating more than I had ever done in training, but I felt quite strong. I sat on the side of the track and caught sight of Chris Bowen – he was looking tense and 'focused', as they would say now. As luck would have it he was in my heat and it was the first two who would go through to the final. I waved at him and he grinned back, then we both got back to the business of warming up.

Dead on the dot of twelve, eight of us found ourselves lining up. The strange metallic voice of the starter, coming from loudspeakers by the side of the track, crackled into life.

'Get to your marks!'

'Set!'

The bang of the gun set us off first time. I got a good start and found myself in the lead. Three-quarters of the way down I felt Chris coming level with me, eased the power up a little and then, looking round, saw that we were clear of the others. I eased down and we crossed the line very close together. It had felt easy, and I was relieved to be in the final without mishap. The dispassionate voice of the announcer informed the crowd that I had won in 10.9 seconds, with Chris on eleven seconds. I was amazed and excited. It had been years since I had had the opportunity of racing on a top-class track in absolutely perfect conditions for sprinting. I had lost count of the number of meetings with rain or a strong wind against. Almost as bad was a strong wind behind, as this would make a good time illegal. The temperature was nudging the eighties and there wasn't a breath of wind.

My two supporters were impressed – but not as impressed as I was.

'I can go faster than that!' I panted.

My personal 'legal' best for the 100 metres was 10.8. I had done 10.4 in France, but that was with the benefit of a gale behind my back.

'I was just saying to Sally here that the country air must be good for you,' Dad said.

'Angie,' I said.

'Oh yes.' Then turning to Angie, he added, 'Sorry, Angie, getting old, that's my trouble. Forgetful. Don't take any notice.'

I gave Angie a sorry-about-that-old-idiot look, but she was all smiles. They were clearly getting on like a house on fire and were munching sandwiches which Mum had made. She never came herself; her nerves wouldn't stand it, she said. Although there was plenty for me, I didn't feel remotely hungry. In any case, within half an hour I was in the 200 metres heats.

There would then be an hour and a half before the 100 final, which was due at three o'clock. I would have a snack before then. I went out on the track to do some stretching.

'Don't overdo it,' Dad warned me, but I ignored him and did some strides down the back straight near to the start of the 200.

I had no nerves as we lined up. I was drawn on the inside lane and could see all the other competitors in front of me. I decided that I would go flat out as if it were the final and then ease back if I found myself in the lead. True to plan, I found myself in the lead as we entered the straight and I eased down all the way to the finish, keeping an eye on the second runner. I crossed the line first. Although not too much out of breath, I was sweating a lot.

The first race had been in virtual silence. Few people were all that interested in the heats. Again I was surprised by the time – 22.3 seconds. It had seemed so easy. Now I was really keyed up for the finals and couldn't think about eating. The 100 final was due at three, so I decided to have a drink of water and sit in the stands for a while. My club were doing well – the 1500 metres had two finalists and we were represented in most of the finals. The club captain collared me and wanted to know how many meetings I could run in for the rest of the season. I pulled a face – he had no idea of weekends on duty – and just replied that I didn't know yet as I didn't have the duty roster for the rest of the season.

A white lie. Athletics seemed a million miles away from my working life. Even being in the London suburb of Crystal Palace seemed strange, with traffic jams and thousands of people.

Dad was getting worried. I was sweating a lot and hadn't had anything to eat and he was convinced I had been overdoing the warm-ups – given that it was the hottest day of the year. With the arrogance of youth, I set off to warm up yet again on the back straight. The final was not due for another forty minutes, but I ran and stretched the muscles and went through the final a hundred times in my mind. I was feeling nervous, but not half as nervous as Chris Bowen looked as we set up our starting blocks at the start of the 100 metres.

Again the strange metallic voice took us to the start. Total silence from the crowd in the main stand – full of relatives and club supporters. The crack of the starter's gun set the eight finalists off in a line. Almost immediately I realized that I had got the best possible start. I could sense nobody near me and I strained every muscle to get into full flight. Halfway down the straight I felt the calf muscle in my right leg cramp up. I knew immediately what it was. A pulled muscle was infinitely more painful, and I had suffered several of those in my time. Instinctively I eased up. I was aware of Chris to my left. I responded – but again the pain in my calf. I knew if I ignored it I would end up tearing it. Chris edged in front. In desperation, with ten metres to go, I pulled all the stops out and caught Chris on the line, but pulled up quickly in a lot of pain. The St John's ambulance crew were at my side at once, putting an ice pack on my leg, the traditional remedy for a pulled muscle, even though I was sure it was just cramp.

Meanwhile the timekeepers were having difficulty, judging by the long wait for the result. I stood up and gingerly tried out my leg. It definitely wasn't a pull, but I was sweating profusely again. I was beginning to realize that I wasn't as fit as I had hoped. In the background I could see Chris pacing anxiously. Ten minutes later we got the result. First, in a time of 10.9 seconds, C Bowen. The rest was lost in a roar from his supporters. He punched the air in delight and immediately came over to me to shake hands. I was disappointed – but pleased for Chris. Later on I was to find that the timekeepers had given us the same time.

Now, though, I had a steep climb to be able to face the 200 metres. Chris was also a finalist and would have high hopes of the double. I met up with my father and Angie in the stand.

She gave me a hug. 'Well done!' she said. 'I thought you had won it.'

My dad was more perceptive.

'Looked to me as though you'd cramped up,' he said, having had plenty of experience of it during his cycling days. I nodded. I should have listened to him. The form I was in, there's no doubt that without that self-inflicted cramp I would have won. We had an hour to sort it out. Suddenly I felt hungry. We went up to the cafeteria behind the beginning of the home straight and I ate a toasted cheese sandwich. Then Dad forced me to swallow some salt, with a couple of cups of tea to dilute it. This was followed by twenty minutes of massage for my sore calf muscle.

His final bit of advice was short and to the point. 'Just stretch – no running in your warm-up.'

This time I didn't argue, and I didn't get on to the track until five minutes before the race was due.

I had been drawn in the outside lane, which was traditionally considered a disadvantage because you had no one to chase. But it simplified matters for me. My plan was to go flat out and hope no one would be able to pass me. There was a strong niggling doubt, too, whether the calf muscle would go again. As we lined up I looked back at the other seven. Chris – ever the sportsman – waved from the inside lane, mouthing good luck.

'And you,' I mouthed back, and then carefully set up my starting blocks.

The race had excited plenty of interest from the crowd and the announcer called for quiet as we got to our marks. The starter's speaker was very near to me on the side of the track and the loud crack of his gun galvanized me into a good start. I ran for my life round the long bend and as I entered the straight I was in the lead. Immediately a roar went up from the crowd. Unlike the 100 final, when for some reason I hadn't been aware of the noise from the crowd, I could now pick out the yelling of individual friends. Afterwards I realized it was because I was well in the lead in the lane nearest them. Angie was yelling herself hoarse – for a day or so afterwards her voice was cracked.

All the frustrations, triumphs and disasters of the last few months seemed to be crystallized in my mind as I came down the home straight. I was angry, determined, desperate and exhilarated all in one. I hardly noticed my leg seizing up as I crossed the line. I collapsed at the side of the track completely exhausted. Angie had run on to the track and was hugging me. I vaguely realized that she was crying, and then that I had won. I also realized that I was far from racing fit. I felt faint, and my pulse was racing. Even ten minutes later I was shaky on my feet. Then came the announcement.

'The result of the 200 metres. First, D Grant, Medway Athletic, in a Championship best performance of 21.7 seconds.'

Chris had come second in a personal best of 22.2, a good five metres behind, but he was over the moon with his efforts – two personal bests and a championship medal. It would be his swan song.

I staggered up to the centre of the stadium to pick up the silver cup and medal. A gang of photographers took my photo, the local reporters were firing questions at me and Angie was hugging me. By the time the county manager came over to ask me if I could represent Kent in the inter-county championships, I had already decided to call it a day this season and concentrate on my job. I was quite honest with the manager. I was simply not fit enough, I told him. I could hardly believe the county record. As it turned out, I was never to run as fast over 200 metres again. It was a combination of perfect weather and my attitude of mind. I had to decide there and then whether to take up athletics seriously or continue as a farm vet.

On the way back home I talked it over with Angie.

'The only way I can really go any faster is to train a lot harder and compete. That means giving up veterinary practice for a few years. I'd have to do a PhD or something like that. Night duties and weekends working are a killer!'

'The trouble is,' she said, 'that you thrive on it, and the most interesting things seem to come in after hours. Even though you get stressed, I think you secretly enjoy it.'

Even as she was talking, my mind was drifting off, wondering how Agnes was getting on. If she couldn't get up, then she would have to be put down. And I knew what the death of his prize cow would do to Roy.

'Of course you're right,' I said, in that half distracted way which women could pick up on instantly, including Angie, who was more perceptive than most.

'You're not listening, are you?' she laughed, half amused, half exasperated. 'So. Penny for them. What are you thinking about?'

'Agnes,' I replied

'Who's she?'

'A downer cow,' I explained, and went on to give her a potted history of what that meant.

She listened, then asked if I'd been to see her to check her progress.

I shook my head.

'We can't be that far away, David. Why don't we just pop in on the way home?' Reading my mind was something Angie was getting very adept at.

I needed no further bidding and took the first available left towards the coast road. Half an hour later, just as dusk was setting in, I drove the Anglia into the Gibbons' familiar farmyard. It was all quiet except for the noise from a few cows out in the fields.

'Sounds like one of them is bulling,' I said, and was just about to explain when Roy appeared at his door. He was surprised to see me.

'Well, young man, how did it go?'

'Second in the 100 and I retained the 200 in a new record.'

'Wonderful! Come on in and have a cup of tea.' They were a teetotal household, but even half a pint of beer would have gone straight to my head. I hardly dared ask how my patient was. Had she had to be put down?

Roy looked at my anxious face and winked at Angie. 'Well,' he said. 'I suppose you want to know about Agnes?'

Katherine couldn't restrain herself.

'Put the poor boy out of his misery, Roy. Agnes got up this afternoon when she heard the others coming in for milking. Dead on the dot of four. She's as right as rain.'

I felt the biggest surge of happiness since I had joined the practice. I jumped up and shook hands with the pair of them while Angie looked bemused, soon, however, joining in the laughter. We trooped outside and into the barn where Agnes would stay for a few days until she was strong enough to join the others. She was standing in a cubicle munching some hay. When she saw me, she stopped eating for a moment before lifting her tail and relieving herself of a very full bladder.

'She always does something like that whenever she sees David.' Roy explained as Angie jumped quickly out of the way.

'Well, that's enough excitement for one day,' I said. 'We had better be making tracks.'

On the way back home I sighed contentedly.

'I can't see you wanting to give this up, can you?' Angie said, putting her hand on my arm.

She was right. It was no contest.

'I don't think so.'

'So, there's your answer about the athletics. You said it

was one or the other. You'll just have to be content with being county champion.' She laughed. 'Or did you have your eyes on the Olympics?' Then I laughed. 'And don't worry. I'll get you training three months before the day next year. Because, come what may, you'll have to defend it. Maybe go for the double!'

'You should be an athlete yourself,' I countered. 'You're more motivated than me.'

When we got back to the Nightingales' I didn't so much walk to the front door as hobble. I felt stiffer than an ironing board. A shout went up as we went in – Keith had arranged a surprise party and quite a crowd had turned up. So much for an early night. But after a few beers, something to eat and a mixture of the Stones, Beatles and The Who, we danced the night away. Well, the rest of them did. I did a combination lurch and shuffle. It was the 'Sixties, after all, and I had just broken the Kent county record. I also knew I had the rest of the weekend to enjoy and it was four in the morning before I finally crashed out, as happy as I had ever remembered being.

Half the next day was spent in bed nursing a sore head. The wine that night hadn't been a patch on the wine we had drunk to celebrate Phil and Sue's engagement, and it showed. I wasn't completely recovered until Monday.

Only Alan expressed anything beyond mild interest in what Keith in his cups had called my 'momentous achievement'. The other partners saw my sprinting as simply a rather eccentric hobby, like train spotting. But there was a rush of work on, so after a few questions and the obligatory Well Dones, it was business as usual.

I'd always found Monday mornings very stressful, but this morning I felt much less wound up than usual. It wasn't long before I realized why. Trying to find time to get fit had been a tremendous stress and I hadn't realized how much it had taken out of me. Now I had given up athletics for another year at least – maybe for good. I had a spell of hard work coming up, but in six weeks' time I was off to Spain with Keith and Jenny, and who knew who else, though not Angie, who was off back to Manchester to get a holiday job and spend the summer with her family. Term was due to finish in a couple of weeks and foreign holidays were out of her reach. But she would be back in the autumn – she had one more year to do before qualifying as a teacher.

The Anglia had taken longer to sort out than I had expected. Nearly two weeks had gone by before Frank told me that it would be delivered later that morning. 'Then I'd like your help,' he went on. 'I'm doing an operation on a bull this afternoon and I'll need you.'

'A bull?' This was news indeed. Had I heard right? Not a bulldog? Did it herald a return to farm work?

He read my mind, as usual.

'I've known Roger Dobson for years. It's his prize bull and he wants me to give the anaesthetic – and Alan and Charles are none too keen anyway! To tell you the truth it will be nice to get out for the afternoon instead of being stuck in here.'

'What's wrong with it?' I asked.

'Bad case of sandcrack.' Frank waited for a second to see my reaction – with a hint of a twinkle in his eye. But I wasn't letting on whether I knew anything about sandcrack or not – though of course I didn't, although I dimly remembered hearing the name.

'Right! Sounds fun to me.'

'Meet you back here around two then.'

I took off shortly afterwards to the east of the practice. This part of Kent was a veritable maze, but I was developing a photographic memory for every turning and hardly needed to look at the signposts – not that they were always much help. In one of the villages I stopped in the shade of a vast horse chestnut tree for a while to look up sandcrack in the trusty *Merck.* There was only a paragraph on it. It was the name given to a defect in the hoof where a split developed longitudinally. In severe cases it would cause lameness and if infection got through the crack it could be potentially disastrous. No wonder Roger Dobson was worried about it. As I read, I vaguely remembered a lecture on it. Now who had covered that in the final year course? I had all my final year notes neatly filed in my flat. If I got my skates on I could look it up. I was curious as to how Frank would anaesthetize the bull. That would be in my notes somewhere too. Most of the large animal operations at college had been done on horses in specialized operating theatres, with hoists to lift the animals about. We had very little by way of sedative drugs to make life easier in field conditions. I looked forward to the afternoon, especially as I wouldn't have sole responsibility.

Frank and I got to his friend's farm at two-thirty and parked up in front of a huge farmhouse with ivy spreading over the walls. I could see our patient in a pen to the side of a great barn. It was warm and sunny and the smell of the farmyard assailed my nostrils, a smell that I had grown to love and which is quite impossible to describe to a townie. Analysed ingredient by ingredient, it would probably sound disgusting. As soon as we got out of the cars, Frank hit the ground running. He had identified a patch of land to cast the bull and now I found out he was going to anaesthetize it with chloral hydrate – a very old anaesthetic which I had seen used at college once. All I remembered was how you had to avoid it spilling outside the vein or it would cause a tremendous inflammatory reaction and infection.

The instruments were placed in a neat pile to the side of the operating area and then the bull was led out with a pole. He was a fairly tranquil beast, called Titan. Within seconds Frank had got into the vein with a huge needle and attached the bottle of chloral. I held it up as Frank supervised the farmhands. Lots of straw bales were placed to the side of the bull so that when he went down he would have a soft landing. Meanwhile, in the quiet of the summer afternoon you could hear the 'glugg-glugg-glugg' as the solution bubbled into Titan's vein. For a few minutes nothing happened and then the bull began to sway. This was the potentially dangerous bit. I had to make sure the needle didn't come out, and I followed the bull about as he tottered and then gently sank to his knees.

'Give him a push, David!' Frank urged.

I did as I was told and Titan rolled over on to his side like a beached whale. While this was going on, Frank was hard at work. The crack extended downwards, but not as far as the bottom of the hoof. He had already shown that it was painful by tapping the hoof with a hammer while Titan was still conscious. Titan had not liked it. Indeed it had looked a comical sight – a slightly built man tapping this huge bull's hoof with a hammer. Now Frank had taken his jacket off, still with the white shirt and immaculate bow tie, and was beavering away on the damaged hoof. The same intense concentration which I had seen when he was fixing a dog's broken leg or consulting in the surgery was equally in evidence here.

As usual, Frank was wearing several different 'hats' while still managing to keep an eye on me while operating. Every now and then he would look up to see if I had the anaesthetic under control. This consisted of pinching the tube to stop the flow of liquid and letting it flow again if the bull showed any sign of pain. Simple, but apparently effective.

He had cut a wedge in the bottom of the hoof to take the weight off the crack, which he was filling with a new acrylic material which he had wanted an opportunity to try out. The whole thing took half an hour, and then it was a question of making sure Titan came round without any problems. It had all seemed so easy.

Not for Frank the tea and scones in the farmhouse kitchen. No sooner was the job done than he excused himself and we set off back to the hospital, where he had a dislocated hip to deal with.

He was in a good mood, having obviously enjoyed his few hours out in the countryside. I asked him if this was the beginning of a return to farm animals

He laughed. 'Absolutely not. It's a young man's game – too much physical work. That's why I had you come along. The fittest vet in the country! Mind you, you're just practising yet. In another year you'll have developed muscles in places you didn't know existed.'

As he spoke he was trying to put a dislocated hip back in a Saint Bernard dog. He put a rope round the dog's midriff and told me to pull against him. Going bright red in the face, he pulled hard on the leg and I had to use all my strength to keep the sleeping dog on the table. I saw the leg click into place and the satisfied smile on Frank's face.

I felt pretty cheerful myself, now that the stress of training was over. With just the job to concentrate on, I found time flashed past and before I knew what had happened it was my last day before the holiday. Keith had reminded me with one of his early morning visits that I had grown used to over the last couple of weeks, testing out his

Spanish holidaywear, sporting yet another new tee-shirt or pair of shorts for my approval.

'For goodness' sake, Keith,' I muttered, as I pulled the sheet over my face. 'What kind of time do you call this?'

'Seven o'clock, you slacker. And tomorrow, don't forget, we're up at five-thirty. Viva Espana, mate,' and with his hands above his head in an approximation of a Spanish dancer, clicking his fingers, he twirled out of my flat.

I went into the practice to learn that my tuberculin test was fixed for the day I got back from holiday. A Ministry of Agriculture vet was going to put me through my paces on one of the farms testing the cows. So within a few weeks I would be a fully fledged large animal vet doing tuberculin testing and other Ministry work. Just right for the summer.

My final afternoon's list presented no problems. While Frank and Peter were slaving away in the hospital, I had a pleasing round culminating in a visit to Roy Gibbons for a couple of pregnancy checks, the inevitable lame cow and a mastitis case. To be followed up, no doubt, by a hefty portion of scones, jam and cream.

As I drove into the Gibbons' farm, I took care to park the Anglia on a dry bit of concrete next to the milking parlour, as I had just given it a good clean. There was still a lot of slurry about in the rest of the yard. Roy hadn't got round to sorting it out. I sighed. Maybe another lame cow would concentrate his mind. It was turning out to be a hot day and I left the windows wide open as I walked to the farmhouse. This was the last call of the day and I had been let off evening surgery, so I wasn't in any hurry.

There was an air of celebration about. Julie's A-level results had been good and she would be off to St Bart's in a few weeks to start nursing training. She was looking particularly lovely: a young girl about to make her start in the world. A few weeks in the sun had brought a healthy glow to her face and she had the happy look of someone who had been taking it easy for a month or two. While Katherine was preparing the food, we got on with the veterinary business first, which I got done in record time. Then it was high tea. Not just cream and scones, but sandwiches of all types, home-made biscuits and ice-cold lemonade. Three quarters of an hour later I looked at my watch. I should really check in before going off. Just in case.

'I'll just pack my things in the back of the car and phone in, if that's all right,' I said, and ambled out into the late afternoon sun. Milking was in process and every five minutes or so a batch of cows would saunter out, crossing the slurry and into the field.

I opened the boot and packed my brown coat and boots away. I smiled at the thought that I wouldn't be needing them for a week and more. Just as I closed the boot, Agnes came lumbering out of the parlour. I recognized her instantly from her size, but also by the distinctive blaze she had down the front of her forehead. For reasons best known to herself, she decided to saunter down between the car and the parlour. None of the other cows had chosen that route. Curiosity perhaps. In the same instant that she caught sight of me, it had simultaneously occurred to me that maybe she wouldn't relish my being there.

With a snort she put on the brakes – both front feet shoving forward at an angle of 45 degrees. Her eyes were bulging even more than usual – my presence alone was enough to induce blind panic. I said nothing and ducked down, hoping she would back out. This simple manoeuvre, however, did not occur to her.

Instead she decided to turn round. In the process, her

enormous rear end squeezed the side of my car, and with a sickening scrunch, I heard it bend inwards. The sound startled her and she squeezed even harder. Her tail was now well inside the open car window and her final act of defiance was depositing a huge cow pat in the middle of the passenger seat. Finally she made it, and trotted out into the field with the other cows, slowing down as soon as she reached them, pausing only to help herself to some lush grass as if nothing had happened.

Roy came out to see what had kept me. He took off his cap, scratched his head and reckoned that the dent could be easily knocked out. He volunteered to get it done by his garage. When he saw the cow pat, he couldn't believe his eyes.

'At least she hasn't got the diarrhoea this time!' and roared with laughter.

There was nothing for it but to clean up. The whole family joined in with spades, scrubbing brushes and disinfectant. Half an hour later, the front seat was clean again and I wearily got in, wondering how I was to break the news.

Reading my mind, Roy said, 'Don't worry. I'll sort it out. The least I can do.'

I set off for base with shouts of 'Enjoy your holiday!'

## *Chapter Fourteen*

The first day of August and I had an appointment with the Ministry vet. It was an incredibly hot day, not a cloud in the sky. The temperature must have been in the nineties. There was a stillness in the air, punctuated by the occasional buzz of a fly. My clothes were sticking to me. It seemed wrong to be wearing long trousers in this heat – I had just got back from Spain, where shorts or swimming trunks were all I ever seemed to wear.

In the end there had only been three of us. Although Jenny and Keith hadn't minded my tagging along, they were always on the lookout for a girl to make up the foursome. About halfway through the holiday it seemed my luck was in. Cheryl and Jenny immediately got on because they came from the same part of the world – Jenny from Liverpool and Cheryl from Manchester. She was small and bubbly, not my usual kind of girl at all, but her giggle had a way of getting everyone laughing. When the girls went off to powder their noses halfway through the evening, Keith gave me the thumbs-up.'

'You're well in there, mate. No problem. Take it from one who knows.'

But Keith didn't know.

Cheryl wasn't staying at our hotel, so we had arranged to pick her up the next morning at eleven before heading for the beach. We had just met up and were on the terrace making plans for the day when suddenly she knocked over her coffee. Seconds later we were being introduced to the madman who was responsible. Terry wasn't really a madman, he just looked like one – hardly surprising, since he hadn't slept for twenty-four hours, having hitch-hiked non-stop from Manchester. Reception had told him where Cheryl was, so he'd rushed out, taken no notice of us, but fallen down on his knees. There and then he asked her to marry him. She burst into tears and said yes.

It turned out they had been going out, on and off, for years, but Cheryl had come to Spain on her own to think things over. When Terry suddenly realized he couldn't live without her, he did the only thing he could think of. Now here he was. And another Grant romance bit the dust.

We agreed to meet up later for a celebration. Perhaps it was the adrenaline, or lack of sleep, or wine on an empty stomach, but by the time we sat down to eat, Terry reminded me of a British football fan whose team had just won the World Cup. He was ecstatic. He was also very drunk.

'None of your foreign muck for me,' he said belligerently as the rest of us ordered paella at a pavement cafe. He abruptly got up and lurched off in the direction of a hamburger stall. The next thing we knew, a fight had broken out and the owner of the stall had Terry pinned to the wall, his arms behind his back. The ground was littered with buns and hamburgers. Spain was then a dictatorship under General Franco, and the police bore no relation to the friendly bobbies who patrolled the Kent countryside in their Panda cars. The arrival of the Guardia Civil was no laughing matter.

'He's the one they should be arresting,' Terry shouted. He had given the owner a 1000 peseta note, he insisted, but 'this bastard' had given him change for only 100. When the stall owner had just shrugged, Terry had tried to grab him, but the stall had given way and sent everything flying. Not that anyone else except us understood Terry's explanation. We tried to put his side of the story to the Guardia Civil, but our knowledge of Spanish was no better than Terry's. In the end we decided that discretion was the better part of valour and settled for explaining the mitigating circumstances, along the lines of: 'Look, don't worry, we'll look after him. He's drunk. He's getting married. He's proposed to this girl, she's said yes, that's why he's happy. This was a mistake, we'll pay for the hamburgers.'

And so that's what we did. How much they understood, I don't know. But the stall owner understood the money bit. It cost an arm and a leg, equivalent today to about fifty pounds. But it was either that or the nick. And not only Terry, but probably us too, as we were his cohorts.

I found it incredibly frustrating not being able to communicate. We had all the hand motions, but no language. The whole episode should have made me hate the place – Terry was a good bloke and I think he really was done – but it didn't. Far from it. It was then that I thought, 'God, I've got to learn Spanish.'

The next day it seemed sensible to 'vamoos', so we said goodbye to Torremolinos and spent the last couple of days exploring the real Spain. It was unlike anything I had ever experienced before, like going back in time five hundred years. Venturing into a fishermen's bar in a quiet village down the coast, we were welcomed as if we were relatives, and sat there all evening drinking red wine for a few pesetas a glass and listening to flamenco music, which none of us had ever heard before. As the men sang and played their guitars, I could only wonder what they were singing about with such passion, veins throbbing in their necks. I became even more determined to learn their language. As the rhythms changed, one of the women moved out from the shadows and began to dance. She was no beauty, and must have been over sixty. A little while earlier she had been serving us with sizzling sausages and spicy fried potatoes to go with our wine, the first time I'd ever had tapas. Yet when she arched her back, stamped her feet and flashed her eyes, she seemed as sexy as a señorita half her age. Although we couldn't understand a word, the smiles and the glasses of wine for the 'extranjeros' said it all. I was hooked.

Back in Kent just a few days later, I drove up the unkempt track to the Manor House. Just like the cobbled streets of that Spanish village, the place had not even nodded towards the 20th century. As in the convent, there were perhaps a dozen or so cows, a few pigs and maybe a couple of hundred sheep. This was how John Bolton and his wife, Mary, made their living. They had a grown-up son, but he had gone to 'Lunnun' to find work in the City.

Most of the manor house was disused and, as in many farms, life revolved around the kitchen. But this too was hardly high-tech, with an ancient Aga occupying central stage. This particular morning, across the equally ancient oak dining table David Thomas, the Ministry vet, was facing me with a cool glass of elderflower cordial in his hand – home-made naturally. Mrs Bolton brought it out from the larder in an old frosted glass bottle, with a marble stopper held in place by a metal clasp. From the condition of the bottle, I should say it had given good service for years.

I had never had elderflower cordial before, but it was delicious, seeming to capture the very essence of summer meadows. It was also wonderfully thirst-quenching and not too sweet.

David Thomas, the Man from the Ministry, was responsible for my certification. I had now been in practice for six months. Before we arrived he had put me through my paces on the theoretical aspects of tuberculosis in cows. Now came the practice. We were to go out and test ten cows. As Welsh as you could be, David was obviously as pleased as punch to be on this remote farm – not unlike many in Wales he told me – and out of the office for the afternoon. He had been working for the Ministry for ten years and was very happy. However, what would make him really happy, he told me, would be a posting to Wales. This didn't surprise me in the slightest. Virtually all the Welshmen that I knew at college were already back there.

We strode out into the yard and the heat hit me like opening an oven door. In spite of the heat, David was dressed for a boardroom lunch, wearing a collar and tie underneath a protective overall. I had remembered from my time on foot and mouth duties what sticklers the Ministry men were for hygiene and disinfection.

Tuberculosis in cows is a serious risk to humans and the Ministry were engaged in a programme to eliminate the disease from the national dairy herd. The simplest way to detect whether a cow was a carrier of the disease was to inject tuberculin into the skin. Tuberculin is a substance made from inactivated bacteria that cause the disease. Although harmless to healthy cows, it would cause a reaction in positive animals – a swelling in the skin where it had been injected. I was shown how to clip up the neck, measure the thickness of the skin and then inject the tuberculin into it, using special syringes. All the cows had to be identified, the measurements of the skin recorded and everything meticulously written into a book. Reactions, if they occurred, would take three days to show up, so a revisit would be scheduled for then and any cows that proved positive would be removed from the herd and slaughtered. The responsibility was enormous, but curiously, worrier that I was, this aspect didn't concern me.

By the end of the week I would get my licence and would be testing countless cows from now on.

On days like today it was idyllic. We might have been anywhere in the world. Only John's Kentish drawl gave any indication of where we were, and then, when I looked back up the hill and saw the old Manor House silhouetted against the blue sky, I was jolted back to the realization that I was back in England in the depths of the countryside. Yet from here I could have made it to the outskirts of London in an hour and a half. Not that I had any intention of doing such a thing.

David Thomas interrupted my daydreaming.

'Well, good luck, old boy,' he said, patting me on the back. 'You should get your licence by the end of the week.'

Although it was only a formality, I felt a sudden sense of elation. Another hurdle crossed. We shook hands and, after carefully disinfecting his protective clothing, he climbed into his car and with a cheery wave headed off back to the office.

Not even time, he said, for a cup of tea.

But I was keen to savour the afternoon in this remote spot.

The kitchen with its stone-flagged floor was surprisingly cool after the fierce heat of the fields. The bottle of elderflower cordial had disappeared and in its place was a large brown teapot, covered by a hand-knitted tea cosy in the shape of a country cottage.

As Mary poured, I asked her husband about the history of the house.

'Some of it dates back to the sixteenth century,' John replied. 'Some say it belonged to the family of Anne Boleyn. The Boleyns certainly came from here and were big landowners, but whether it's true or not, it's hard to know.'

I sat lost in thought, thinking of all the generations of farmers, their wives and hands who had sat in this very room, their concerns not so different from those of the Boltons and farmers like them.

'Of course,' said Mary, 'we don't use a third of it – can't afford to. These big rooms, nice in summer, take a lot of heating come the winter.'

The land and the house had been in the Bolton family for generations, but Jim, their son, showed no interest in taking it over and now they were thinking of selling up.

'We're not getting any younger,' Mary explained.

'Though Lord knows what I would do,' John added, staring into his teacup.

I looked at the two of them. To all outward appearances they seemed quite simple folk. No pretensions whatsoever, yet they owned what could be a spectacular house, not to mention the farm itself. I'd put them in their early sixties, although a life of graft on the land could easily have made them look older than they were.

I imagined some tycoon buying the place and restoring it – but it was very isolated, with just a small village over half a mile away with one pub and a post office. The wholesale gentrification of the countryside was many years away. I haven't dared go back there since.

I left the two of them, saying I would see them on Thursday and drove to the village post office. It was nice to be back in the Anglia – Roy had been as good as his word and the dent caused by Agnes had been fixed. Since getting the car back, I was driving it with kid gloves.

There was a heat haze on every undulation of the country lane. I made my customary phone call back to base. But it was all quiet. Alan explained that for a month or so the farmers would be too busy with harvest to worry over much with their stock. In any case, with the animals out in the warm sun, and Dr Green and Mother Nature working their miracles, nothing much seemed to go wrong with them.

The days would be long and quiet and I could feel the tension gradually easing away from me. The holiday had been a marvellous tonic, too, and I had already bought a book to teach myself Spanish. I dawdled back into town listening to the new number one, 'Hey Jude' by the Beatles.

At the end of the week my LVI certificate dropped on to the mat. It was contained in a neat green plastic folder which I kept at the hospital. A special rubber stamp was made with my name and LVI after it. I had arrived! Now I could really start to earn my keep. I immediately found myself doing at least one test a week, or blood sampling numerous cows to check if they had brucellosis, another disease that, along with tuberculosis, transmits to humans and which I could now test for.

My face, already brown from lying in the sun in Spain, took on the same deep tan of the farmers. For the next few months the weather seemed to alternate between glorious during the week and tanking down at the weekend, to the utter frustration of just about everybody except me. For almost every weekend that August I found myself on duty, so I welcomed the rain and spent most of the time chatting with Keith when Jenny was working, or whoever I could find in the Nightingale household. Keith was going through a flower-power phase, and walking past his door you were assailed with the aroma of burning joss sticks. His hair had grown, and the old familiar 'Wotcha, mate' had turned into 'Hey, man'. But he was still good for a laugh.

The summer passed quickly and I couldn't wait until the beginning of the autumn term and the return of the students for their final year. When they did arrive, it was over a particularly wet duty weekend. Since about four in the afternoon on Friday, it had poured down. Wet and bedraggled students began appearing at the front door. Rooms began to blare out music. I caught up with the gossip, drinking endless cups of coffee and waiting for the phone to ring.

For the first time in a long time I had not had to do anything since Saturday lunchtime, and by six on Sunday evening I was beginning to get edgy. Was the phone out of order with this incessant rain?

I rang in to Charles – but it was all quiet. Quiet, that is, apart from a thunder storm which blew up. I tried listening to music, but flashes and great claps of thunder made it impossible. Huge black clouds obscured the sky – it was dark and foreboding.

In between a couple of crashes of thunder there was a knock at the door – and there was Angie. I'd sent her a post-card from Spain and she'd sent me one from Blackpool, but we hadn't spoken since the end of the summer term. We hugged each other, but before I could say anything, I could just hear the ringing of the phone over the noise of the storm.

It was Charles's wife, Penny. An urgent case. Bob Adams had phoned in. He had been getting his cows in, due to the weather getting so bad, and one of them had gone down with the 'staggers'. Collapsed in the road and convulsing. The police were on the scene as she was blocking the narrow one-track lane. Could I get there as soon as possible?

'Can I come too?'

It was Angie.

'Of course,' I answered, feeling my face lit by a huge smile, and we dashed out to the car.

The rain was truly torrential, as if the heavens were making up for the hot high summer days that had put smiles on all the farmers' faces. As we drove through the storm, I couldn't help thinking of those farmers who hadn't got their crops safely in.

Although it was only about seven o'clock, it was as dark as a winter evening. Every now and then the whole sky would be lit up for an instant, to be followed by the deafening crash of thunder. Even with the windscreen wipers going full pelt, the visibility was terrible. A journey that would normally take fifteen minutes took just over half an hour. I kept thinking of the poor animal thrashing about in the road and getting a soaking into the bargain. We hardly spoke during the drive, as I had to concentrate just to keep the car on the road. Familiar roads and lanes became distorted. Fortunately we were the only travellers abroad – no one who didn't have to would be mad enough to venture out. I had to stop several times because the windscreen wipers couldn't cope with the downpour.

Coming to the top of a hill, we could see nothing, although I knew the Weald stretched out from here with a wonderful panoramic view.

'You wouldn't believe it,' I shouted through the thwack-thwack of the windscreen wipers and the drumming on the roof, 'but the view from here is just amazing. On a clear day you can see right over the Weald to the coast.' As it was, it was all I could do to see the front of the car. Trees loomed up out of the spray like ghosts. Then, just at that moment, there was the biggest flash of lightning I had ever seen and for a couple of seconds the whole vista was displayed for us. It had an awesome beauty.

Angie began to say something, but her words were drowned out by a frighteningly loud clap of thunder. We were obviously in the eye of the storm.

'I reckon we must be about there,' I said, as we rounded a bend, and almost immediately a flashlight flagged us down.

'Road's blocked. You'll have to turn back.' A completely soaked policeman about my age leaned through the window.

'I know,' I replied. 'I'm the vet.' For an instant I thought he didn't believe me, as he looked first at me, then at Angie.

'Sorry, sir, didn't recognize you. Right – she's just round the next bend – follow me!'

The cow, Jessie, was lying on her side across the road. A police car had the lights on her and there was a queue of several cars behind. At first sight I was convinced she was done for, no sign of life at all, but a sudden clap of thunder had the effect of making her thrash about. I could just make out Bob lying in the road with a large blanket, trying to protect her head every time she went into a convulsion.

I got out of the car to open the boot. Immediately I was soaked to the skin. With the help of the policeman's torch, I got the bottle of magnesium out and connected up the giving set. I waded over to my patient. A quick look at the milk vein told me that I couldn't use it. The whole of her abdomen was completely caked-up in thick mud. I would have to get into the neck vein. Using the headlights of the cars and the policeman's torch, I leaned over the cow's shoulders, keeping as far away from the flailing legs as possible. I was suddenly aware that Angie was beside me.

There was no point telling her to get into the car – she was completely soaked through, but was desperate to help. Using a rope round the cow's neck, the huge jugular vein came into view. Another clap of thunder caused another convulsion, and when it subsided I jabbed the needle in. A gushing of blood came back and I quickly attached the giving set.

'Hold the bottle as high as you can,' I yelled to Angie.

Meanwhile, Bob and I lay down on top of the cow, holding her down and trying to keep her head still while the magnesium was doing its stuff. We held on with grim determination. With my right hand holding the needle steady, I prayed for the treatment to take effect.

Just at that moment an irate voice that reminded me of Captain Mainwaring of *Dad's Army* came out of one of the cars held in the queue.

'Now look here! How long is this going to take?' he barked.

I looked up at Angie, who was bravely taking the full pelt of the rain in her face, and shook my head. I decided to ignore the question. Over the next ten minutes I let the cow have the full bottle. The convulsions stopped and she lay quite still, completely exhausted. Bob got up and with one of the hands went to get a gate and a tractor. My experience with Agnes was paying dividends. Now we could start to move her. With the cow roped down, we towed her very slowly down the road to the farm entrance about twenty-five yards away, followed by a convoy of half a dozen cars and the police.

Once Jessie was off the road, the road was clear to traffic, yet none of the cars drove off, except Captain Mainwaring's. Some got out with umbrellas to see what would happen next. I decided to untie the cow, roll her on to a grass verge and prop her up with straw bales. But all of a sudden, without warning, she struggled to her feet. Bob had a halter round her in a flash and walked her to the warm, dry barn. A ripple of applause came from behind us and several of the drivers came and shook my hand – they had never seen anything like it.

The three policemen, Angie and I went into Bob's place. It was a huge, modern house with goodness knows how many bedrooms. We were welcomed by his wife, Chris, and two of their older children.

'You'll need a shower,' Chris said to Angie and me. 'And you can borrow some dry clothes.' She was a large, matronly lady and, as if reading my thoughts, she laughed, 'Don't worry, one of the girls will have something to fit you.'

Twenty minutes later, dry and warm in an old pair of tweed trousers of Bob's and with a mug of tea in my hand, I felt completely refreshed. Angie was in a bright blue tracksuit, property of the Adams' elder daughter, which brought out the blue of her eyes. I had to admit she looked lovely, with the rosy glow of summer in her face.

'Thank God you arrived when you did,' Bob said. 'Another five minutes and she would have been a goner for sure – and she's one of my best cows!'

I grinned at Angie – she knew I had heard that one before.

'And you too, Mrs Grant,' added Bob. 'Thanks for your help too. Quite a performance that was, and no mistake.'

Angie and I caught each other's eyes and laughed, but before getting the chance to set the record straight about our marital status, Chris called me to the phone.

It was Charles.

'Well, David? Did you save the cow?' The familiar military tone boomed down the line.

'Just about.' I replied, and was going to give him a blow by blow account, but he cut me short. His mind was elsewhere.

'Jolly good.' he said, followed by the throaty rasp in his voice that signalled something difficult was on its way. But I was wrong

'Now look here. It's Miss Heskins. Or rather Horace. Apparently he's in a bit of a state with the thunder and she reckons he's heading for another heart attack.' Another rasp, and I could swear I could hear him thumping his side pocket.

'I said you'd pop in to attend to him.'

'Pop in? Where does she live?'

'Not far from where you are now, actually,' and he proceeded to give me directions.

I said I would be there in fifteen minutes. Angie and I said our goodbyes to the Adamses, ran out with borrowed umbrellas and jumped in the car.

Miss Heskins lived in the next village – on the way home. The storm finally appeared to be abating; I could see quite well as we drove along, with the rain not quite so vicious and fewer crashes of thunder. We eventually found Miss Heskins' cottage after driving past it a couple of times. It was one of four ex-farm workers' cottages in a low terrace. The path to the front door was lined with bedraggled hollyhocks beaten down by the storm. The porch was covered in roses, and just visible above the front door was its name, 'Windrush'.

Miss Heskins opened the door before I even had time to knock. Horace was under the kitchen table. He had apparently been there all afternoon and had refused to come out even for his food. I got down on all fours and peered at him. All I could see were two widely dilated eyes. I reached under the table and pulled him out. He was panting like a dog.

'Oh, you poor moggie.' Angie said as she bent down and stroked his head. He made no response. He let out a loud plaintive miaow as soon as he saw his owner, but otherwise seemed all at sea. I opened my bag, found the thermometer and took his temperature. Surprisingly it was normal, even with all that panting. I went over him but couldn't find anything wrong.

'Is he normally like this with storms?' I asked Miss Heskins.

'I don't think we've ever had one of this magnitude,' she replied. 'But I suppose he was a bit het up last time – but not as bad as this.'

'Well,' I said. 'It looks as though he's cracking up. I think the best thing to do is give him a tranquillizer and wait for a while to see if he goes to sleep.'

I rummaged around in the bag for a syringe and needle, hoping to find a bottle of acepromazine – or acp as we called it for short – which was the only routine tranquillizer I had available. I found a bottle, but it was the one for cows and horses. I had visions of having to go back to the hospital, when I came across a bottle of distilled water. I did a quick mental calculation and diluted the acp down. With Angie and Miss Heskins talking to Horace, I gently slid the needle into the muscle in his back leg and gave him an injection which I reckoned would last the rest of the night.

We sat down and another cup of tea was made. We were ushered into the lounge with its oak beams and open log fire, and an alcove already piled high with neatly stacked logs ready for the long winter nights.

When Miss Heskins disappeared to the kitchen to fetch a plate of chocolate digestives, Angie prodded me in the ribs.

'You must drink tea all day.' she whispered. 'Just what

are the symptoms of a tea overdose?' I just grinned. I looked around. The cottage was very neat. A collection of Hungarian china animals was displayed on the sideboard and on the table beside a high-backed chair was an old black and white photo of two young men in service uniform in a plain ebony frame. Across the picture was written the words, 'Dora, with love.'

'That's my brother Alec, and his best friend,' Miss Heskins explained when she returned bearing the biscuits.

'RAF?'

She nodded.

'When was it taken?'

'1941. They were both fighter pilots. Eric and I were engaged.' She paused again. 'My brother's friend.'

Neither Angie nor I dared to ask more, but we didn't need to. In a small voice Miss Heskins continued.

'They were both shot down within weeks of each other. Battle of Britain, you know.'

'Oh – I'm so sorry.' Angie and I both said it at the same time.

Miss Heskins looked down at Horace lying in her lap, who was starting to get sleepy. The panting had stopped.

'I think I can put Horace to bed. Fortunately the thunder seems to have stopped.'

She was right – the storm had stopped as suddenly as it had erupted. Sedated Horace was a dead weight, so I carried him upstairs and put him in his basket at the bottom of Miss Heskins' bed. There were further photographs of her fiancé in the bedroom. I suddenly felt overwhelmed with sadness for this now old lady living on her own, with just an old cat for company, as she had done for nearly thirty years. A whole lifetime of grieving. When we came back downstairs, I could see the hint of a tear in Angie's eye too.

'I'm sure he'll be all right now,' I said. 'And thanks for the tea.'

I was on the point of saying, 'Ring us if you're worried,' but stopped myself. Instead I told her I would ring tomorrow morning after surgery to make sure he was back to normal.

We trudged out into the warm and clear air. Everything had a fresh smell about it after hours of deluge.

'You must bring your young lady for tea again,' said Miss Heskins with a brave smile.

'We would love to,' Angie replied, with that gentle, warm smile that I was realizing just how much I'd missed over the summer.

'Blast,' I said as we set off for home. 'I've forgotten to ring Charles.'

It would have to wait until we got home. No phone boxes out here. But now that the rain had stopped, it would only be ten minutes before we got back.

'What an amazing night!' Angie said, breaking the silence. 'That was better than any party or film. From convulsing cows to mortified moggies. I had no idea what you got up to when you disappeared into the night.'

'People wouldn't believe me if I told them.'

It was getting late as we arrived home. Keith and Jenny were just leaving having had an evening in.

'Hey man,' Keith said as we passed in the hall. 'Nice togs. Ever thought of being a fashion model?' I had completely forgotten that I was still wearing Bob's clothes: braces holding up trousers that were so short they rode a good four inches above my socks. Miss Heskins had been either too distraught or too polite to notice.

'You wouldn't believe what we've been up to,' began Angie, and started to tell them the story of Jessie and the blocked road.

Keith's eyes popped out and his jaw dropped. But he would have to wait until tomorrow for the whole story. I was just too tired. We bade them goodnight and went in.

# *Chapter Fifteen*

With my LVI certificate in my pocket life became more structured and I began to realize that much of the farm work was routine preventative medicine.

I was involved in tuberculin tests every week now, and also blood testing cows to see if they had been exposed to brucellosis, as an eradication campaign was underway. I also vaccinated sheep, pigs and calves. Allied with castrations, debuddings, cleansings and fertility work, I had to admit a lot of it was fairly mundane. But it had its compensations. The biggest of these was being out in the fresh air on the farms in the sunshine. I had never felt healthier and looked better. I learned to cherish and use my time off.

I hardly knew the town at all, but now that there were fewer tourists it took on an even greater charm. Keith and Jenny and Angie and I started to seek out the restaurants and centuries-old pubs and hostelries, sitting in courtyards where coachmen would have brought weary travellers newly arrived from the continent before the final day's journey to London. We could walk to the centre in twenty minutes, and in parts of it we could almost feel the history as we strolled along the narrow cobbled lanes and streets.

Night duties no longer held me in dread, although when I was on duty I rarely slept well – something which hasn't changed more than thirty years later. But the ring of the telephone in the middle of the night didn't cause palpitations and an adrenaline rush like in the early days. More likely than not I would curse, look at the time and answer the phone within a couple of rings. It would usually be one of the partners' wives, as they took the calls. Nowadays you can use machines to monitor calls and take messages, but then you had to answer every one when it came, even though a good percentage of them weren't urgent at all. Mobile phones simply did not exist. Not even bleepers.

In those days vets' wives were a bit like vicars' wives. Unpaid receptionists. Often a job advertisement would stipulate married male vets. At least I was in a progressive practice and didn't have to worry about the on-call arrangements.

Routine though much of my day-to-day work had become, I enjoyed virtually all of it – except the fertility work. Countless rectal examinations in reluctant cows were a little boring and made my arm ache. Those with womb infections would have to be washed out and it was never a subject which had caught my fancy at college. And in the heat of summer there were the flies to contend with. They had an in-built ability to molest when I only had one hand available to swat them – the other one being up the rear end of the cow.

A few months later, in the depths of winter, I would find myself looking back on these lazy, hazy days of summer with longing, although I had yet to appreciate the fact. The truth was, I was getting just a little complacent. My confidence had soared and I needed to get a perspective on my limitations.

It was to come in the shape of a horse owned by a local personality, Geoffrey Norman, who owned a country club on the outskirts of town. He had just two animals, a sleepy old German shepherd that must have been getting on for fifteen, and a ten-year-old gelding which he used to ride every day. I had seen Jaspar grazing in the fields on either side of the drive that led up to the club, where I had been several times both on business and pleasure. Geoffrey wasn't really a horsey type. It was just that a horse fitted into his idea of the place – it looked right grazing in the fields that surrounded the club – and learning to ride had seemed the next logical step. He wasn't a man to have something and not use it.

Unlike the typical horse owner, he professed no knowledge of veterinary matters, which made him an easy client. Until this occasion, the only contact I had with Jaspar was to give him a shot against equine influenza. He was a big, fine-looking bay, and spirited. I had managed to get the vaccine in – but only just, as he reared up and flailed with his front hooves.

My theoretical lectures at college had been excellent, but I had no practical experience, which was why my day's outing at the point-to-point had been a miracle. Also, the majority of horse owners almost certainly knew more than I did and, from the stories I had heard, were as temperamental as their four-legged friends. Jaspar, like Nero, had the effect of making the hairs on the back of my head stand on end.

So it was a very worried young veterinary surgeon who drove along the driveway through Geoffrey Norman's park at seven o'clock. The shadows of the trees cast long shadows across the drive. It was late September and the evening was already beginning to draw in. Jaspar had jumped a fence and gashed his neck. It would need stitching.

Jaspar was standing in his stable with his head over the door, looking out at the open countryside. I just about managed to see the extent of the wound before he darted into the dark recesses at the back. For a second I considered whether it wouldn't be better left to heal naturally on its own. A hitherto hidden sense of bravura urged me to banish such a thought from my mind and stitch it – it would only need three or four, I told myself.

'We'll have to stitch that,' I informed Geoffrey, with an air of authority. I asked him to bring the horse out into the open and went back to the car to set up the instruments that would be needed.

The stitching wouldn't be the problem, I began to realize, looking at Geoffrey's attempts to lead Jaspar out. It would be the restraint and giving the local anaesthetic. I rummaged around the boot and picked up the twitch. This was a pole with a loop of rope in the end of it. What you were supposed to do was trap a bit of the horse's upper lip in the rope and twist it until it was hurting the horse enough for it to stand still and ignore what the vet was doing. Then, if it worked, you could get away with giving injections of local anaesthetic without the horse jumping about and causing mayhem.

I looked at my client. A slight, city-slicker type, I doubted somehow whether he would be able to hang on to the twitch, which would be his job while I stitched. In any case, this had always struck me as a crude device and potentially cruel in unskilled hands. What I needed was a potent tranquillizer which was easy to give. I didn't have such a thing – just the acp which had given Horace the best sleep in a thunderstorm he had ever had. That would have to do. No distilled water this time. I drew up a hefty amount.

Horses are highly intelligent animals, and as soon as Jaspar saw the syringe and needle it obviously brought back memories. Unpleasant memories. He began to back away and sway about, which had the effect of almost lifting

Geoffrey off his feet as he gamely held on to the halter.

Eventually, with my left hand on the halter to steady Geoffrey, and with my right hand wielding the syringe, I managed – just – to get the injection in. By now all three of us were sweating profusely. I flopped down on a grass bank to rest and wait for the tranquillizer to take effect. The sun was just going down and the sky resembled a beautiful painting by Turner, with just a few fiery clouds rising up into the blue like a magical mountain range. Although the day had been warm, there was a chill in the air now that the sun had gone down. Behind me, the grass bank sloped gently down to a stream which ran through the grounds. Sheep belonging to a neighbour grazed this field and several of them were idly drinking from the stream.

This idyllic scene should have been relaxing, but for the prospect of dealing with this frisky gelding, which after twenty minutes only showed the merest hint of being sleepy. A slight drooping of the eyelids, perhaps. A gentle swaying when he changed posture. Enough to persuade me to set about the next stage in the procedure.

I drew up a syringe full of local anaesthetic and selected the smallest needle I could find. Talking very quietly to Jaspar, I went up to him and slid the needle in to the side of the wound. I managed to get a couple of cc in and then did the same on the other side. This time he reared up and a couple of hooves whistled across the top of my head. Geoffrey lost control of him and he cantered off with a wobble.

'If you can catch him, it shouldn't be difficult to finish the job,' I said, failing to keep a hint of anxiety out of my voice. It would very soon be dark and I might have to do the operation under torchlight. There was no light in the loose box.

'He's had all the local – it will be numb in a matter of five minutes,' I explained.

Ten minutes later Geoffrey brought an even sleepier Jaspar back to the grassy verge. I threaded a stitch-up needle with nylon and quietly crept up behind Jaspar to put the stitches in. The first went in easily and the wound closed up nicely. But the second one seemed to catch a nerve. Jaspar caught me with his head and knocked me flying. I rolled over backwards, slid down the grass bank and landed in the stream. A startled sheep scuttered away and then stopped to stare at me through the gloom, as though I was mad. Jaspar stood at the top of the verge half asleep, seemingly totally unaware of my presence. I decided he had won this particular battle. I tottered back up the bank with a sore jaw and a very wet backside and pronounced that the wound was closed enough to have a good chance of healing. I prepared two more injections. First, the anti-tetanus jab and, second, the penicillin. It was totally dark by the time Jaspar was led into his stable for the night.

Geoffrey's private quarters were at the rear of the country club. I had been there before, so I made my way in to clean up. My shoes were soaking, but fortunately I had a pair of running shoes in the car. My trousers weren't too bad and would do until I got home. As I walked in, Geoffrey's telephone rang. Instinctively I knew it was for me. Frank's wife this time. Another horse call. I couldn't believe it. In all the time on duty at the practice I hadn't had an equine emergency. Now two on the trot. This time a colic. Major Hamilton-Jones had called in. His usual vet was away at some congress or other – would we mind attending on this occasion as it was an emergency? The horse was in acute pain and rolling about.

It was as though I was on my first-ever night duty. That familiar adrenaline rush, stress and anxiety, all rolled into one, came flooding back.

As I started up the Anglia, Geoffrey's old German shepherd woke up and lumbered after the car, barking furiously and showing what remained of his teeth. I looked in the rear mirror and saw the silhouette of the ancient dog, satisfied with having seen me off, standing in the drive and looking round at his master, wagging his tail for approval.

'Calm down!' I told myself as I drove back to the main road. I would take it logically step by step. If I wasn't sure, I would call in for help. Charles was sure to be in and he would come out if needs be. He was always offering, and so far I had never had to take him up. I thought back through my notes. They had been excellent and covered everything. So what did I have to worry about? Quite simply, lack of experience. That was it, I decided, as I arrived at Major Hamilton-Jones' palatial residence, where the gravel was so thick I had to put the car into second gear.

The major was waiting in the semi-circular drive as I arrived. Lights flooded the house. He was just a silhouette and looked like one of the statues that flanked the front door.

'Thanks for coming so soon. Really appreciate it.'

He was in his early forties and had the easygoing nature and impeccable manners that seemed to go with being an army officer, though the house suggested that he didn't just live on his income.

'My daughter Jessica's with the patient,' he told me as he led the way round to the stables at the right of the house. 'She's more up on this sort of thing than I am.'

He indicated the stable and disappeared back into the house.

Carrying my bag and stethoscope I walked to the stable, which was well lit in contrast to Jaspar's quarters. I was confronted with a pony standing quietly and bathed in sweat, being attended by a teenage girl wearing a sweater and jodhpurs with long boots. Her hair was in a ponytail and she wore steel-rimmed glasses which she continually pushed up her nose whenever she spoke.

'It's a case of spasmodic colic,' were her first words on seeing me. 'Hugo normally treats Blaze with a painkilling injection and a sedative.'

I looked at the pony standing quietly. I was about to say that it didn't look like colic to me when another attack started. Blaze started to kick at his belly, looking round, and then fell to the ground, rolling and kicking his legs in agony. It lasted about two minutes and then, as suddenly as it started, it stopped. As we stood watching, great rumbling sounds emanated from the abdomen.

'So this has happened before?' I asked, quite calm now and trying to get a history.

'Yes, several times. I rode him a lot today and he drank a lot of water when we got back. I'm sure that's the cause. Have you got the pethidine?'

I ignored this remark and proceeded to examine the pony. He was sweating profusely as I took his pulse, which was racing a bit but quite strong. Good, I thought to myself – at least he doesn't appear to be in shock. A look at his mucous membranes confirmed this. I didn't need the stethoscope to hear the loud rumblings coming once again from his abdomen.

'I'll just get some pethidine and a sedative,' I told the girl, and went back to the car to load up the syringes. On my return she pushed her glasses further up her nose. I was in for more.

'Shouldn't you do a rectal examination to rule out an obstruction?'

'It had occurred to me, but I would prefer to get some pain relief first to try to ward off the next attack.' I was rather pleased with this, but Jessica looked doubtful. She opened her mouth to say something, but then thought better of it.

In any case, I had already given the first of the two injections.

We waited ten minutes for the injection to take effect and then I repeated the earlier examination. The pulse had settled down and there was no doubt about it – there was a definite improvement.

'He should be ready for that rectal now, don't you think?' said Jessica as she stood behind her pony.

'Yes, maybe that's a good idea,' I said, but just at that moment Blaze lifted his tail and deposited a large lump of manure on Jessica's foot.

'But then again, maybe it isn't!' I grinned at her, but got no response. This determined young lady did not seem to have a sense of humour.

'I'll head on back. I think things are on the mend.'

'Aren't you going to stay? Hugo usually does, until he's quite sure of a complete recovery.'

'I'm sure he does – but you can call me if there's a deterioration – it's less than twenty minutes away.'

And with that I packed up my bag and bade her goodnight.

It was just after midnight when I got in. I realized that I hadn't eaten – or done the shopping for that matter. I was dead beat, having been on the go since seven-thirty that morning. I looked in the fridge. One egg, half a pint of milk, some margarine and nothing else. I had intended to eat a

Chinese take-away, but events had overtaken me. Serves me right for being disorganized, I thought. I crashed out more tired than hungry. It would be egg on toast for breakfast.

The phone went just after four in the morning. The worst possible time. Woken from the deepest part of my sleep, I always felt wretched. I felt particularly so when I heard the dread news that the Hamilton-Jones' pony had had a relapse.

Cursing, I was out of bed, instantaneously wide awake, dressed and into my car within five minutes. Twenty minutes later I was back with my colic case, although now it didn't seem like a colic case at all.

The pony was standing, resting and occasionally shifting his feet. Jessica barely acknowledged me.

'He's perked up in the last ten minutes. I've been taking his pulse every fifteen minutes,' and she produced a graph of the last four and a half hours.

I went over him and couldn't find anything wrong.

'I thought he ought to have repeat injections,' said Jessica, pushing her glasses even further up her nose.

I thought for a minute.

'The sedative injection won't need repeating for several hours yet and I'd prefer not to overdo it with the pethidine. It would be better if you keep the graph up until nine in the morning and then phone in.'

She nodded keenly.

'Truth is,' I added, 'you're doing such a splendid job, you don't need me here.'

I packed up for the second time that night, arriving home at five in the morning. Starving hungry by now, I had my meagre breakfast and tried to get some sleep, but sleep wouldn't come. The two horse cases had taken most of the night and not filled me with confidence. Maybe horses and me didn't mix, I thought to myself as I got dressed. A very wet bottom reminded me that a trip to the dry cleaners would be necessary during my lunch hour. I hunted around for my one spare pair of trousers, put them on and drove into work.

I arrived at the hospital just before nine. There was already a message from Jessica, thanking me for my help. The pony seemed much better – but she was getting 'Hugo's' specialist opinion this morning as he was back from the congress.

'You're welcome,' I thought – maybe a bit uncharitably. I had this feeling I didn't have what it took to be a successful horse vet. Years later I feel that, as in all things to do with animals, all I needed was to be seeing lots of cases in a dedicated horse practice. With only a few cases every now and then it presented a far-too-steep learning curve. I had enough on my plate with farm animals and companion animals.

* * *

The summer ended as quickly as it had begun. Autumn took on a beauty I had never seen before. Continuously exposed to the country lanes, I saw colours that I had never appreciated before. Lanes which had once danced with lacy cow parsley were now cobwebbed in old man's beard – wild clematis. On the Weald, beech stands turned miraculous shades of red and gold.

Work accelerated, as the harvest had finished and all the common diseases reared their heads. But they were by now for the most part familiar diseases with standard treatments. At last I felt that on many occasions I matched the others –

for my treatments were identical to theirs. I had my favourite farms. I positively looked forward to visiting them. By now I knew the families of the farmer and as often as not the families of the farmhands too.

As far as small animals were concerned, I was continually learning snippets from the masters, whom I generally held in awe. I was getting better on the medical side but hadn't done any surgery. It would have to wait, I decided. It takes a few years to get really experienced. I'd be there in five years. Little did I know!

It was one morning late in November. I had woken early, while it was still dark, worried about where I was going in my life. More specifically, where I was going with Angie. She had grown on me and we were in a routine, with many nights out as a foursome with Keith and Jenny. Whereas they had become closer and closer since our holiday, and an engagement seemed imminent, I still couldn't commit myself to Angie. In a way I wanted to. She was a wonderful girl. Beautiful, funny, caring, sensitive, generous. But I still found myself eyeing up other girls. And the idea of being tied to just one person terrified me. Looking back now, I suppose I just wasn't in love with her. As it was, I hid my head in the sand and hoped the problem would go away. We could just go on as we were. It wasn't as if Angie was handing out ultimatums. Maybe the issue would have to be addressed when Angie qualified in the summer. We could leave it to then.

Or so I thought.

Time had flown by and in another few weeks the students would be away, with just two terms left to qualification. Angie and I were sitting watching television in my flat on a night off when the subject of Christmas came up.

'So. What are we going to do?' she asked

My heart lurched. *We?* Christmas?

'Why don't you come up to Manchester? It's about time you met Mum and Dad. And I can't see them coming down here.'

Another lurch of panic. I could feel my mouth go dry. This was serious stuff. Parents. Although she'd met my Dad at Crystal Palace, I'd never thought of taking her home to meet Mum, even though it was less than an hour away. I knew that for Mum that would mean only one thing: wedding bells. Her mother would think the same. If I went up there, I might as well be buying an engagement ring. It was the first step on a conveyor belt that I knew I then couldn't stop, which would end up in a church. I just wasn't ready. I gave an exaggerated sigh.

'But I'm certain to be on duty.' However true, it must have sounded like a lame excuse.

Angie had been lying on the settee with her head resting in the curve of my arm. I felt her go tense. After a minute or two, she got up to make a cup of hot chocolate. I stayed watching the television, but I might have been watching clothes in a washing machine for all the notice I took. Minutes passed.

'You all right, Angie?'

No reply.

I got up and went into the kitchen in time to see her wipe her eyes on her sleeve.

She knew what I had been thinking. Probably the suggestion had been a test of my commitment. And now she knew the answer. There was no point dressing it up, pretending that wasn't what I meant.

I took her in my arms.

'Don't cry. Please don't cry.'

She smiled bravely.

'I'm just not ready, Angie.'

She nodded and turned her head away.

'Look, I know that I'm probably being stupid,' I went on, 'and you know how I feel about you.'

'Do I, David?' She turned back to me and looked at me directly with those honest blue eyes. 'Perhaps I do. But I don't know what you want from me. I do know that it's not the same as I want from you.'

Then she pulled away. 'So. There it is.'

I suddenly couldn't bear the thought of losing her.

'Can't we just be friends?'

She sighed and raised her eyes.

'No clichés, please, David.'

'Sorry.'

'Look. I don't know. It'll take time. I just don't think I can cope with seeing you. For the time being anyway.' She walked to the door, not looking back. 'Let me know if you change your mind.'

I stared at the two steaming cups of hot chocolate and poured both of them down the sink.

I was suddenly aware of how cold my flat was. I lit the fire and slumped in front of the television, feeling very sorry for myself.

Falling back on established patterns, I immersed myself in my work. It wasn't difficult – each day kept me too busy to contemplate my future. Keith and Jenny were sympathetic, although Keith thought I was mad to risk losing Angie. And anyway, they were too busy discussing arrangements for their own wedding, which was planned for the spring.

Angie and I somehow managed to keep out of each other's way, although it was difficult living in the same house. The familiar knock on the door had stopped. Mrs

Nightingale knew what had happened and invitations to join the students for supper stopped coming. From my flat I would hear laughter as the students neared the end of term and Christmas festivities were in full swing. I felt very sad and alone.

One day a Christmas card appeared under the door with a little note saying she had gone home early. A bulky parcel, with instructions not to open until Christmas Day, she'd left propped up outside.

More Christmas cards arrived. One from Bob. He had landed a superb job in a mixed practice in Wiltshire. He had never got over his infatuation with Chantal and had kept in touch. She had just told him that she had got engaged to an airline pilot. 'Fast worker, eh David?' he wrote. I could sense his sadness. But it didn't surprise me. When all was said and done, she was a terrible flirt. I'd even spotted her kissing Phil, long after they had stopped seeing each other and only a few days before he got engaged to Sue, and when she was meant to be going out with me. Another airline pilot. The hours might be just as difficult, but when it came to glamour, vets obviously came a poor second to pilots.

I was surprised to find that I had some grateful small animal clients. I had now a grand collection of six bottles of Grant's whisky and still counting. These were added to the Nightingale household, which was gearing up to a mammoth celebration for the engagement, when Sue would be introduced to the wider family. Now that Angie had gone, I was once more welcomed back. At least I wouldn't be lonely at Christmas.

What I had told Angie turned out to be only too true. As the only single person in the practice, I would be expected to do at least a couple of days over the festive season. I broke it to my mother the week before when I took my parents their presents. She clattered around the kitchen not saying anything, but I knew she was upset to have Christmas for the second year running without me around.

A few weeks earlier, Frank had warned me to keep the Friday before Christmas free. A tradition, he explained. The only time in the year when the farmers and the vets got together for a social. Finally it was here.

No one was driving, as it was clear this was a boozy night out. The partners had organized a cab. I was the last to be picked up and we were soon headed out of town to a pub with a dance hall. Just about the entire local farm workforce was already there, and within minutes of arriving we each had a pint of best bitter in our hands.

I recognized a surprisingly large number of those present, including Rupert Charlton-Jones amongst a crowd of farmers' sons about his age. There were no women around. Just as I had suspected, it was a stag night. Right away we were part of more than a hundred farmers, all laughing and joking and talking shop. Several came over offering to buy drinks and bring us up to date about our various patients. It was obvious that, as guests, we weren't expected to put our hands in our pockets. I was beginning to wonder about food when a huge buffet appeared, which was demolished very quickly in expectation of the highlight of the evening.

The entertainment, I'd been told, was to consist of a comedian and some dancing girls. Sounds like fun, I said to Alan. He smiled indulgently and patted me on the back.

The vets were given pride of place in the front row, though I noticed that some of the older ones preferred to hang around at the back near the bar. It was the same with the older farmers, who held back while the front seats were taken by the younger contingent. The hospitality was overwhelming. I loved a pint of the best Kentish brew, but my stomach was beginning to inflate and I started taking sips, knowing that emptying the glass would just signal it to be filled.

About an hour into the proceedings, a short, squat man appeared in a bright blue suit and a microphone. He started the ball rolling with some jokes that matched the colour of his suit, delivered in some very ripe language in an earthy cockney accent. The response was riotous – the bluer the jokes, the greater the noise. Then, to a round of raucous cheers and wolf whistles, nearly drowning out Shirley Bassey singing 'Big Spender', from the back of the hall the dancing girls appeared, dressed in long silver boots, figure-hugging tops that revealed their midriffs, and skirts the size of pelmets.

Another pint was thrust into my left hand. A sudden blare of Tina Turner and the girl at the front strutted across the 'stage' and down to where the audience had assembled. To the pounding rhythm of the music, she began to strip down to her underwear, which consisted largely of tassels and a G-string. I had never seen a striptease and wasn't sure how to react. I didn't want to do the wrong thing with the partners' eyes watching me. But she was surprisingly attractive, very tall, particularly in those high-heeled boots, and with a figure that made her a natural for this kind of job. She was now weaving through the audience, dropping bits of clothing as she went, much to the delight of the recipients.

Then I looked again. Were my eyes deceiving me, or was she sitting on Alan's knee? To a great cheer, she removed his tie and stole off with it. Next thing she was making straight for me – it seemed that the vets had been selected as targets. Before I could think what to do, she had sat down on my knee. I was still holding two pints of bitter, and to avoid them spilling over her I held out my hands horizontally. The effect was apparently very comical.

As she wriggled and writhed in time to the music, the tassels on what remained of her top came close enough to tickle my nose. One of the farmers shouted out, 'Watch him, darling – he's the fastest vet in the county!'

Using Alan's tie, she snared my head and pulled me towards her. I thought I was going to suffocate. The audience thought this was hilarious and, just when I thought things couldn't get worse, I was released while she resumed dancing. She turned to Rupert, who had been laughing with the rest of them and was sitting next to me. He must have been far worse for wear than I was, because somehow he had his shirt removed. Very red faced, he managed to get it back on by the time she had finished the dance. I wondered what he would tell his mother when he got home.

Then the comedian was back on. While every one was laughing, I managed to off-load some of my beer into Rupert's glass and drink slowly from the other one.

There were three girls in all and each had more or less the same routine. They didn't take all their clothes off, concentrating on making fun of any likely looking targets in the front row. The vets were now left alone and the girls were concentrating on the young farmers, several of whom after an hour of this entertainment were minus their shirts and trousers.

After this was over, it was back to talking and joking. I had lots coming up to ask how I was settling in, offering to buy me a drink, even asking advice about their cows. I talked to Ken Griffin and Harry Myers, not to mention the regulars, the farmers who I now counted among my friends. Even Richard Dell gave me a nod, which I knew was as close as he would come to any kind of acknowledgement. I knew that this had been some kind of rite of passage and I had come through. I had been accepted. I was one of them and, not only that, I had held my beer and been a good sport.

The evening eventually came to an end and we were just waiting for our cab when a young farmer I barely knew, decidedly the worse for wear, decided I was his best friend. He gave me a bear hug, causing me to spill the pint of bitter I had been nursing for the last hour. All over Frank's camelhair coat.

The young man didn't even register what had happened. I was mortified. Frank and Alan dropped me off at the Nightingales' before continuing on home. Charles lived in the opposite direction.

Frank and Vivien were off on a skiing holiday the next morning, so I apologized again and said I'd see them on New Year's Eve when they got back.

'That's if I'm not sacked by then.'

Alan laughed. 'No chance – you're just practising, so far.'

Christmas Day arrived and was a doddle. No farm calls and only a couple of small animal clients in the morning. I had turkey and Christmas pudding with the Nightingales, with ginger beer to wash it down, and wore the warm shirt that Angie had bought for me. I was very tempted by the wines that Phil and Sue had brought in from France, but if I did have to go out I'd need all my wits about me.

Night fell, and the winds sprang up from the East. The fine cloudless day led to a bitterly cold night, with the weather coming straight from Siberia. The weather forecast said to expect snow. The family settled down in front of the roaring fire. The phone didn't ring and I fell asleep in front of the television, being woken by the National Anthem. I staggered back upstairs into my own bed.

Boxing Day dawned bleak and windy, but still no snow, although there was more than a hint of it in the air. Frank had warned me that when it snowed in these parts it really went for it, with villages being cut off at times. The trusty Anglia started first time and I set off for a mini-round towards the coast. A couple of cleansings, a mastitis, nothing too arduous.

The first few flakes of snow began to fall – slowly and gently – hardly settling. The final call of the morning was at Jed Dickens' place. He had actually requested that I have a look at one of his lame cows – having decided, for whatever reason, that I wasn't such an incompetent after all. Maybe the social had done it – having a beer and a laugh together. He'd been dressed like a character from an Ealing comedy in a suit that must have been made in the 'Thirties, and we had exchanged a cheery wave. It was 'David' now. When I had injected his cow with antibiotic he apologized for not asking me in for a drink.

'You'd better get back into town, David, or you'll be spending the night with me and the cows. I'm not saying as you wouldn't be welcome, but who knows when you'd get out again. We're gonna 'ave a blizzard. No mistake. When it blows like this, we get cut off.'

He gestured up to a sky the colour of anthracite, which was obviously laden with snow. I phoned in to Alan to see if anything had come in. Helen answered the phone.

'Got a call for you, David. A bullock on Jim Shearer's got out early this morning and he's found it collapsed in a field near the main road. He says it's blizzarding down. Can you see if you can reach it? Alan's been landed with a prolapsed uterus. Goodness knows when he'll be back.'

I set off at once, bidding Jed a Happy New Year.

Amazing what a few beers and scantily dressed women can achieve, I thought.

The main roads were fine, but the snow was slowly building up at the sides and few people were venturing out.

I was at Jim's three-quarters of an hour later. His farm was just off the main road and I reached the farmhouse without too much difficulty as it was downhill. I hardly recognized him as he came out to greet me at his front door. He was wrapped up in a thick duffel coat. I got out of the car and was immediately hit in the face by a penetrating icy blast. I put my boots and brown coat on and realized that I wasn't well prepared for Siberian conditions. But there was nothing I could do about it now. We set off in Jim's tractor to get to the bullock, stopping on the way to pick up a gate.

'What's that for?' he asked.

'You'll see,' I answered, with the benefit of a two-case experience.

We found the bullock half immersed in snow and still alive, but weak. It took twenty minutes to manhandle him on to the improvised sledge and get him back to a warm barn with his mates. Now the blizzard really took off. We could hardly see where we were going. Somehow we got him back inside and I could take a look at him. His temperature didn't register on the thermometer. He was one of the smaller, weaker ones of his group and it seemed that it was just a case of exposure – my first admittedly – and what he really needed was warmth and food. I gave him a shot of antibiotic to ward off pneumonia and left the nursing to Jim. He had already got blankets wrapped round and was propping the bullock up in huge quantities of straw.

It was me that needed attention now. My hands were bitterly cold without the benefit of gloves and I was shivering. The car started first time and I put the heater on full blast and inched out of the drive. I just made the main road and swung in the direction of town. Visibility was down to twenty feet, but amazingly there were still a few lorries coming from the Channel ports and I could follow their tracks in the snow. The main road was by now down to single tracks and I drove with my nose on the windscreen, almost praying that I would make it home.

An hour later, the hospital came in to view and with a sigh of relief I stopped in the car park. I walked down the path by the hospital which led home but couldn't resist popping into the Spotted Cow, where I knew a roaring fire would be going. As soon as he saw my blue face and shivering body, Theo paused.

'The usual, Dave?'

'No. Make it a whisky,' I said. 'Grant's'. And I sat in front of the fire to thaw out.

Over the next half an hour the door would open and let another customer in with a flurry of snow. I had never experienced anything like this. It was just amazing.

I rang Alan to let him know where I was.

'There'll be no more calls today,' he said. 'We can't get out and they can't get in! It will have to be advice over the phone. It's set to get worse!'

Like me, he was an avid weather watcher.

'You might as well stay where you are,' he added. 'I'll hold the fort and we'll see how things are in the morning.'

I downed the last drops of the whisky with a clear conscience.

'I'll have that pint now,' I said to Theo, and settled down with a happy sigh in front of the log fire.

'By the way, did you know that Tony's getting married to that nurse of yours?' said Theo.

'It's news to me!' I said. 'She hasn't said anything to us.'

'Just happened, that's why. They decided yesterday – Christmas Day.'

We toasted the happy couple and had another drink on the house.

An hour later, with two borrowed sweaters belonging to Anthony, I set off for home – only two hundred yards away. I could only see ten yards in front of my face and was walking in snow up to my knees, but I finally made it and went straight for the Nightingales' roaring fire.

I walked into a Boxing Day meal, which turned into a double celebration as Keith and Jenny were now officially engaged. First Anthony and Jackie and now these two. Even though it was all on the cards and I said the right things, I felt well and truly left out. I had an overwhelming temptation to phone Angie, but resisted it. A little voice in the back of my head told me to think about it in the cold light of day – not now.

Knowing that I couldn't be called out let me sleep as I had hardly done all year. For the first time since I had started work I slept twelve hours. I looked out of the window when I woke and couldn't see anything. I opened the door and it was still blizzarding down, with a couple of feet of snow. I had the day off again.

The weather didn't improve until New Year's Eve, when we had a beautiful sunny day without a cloud in the sky. The ground was still white with snow. There had been no traffic to turn the roads into sludge. A trickle of small animal clients began to make their way to the hospital. It was just Alan, me and Frank who had come back from Austria looking relaxed and tanned, though he said there was more snow here than there was in Innsbruck. Charles was stuck in his village and Peter had the day off.

Most of the outlying villages were still impossible to get

to, so a leisurely end to the year was in prospect. Evening surgery consisted of two clients – at this rate we would go bankrupt!

I phoned Charles and Peter to wish them Happy New Year – they had been so helpful all year. In fact, everyone had. I was so lucky, I thought. Pauline interrupted my thoughts.

'Can you pop up to the library to see Mr Archer and Mr Jenkins before you go?'

'Now what?' was my immediate thought. Bad news? No, surely not. But she'd said library, not X-ray room. Perhaps it was to do with Jackie's engagement. Perhaps they wanted me to organize a present.

I walked into the library, wondering what it was all about.

Alan shook my hand, and then Frank.

'David,' Frank began, 'you've been a very cheerful colleague all year and you've become a very valuable member of the team. If you're happy to stay, we're proposing to increase your salary to £1,750.'

I stood there open-mouthed and gasped.

'I'm more than happy!' I said.

They both grinned and wished me Happy New Year.

I left them discussing the practice business and set off. There was a party tonight and tomorrow I was off. A quick visit to my parents, then I'd planned to meet up with Bob to celebrate his new job.

I grinned to myself as I put the Anglia into gear. As I turned the corner of the road, I saw Mr Sarabini waiting at the kerb, about to cross the road with Nero in tow.

Even the sight of Nero's unlovely face couldn't spoil the day.

I wound down the window.

'Happy New Year, Mr Sarabini!' The words echoed across the empty street.

His face lit up.

''Appy New Year! No bad feelings, eh?' he said, indicating Nero.

'No bad feelings. How's business?'

'Never better.' He searched for the word. 'Booooming. This the life, eh?'

I laughed, and drove off through the snow-covered streets.

'Yes,' I said out loud. 'This is the life.'